THE HISTORY OF IMPERIAL CHINA
A Research Guide

by
Endymion Wilkinson

Published by
East Asian Research Center
Harvard University

Distributed by
Harvard University Press
Cambridge, Mass.
1974

The East Asian Research Center at Harvard University
administers research projects designed to further
scholarly understanding of China, Japan, Korea,
Vietnam, and adjacent areas. These studies have been
assisted by grants from the Ford Foundation.

Library of Congress No. 72-93955
SBN 674-39680-4

CONTENTS

Part II. Traditional Chinese Historical Writing
and Main Categories of Primary Sources

TABLES

PREFACE

The present Guide has been put together primarily to meet the needs of students of Chinese history, and in particular socioeconomic history. Because of the necessarily somewhat broad coverage of primary sources and the reference aids to them in Chinese, Japanese, and Western languages, students of other aspects of Chinese traditional culture may also find it useful.

The time span covered is from the earliest times to approximately 1911, but within these broad limits I have concentrated on the sources and research aids for the study of imperial China from the third century B.C. to the eighteenth century.

The special problems of the sources for pre-imperial history (pre-third century B.C.) are alluded to in section 11.2 and several of the major types of these sources (archaeological, epigraphical, and literary) are briefly discussed, but the main focus is on the later periods.

Although the Guide covers sources produced down to the early twentieth century, no attempt has been made to deal with the many new types of sources available for the study of nineteenth and twentieth-century Chinese history for the simple reason that several adequate guides already exist. The reader is referred in the first instance to A.J. Nathan, *Modern China, 1840-1972: An Introduction to Sources and Research Aids* (Michigan, 1973); J. Chesneaux and J. Lust, *Introduction aux études d'histoire contemporaine de Chine, 1898-1949* (Paris, 1964); and to P. Berton and E. Wu, *Contemporary China: A Research Guide* (Stanford, 1967) for the post-1949 period.

In Part I, "Research Hints," some of the main problems liable to be encountered in research are discussed and solutions are suggested. This is by no means an exhaustive discussion of research problems (the absence of a separate section on weights and measures and statistics in general being one of the most obvious omissions), but a judicious use of the subject index should lead to research aids for problems not discussed separately in Part I, but alluded to in other sections.

In Part II the major types of traditional historical writing (sections 14-17) as well as the main categories of primary sources (sections 13 and 18-32) are briefly introduced. The objective throughout has been to be suggestive rather than exhaustive, but for those sources which have been included every attempt has been made to give the available research aids, whether in Chinese, Japanese, or Western languages.

Throughout the Guide the emphasis is placed on those sources and research aids which are of practical use to the student of Chinese history. Thus no attempt has been made to cover the full range of historical writing in traditional China, since to do so would merely be to compile an anti-quarian list.

The language requirements for the serious study of Chinese imperial history are formidable: modern Chinese, classical Chinese, and Japanese are all indispensable. The present Guide assumes a knowledge of all three, but wherever possible translations into Western languages and Western-language research aids have been included. The aim has been to make this Guide useful to the student of Chinese history who has only begun his studies as well as to more advanced students wishing to round out their knowledge of the main types of primary sources in different periods.

Hanyu pinyin (the system of romanization used in the People's Republic of China) has been used throughout. In the future students are more and more likely to begin their studies with this normative system rather than with Wade-Giles or the other Western systems. For the convenience of those not yet familiar with *pinyin*, a *pinyin*/Wade-Giles conversion table will be found after the acknowledgments.

Publishers are not given unless there is a good reason such as the need to distinguish editions.

The Guide is being issued in a preliminary edition in the hope that those working in the field will contribute ideas and expertise to improve and correct it, in order eventually to produce a much more substantial work. In its present form the Guide is merely offered as a frame and as a starting point. All corrections and suggestions for improvement will be gratefully acknowledged and should be addressed to the compiler at The

History Department, School of Oriental and African Studies, University of London, London W.C.1, England.

E.P.W.

August 1972

ACKNOWLEDGMENTS

I am very grateful to the following people who read through parts of the first draft and offered their advice or encouragement: T. Connor, Harvard University; R. Edwards, Harvard University; M. Elvin, Glasgow University; J.K. Fairbank, Harvard University; W.J.F. Jenner, Leeds University; D.C. Lau, London University; J.T.C. Liu, Princeton University; P. van der Loon, Oxford University; D. McMullen, Cambridge University; F.W. Mote, Princeton University; D.C. Twitchett, Cambridge University; and S. Wu, Boston University.

In particular Mr. Connor, Mr. Jenner, Mr. Lau, Mr. van der Loon, Mr. McMullen, and Mr. Mote offered a great many useful comments and suggestions, many of which I have followed.

Needless to say none of the above can be held in any way responsible for the numerous errors of omission and commission which doubtless appear in the text.

I should also like to express my thanks to the History Department of the School of Oriental and African Studies, University of London, for making a typing grant to get the first draft into shape. The present preliminary edition was prepared during a summer's work at the East Asian Research Center, Harvard University. I am very grateful to Professor Dwight Perkins and the Director, J.K. Fairbank, for generously extending the invitation and putting the facilities of the Center and the Harvard-Yenching Library at my disposal. Without all the hard work put in by the Center's editorial staff, in particular Mrs. Anne T. Stevens, this Guide would probably still be caught in some limbo between first typescript and camera copy.

I should like to thank Professor D.C. Lau and Professor L.S. Yang who pointed out numerous errors (mainly incorrect characters) in the first printing. Most of these have now been corrected in the second printing.

E.P.W. (Tokyo, 1974)

HANYU PINYIN/WADE-GILES CONVERSION TABLE

Pinyin	Wade-Giles	Pinyin	Wade-Giles	Pinyin	Wade-Giles
a	a	chu	ch'u	er	erh
ai	ai	chuai	ch'uai		
an	an	chuan	ch'uan	fa	fa
ang	ang	chuang	ch'uang	fan	fan
ao	ao	chui	ch'ui	fang	fang
		chun	ch'un	fei	fei
ba	pa	chuo	ch'o	fen	fen
bai	pai	ci	tz'u	feng	feng
ban	pan	cong	ts'ung	fo	fo
bang	pang	cou	ts'ou	fou	fou
bao	pao	cu	ts'u	fu	fu
bei	pei	cuan	ts'uan		
ben	pen	cui	ts'ui	ga	ka
beng	peng	cun	ts'un	gai	kai
bi	pi	cuo	ts'o	gan	kan
bian	pien			gang	kang
biao	piao	da	ta	gao	kao
bie	pieh	dai	tai	ge	ke, ko
bin	pin	dan	tan	gei	kei
bing	ping	dang	tang	gen	ken
bo	po	dao	tao	geng	keng
bu	pu	de	te	gong	kung
		dei	tei	gou	kou
ca	ts'a	deng	teng	gu	ku
cai	ts'ai	di	ti	gua	kua
can	ts'an	dian	tien	guai	kuai
cang	ts'ang	diao	tiao	guan	kuan
cao	ts'ao	die	tieh	guang	kuang
ce	ts'e	ding	ting	gui	kuei
cen	ts'en	diu	tiu	gun	kun
ceng	ts'eng	dong	tung	guo	kuo
cha	ch'a	dou	tou		
chai	ch'ai	du	tu	ha	ha
chan	ch'an	duan	tuan	hai	hai
chang	ch'ang	dui	tui	han	han
chao	ch'ao	dun	tun	hang	hang
che	ch'e	duo	to	hao	hao
chen	ch'en			he	he, ho
cheng	ch'eng	e	e, o	hei	hei
chi	ch'ih	ei	ei	hen	hen
chong	ch'ung	en	en	heng	heng
chou	ch'ou	eng	eng	hong	hung

Pinyin	Wade-Giles	*Pinyin*	Wade-Giles	*Pinyin*	Wade-Giles
hou	hou	kun	k'un	min	min
hu	hu	kuo	k'uo	ming	ming
hua	hua			miu	miu
huai	huai	la	la	mo	mo
huan	huan	lai	lai	mou	mou
huang	huang	lan	lan	mu	mu
hui	hui	lang	lang		
hun	hun	lao	lao	na	na
huo	huo	le	le	nai	nai
		lei	lei	nan	nan
ji	chi	leng	leng	nang	nang
jia	chia	li	li	nao	nao
jian	chien	lia	lia	ne	ne
jiang	chiang	lian	lien	nei	nei
jiao	chiao	liang	liang	nen	nen
jie	chieh	liao	liao	neng	neng
jin	chin	lie	lieh	ni	ni
jing	ching	lin	lin	nian	nien
jiong	chiung	ling	ling	niang	niang
jiu	chiu	liu	liu	niao	niao
ju	chü	long	lung	nie	nieh
juan	chüan	lou	lou	nin	nin
jue	chüeh	lu	lu	ning	ning
jun	chün	luan	luan	niu	niu
		lun	lun	nong	nung
ka	k'a	luo	lo	nou	nou
kai	k'ai	lü	lü	nu	nu
kan	k'an	lüe	lüeh	nuan	nuan
kang	k'ang			nuo	no
kao	k'ao	ma	ma	nü	nü
ke	k'e, k'o	mai	mai	nüe	nüeh
ken	k'en	man	man		
keng	k'eng	mang	mang	o	o
kong	k'ung	mao	mao	ou	ou
kou	k'ou	mei	mei		
ku	k'u	men	men	pa	p'a
kua	k'ua	meng	meng	pai	p'ai
kuai	k'uai	mi	mi	pan	p'an
kuan	k'uan	mian	mien	pang	p'ang
kuang	k'uang	miao	miao	pao	p'ao
kui	k'uei	mie	mieh	pei	p'ei
				pen	p'en
				peng	p'eng

Pinyin	Wade-Giles	Pinyin	Wade-Giles	Pinyin	Wade-Giles
pi	p'i	san	san	ti	t'i
pian	p'ien	sang	sang	tian	t'ien
piao	p'iao	sao	sao	tiao	t'iao
pie	p'ieh	se	se	tie	t'ieh
pin	p'in	sen	sen	ting	t'ing
ping	p'ing	seng	seng	tong	t'ung
po	p'o	sha	sha	tou	t'ou
pou	p'ou	shai	shai	tu	t'u
pu	p'u	shan	shan	tuan	t'uan
		shang	shang	tui	t'ui
qi	ch'i	shao	shao	tun	t'un
qia	ch'ia	she	she	tuo	t'o
qian	ch'ien	shei	shei		
qiang	ch'iang	shen	shen	wa	wa
qiao	ch'iao	sheng	sheng	wai	wai
qie	ch'ieh	shi	shih	wan	wan
qin	ch'in	shou	shou	wang	wang
qing	ch'ing	shu	shu	wei	wei
qiong	ch'iung	shua	shua	wen	wen
qiu	ch'iu	shuai	shuai	weng	weng
qu	ch'ü	shuan	shuan	wo	wo
quan	ch'üan	shuang	shuang	wu	wu
que	ch'üeh	shui	shui		
qun	ch'ün	shun	shun	xi	hsi
		shuo	shuo	xia	hsia
ran	jan	si	szu	xian	hsien
rang	jang	song	sung	xiang	hsiang
rao	jao	sou	sou	xiao	hsiao
re	je	su	su	xie	hsieh
ren	jen	suan	suan	xin	hsin
reng	jeng	sui	sui	xing	hsing
ri	jih	sun	sun	xiong	hsiung
rong	jung	suo	so	xiu	hsiu
rou	jou			xu	hsü
ru	ju	ta	t'a	xuan	hsüan
ruan	juan	tai	t'ai	xue	hsüeh
rui	jui	tan	t'an	xun	hsün
run	jun	tang	t'ang		
ruo	jo	tao	t'ao	ya	ya
		te	t'e	yan	yen
sa	sa	teng	t'eng	yang	yang
sai	sai				

Pinyin	Wade-Giles	Pinyin	Wade-Giles	Pinyin	Wade-Giles
yao	yao	ze	tse	zhu	chu
ye	yeh	zei	tsei	zhua	chua
yi	i	zen	tsen	zhuai	chuai
yin	yin	zeng	tseng	zhuan	chuan
ying	ying	zha	cha	zhuang	chuang
yong	yung	zhai	chai	zhui	chui
you	yu	zhan	chan	zhun	chun
yu	yü	zhang	chang	zhuo	cho
yuan	yüan	zhao	chao	zi	tzu
yue	yüeh	zhe	che	zong	tsung
yun	yün	zhei	chei	zou	tsou
		zhen	chen	zu	tsu
za	tsa	zheng	cheng	zuan	tsuan
zai	tsai	zhi	chih	zui	tsui
zan	tsan	zhong	chung	zun	tsun
zang	tsang	zhou	chou	zuo	tso
zao	tsao				

ABBREVIATIONS

BMFEA	*Bulletin of the Museum of Far Eastern Antiquities*
BSOAS	*Bulletin of the School of Oriental and African Studies*
FEQ	*Far Eastern Quarterly*
HJAS	*Harvard Journal of Asiatic Studies*
JAS	*Journal of Asian Studies*

PART I. RESEARCH HINTS

1. Guides and Reference Works

1.1   Manuals, bibliographic guides, and syllabi

There are no manuals of historical method for the student of Chinese history in a Western language although the section on China by O.B. Van der Sprenkel in *Handbook of Oriental History,* ed. C.H. Philips (London, 1951, 1963) contains useful brief discussions of Chinese names and titles, place names and geographical terms, calendars and systems of dating and dynasties and rulers (pp. 155-216). H. Franke, *Sinologie* (Bern, 1951) contains much useful information on Chinese historical studies in the form of a guide to the state of the field, but is already badly out of date.

The American Historical Association's Guide to Historical Literature (New York and London, 1961) contains titles of some 600 primary and secondary sources for Chinese history to 1911 (pp. 106-116, 258-298) with brief annotations. The arrangement is by periods and by topics. The selection is marred by the almost total failure to include references to the Japanese secondary literature.

Chun-shu Chang, *Premodern China, A Bibliographical Introduction* (Michigan, 1971) is a useful guide to Western language literature (mainly English) which effectively updates the older *China: a Critical Bibliography,* ed. C.O. Hucker (Tucson, 1962). Both Chang's and Hucker's bibliographies are clearly organized and both cover the whole stretch of Chinese studies or sinology, rather than Chinese history in the narrow sense. It goes without saying that the Western student of Chinese history should be familiar with the secondary literature in these two bibliographies before going on to more advanced studies.

For bibliographies of secondary works in Western languages (rather than bibliographical guides), see section 10.6 below.

L.S. Yang, *Topics in Chinese History* (Cambridge, Mass., 1950) contains a syllabus on Chinese history and bibliographic entries on Chinese sources for the whole range of sinology; although somewhat out of date, this is a carefully selective and well-ordered list of primary sources. J.M. Gentzler, *A Syllabus of Chinese Civilization* (New York, 1968) is an elementary but useful syllabus designed for students with little or no background in Chinese.

Two language guides are worth consulting: G.A. Kennedy, *ZH Guide to Sinology: A Guide to the Encyclopaedia Tz'u-hai* (New Haven, 1953) which deals with many basic language problems liable to be encountered, as does the topically arranged *General Knowledge about Chinese Culture* (**Zhongguo wenhua de changshi** 中國文化的常識 ; Hong Kong, 1966) which was taken from a guide and source book for Chinese first-year university students: Wang Li 王力 , ed., **Gudai hanyu** 古代汉语 (Peking, 1964-1965).

1.1.1 Chinese

Rather than give the many Chinese readers and manuals of historiography which began appearing in large numbers after the pioneering work by Liang Qi-chao 梁啟超 , *Techniques of Research in Chinese History* (**Zhongguo lishi yanijiufa** 中國历史研究法 ; Shanghai, 1922), two more recent Chinese readers are listed as well as two Japanese introductory works. Zhang Shun-hui 張舜徽, *Introduction to Major Sources of Chinese History* (**Zhongguo lishi yaoji jieshao** 中国历史要籍介绍; Wuhan, 1956) was based on lectures prepared for students at the Central China Normal College; for this reason perhaps, the book is written in a simple style and starts with the essentials. Zhang discusses the major sources and also gives advice on how to read them, a topic dealt with in much greater detail in his *Techniques for the Collation and Study of Sources of Chinese History* (**Zhongguo gudai shiji jiaodufa** 中国古代史籍校读法 ; Shanghai, 1962). Another excellent introduction to the major categories of Chinese historical sources (traditionally defined) is Hao Jian-liang 郝建樑 and Ban Shu-ge 班书阁 , *Introduction to Important Sources of Chinese History with Selected Readings* (**Zhongguo lishi yaoji jieshao ji xuandu** 中国历史要籍介绍及选读 ; Shanghai, 1957; reprinted Hong Kong, 1970). The authors have selected readings from pre-Han sources (pp. 1-33) and from the Standard Histories (pp. 34-194) and added informative introductions to each excerpt as well as introducing many other important historical sources and reference tools. Here again the work was compiled for beginners and therefore the introductions are written in an easy style and do not assume any prior knowledge.

1.1.2 Japanese

Both the Japanese works discussed below are somewhat more systematic in their coverage of historical sources and they were both written for students at a more advanced level than the two excellent Chinese introductions discussed above. The first, compiled by the Society for Oriental Studies (Tōhō gakujutsu kyōkai 東方学術協会) is entitled *Introduction to Chinese Historical Studies* (**Chūgoku shigaku nyūmon** 中国史学入門; Kyoto, 1951). The first chapter, by Miyazaki Ichisada 宮崎市定, "General Introduction to 'Introduction to Chinese Historical Studies,'" (Chūgoku shigaku nyūmon sōron 中国史学入門総論) succinctly runs over the major categories of primary sources and essential reference works. It was reprinted in his **Ajiashi kenkyū** (Kyoto, 1963), III, 29-49.

The second Japanese introduction or manual was originally compiled as a bibliographic guide to accompany an encyclopaedia of world history, although it was later issued as a separate book: *Bibliography of Primary and Secondary Sources for Oriental History* (**Tōyō shiryō-shūsei** 東洋史料集成; Tokyo, Heibonsha, 1956). It was also published as vol. 23 of the *Encyclopaedia of World History* (**Sekai rekishi jiten** 世界歴史辞典; Tokyo, Heibonsha, 1951-1956). This Tokyo work is more up to date in its secondary sources than the Kyoto *Introduction,* but it is arranged less as an introduction to historical sciences and more as a bibliography; it does, however, have sections on the major types of primary sources, reference tools etc. (pp. 1-4, 108-109). For annotated guides to the whole range of Chinese primary sources, see sections 3 and 4 below. Bibliographies of Chinese, Japanese, and Western secondary sources are listed below in sections 10.2, 10.4, and 10.6.

Note the following guides to neighboring areas: D. Sinor, *Introduction à l'étude de l'Eurasie centrale* (Wiesbaden, 1964); H. Webb, *Research in Japanese Sources: A Guide* (New York, 1961); R. Marcus, ed., *Korean Studies Guide* (Berkeley, 1964); S.H. Hay and M.H. Chase, *Southeast Asian History: A Bibliographic Guide* (New York, 1962).

1.2   Guides to reference works

The single indispensable work is Teng Ssu-yü and Knight Biggerstaff, *An Annotated Bibliography of Selected Chinese Reference Works,* 3rd rev. ed. (Cambridge, Mass., 1971). It covers Chinese studies in general and arranges Chinese reference works of all periods (with lengthy and meticulous annotations) under the following categories: (1) bibliographies, (2) encyclopaedias, (3) dictionaries, (4) geographical works, (5) biographical works, (6) tables, (7) yearbooks, (8) sinological indexes. The serious student of Chinese history is advised to get a copy of this work at an early stage in his research.

The only book dealing specifically with reference works for the student of Chinese history is unfortunately uncritical in its selection and mainly bibliographic in its annotations: Tseng Ying-ching 曾影靖, *Research Tools for Chinese History: An Annotated Bibliography* (**Zhongguo lishi yanjiu gongju shu xulu** 中國歷史研究工具書敘錄 ; Hong Kong, 1968). There is no index.

Most of the guides to historical studies listed above contain a chapter on reference books.

1.3   Japanese historical encyclopaedias

Japanese historical studies of Asia are characterized by a unique and indispensable feature: the huge historical encyclopaedias and historical dictionaries which contain short articles on all aspects of Asian history, personalities, periods, places, institutions, and events in a readily accessible form. The first of these great encyclopaedias was the *Encyclopaedia of Oriental History* (**Tōyō rekishi daijiten** 東洋歷史大辞典), 9 vols. (Tokyo, Heibonsha, 1937-1939). The entries are arranged phonetically by Japanese syllabary with vol. 9 an index. Many of the articles provide excellent summaries which indicate the level reached by the firmly textually based studies of Chinese history in Japan before the war. This encyclopaedia has largely been superseded (as have most of such prewar works) by a completely new one brought out by the same publishers: *Encyclopaedia of Asian*

History (**Ajia rekishi jiten** アジア歴史辞典), 10 vols. (Tokyo, Heibonsha, 1959-1962). Here again the entries are comprehensive, easy to locate, and extremely convenient to use as a starting point for research, in that references are given to primary and secondary sources at the foot of each article. Entries are arranged phonetically by Japanese syllabary. Vol. 10 contains tables and indexes, including a stroke-order index *and a Wade-Giles index* (not as full as the stroke-order index).

There is a single volume encyclopaedia of Asian history which is handy to use, but of course contains only a fraction of the material to be found in the big multivolume works: *Encyclopaedic Dictionary of Oriental History* (**Tōyōshi jiten** 東洋史辞典), compiled at the Oriental History Seminar, Department of Letters, Kyoto University (Kyoto, 1961). A useful feature of this work is the inclusion of tables and appendices of coins, dates, official posts, etc.

The popularly written and profusely illustrated articles on China in such works as *Outlines of Oriental Cultural History* (**Tōyō bunkashi taikei** 東洋文化史大系), 8 vols. (Tokyo, Seibundō Shinkōsha, 1938) are well worth reading as are the articles on Asia and China in the huge and well illustrated *Encyclopaedia of World History* (**Sekai rekishi jiten** 世界歴史辞典), 24 vols. (Tokyo, Heibonsha, 1951-1956) and in the multivolume *Outlines of World History* (**Sekai rekishi taikei** 世界歴史大系), 17 vols. (Tokyo, Seibundō Shinkōsha, 1958).

Vol. 23 of the **Sekai rekishi jiten** is the indispensable annotated guide to primary and secondary sources, already referred to, *Bibliography of Primary and Secondary Sources for Oriental History* (**Tōyō shiryō shūsei).**

2. Dictionaries

There are many Chinese-Western language dictionaries available including Couvreur, Karlgren, Giles, and Mathews. It is advisable, however, to start using the much fuller Chinese-Chinese and Chinese-Japanese dictionaries as soon as possible. In addition there are a limited number of special-purpose dictionaries (e.g. of Taoist terms or of legal institutions) which can sometimes be essential; their titles are listed at the end of this section. Standard dictionaries of modern spoken and written Chinese are not included.

S. Couvreur, *Dictionnaire classique de la langue chinoise* (1890; 3rd ed. 1911; 1930; Taipei reprint, 1963) has the great advantage of limiting the coverage (one knows what one is getting) and also of giving examples of usage (in this case, of course, of the classical language).

Bernard Karlgren's *Grammata Serica Recensa* (Stockholm, 1957; reprinted Göteborg, 1964) is a summary in dictionary form of the author's extensive researches in the phonology of Zhou and Tang Chinese. It has the great advantage of systematically giving the meanings of each character as found in each of the Zhou texts and corpus of inscriptions used by the author. A further advantage of this work is that the reconstructions of early pronunciations can be very useful to the historian faced with Chinese versions of foreign names in Tang or earlier writings. The dictionary is arranged and indexed by phonetic elements of characters.

H.A. Giles, *Chinese-English Dictionary* (Shanghai, 1892; 2nd ed. 1912; Taipei reprint, 1964) is useful as representing "Mandarin" of the late nineteenth century; although arranged by radicals, the author has adopted the infuriating habit of placing phrases sometimes under their first character and sometimes under their second or later characters.

R.H. Mathews's *A Chinese-English Dictionary Compiled for the China Inland Mission* (Shanghai, 1931), rev. ed: *Mathews's Chinese-English Dictionary* (Cambridge, Mass., 1943) is a much reviled but nevertheless a much-used dictionary; it covers indiscriminately many different styles of Chinese; it is awkwardly arranged and many of the definitions give a spurious sense of accuracy. To date, however, it remains the single most comprehensive Chinese-English dictionary (even though it has not been updated since the 1930s).

Everyone has his own favorite dictionaries; the student should test the ones mentioned here, then shop around and find those which fit his needs best.

In traditional China, character dictionaries *(zidian* 字典 *)* existed in very large numbers. As time went by the compilers of such dictionaries were able to build on the labors of their predecessors and by the Qing dynasty enormous quantities of characters were included. The largest of the traditional character dictionaries was completed in 1716: Zhang Yu-shu 張玉書 and Chen Ting-jing 陳廷敬 , *Kangxi Character Dictionary* (**Kangxi zidian** 康熙字典 ; Shanghai, Commercial Press, 1933, punctuated edition, and many later reprints). It contains 47,035 characters which are arranged by the 214 radicals. The reading is given after each character (taken from standard rhyming dictionaries and from commentaries), followed by the meaning (usually drawn from previous dictionaries and commentaries), followed by examples drawn from early literature (sources cited). The editors seldom ventured their own opinions on readings and definitions. In 1831 a supplement corrected 2,588 mistakes, mainly of citation: Wang Yin-zhi 王引之 , **Zidian kaozheng** 字典考證. This supplement was printed as an appendix to the Commercial Press edition (1933) and also to the Zhonghua Shuju edition (1958).

A modern version of the **Kangxi zidian** was compiled by Xu Yuan-gao 徐元誥 and others: **Zhonghua da zidian** 中華大字典 (Shanghai, Zhonghua Shuju, 1915 and many later editions). It contains slightly more characters (48,000) than the **Kangxi zidian** and is probably easier to use.

The meanings of individual characters are, of course, dealt with in the large modern dictionaries which include both characters and phrases (see below).

Besides character dictionaries *(zidian* 字典 *)*, phrase dictionaries *(cidian* 詞(辭)典*)* were compiled in old China in very large numbers, chiefly for the purpose of aiding literary composition. These are of great service to the historian, for they frequently cite a given phrase as it was used in many different contexts at many different times. The most comprehensive of these encyclopaedic dictionaries quoting phrases, rhymes, synonyms, antonyms, and literary allusions was compiled under imperial auspices and presented in 1711 and (supplement) 1720: Zhang Yu-shu 張玉書 , **Peiwen yunfu**

佩文韻府 (Shanghai, Commercial Press, 1937, and many later reprints). All phrases are arranged under the rhyme of their last character. Each phrase is followed by a very large number of quotations (with sources) showing the different uses of the phrase but no definitions as such are given. Even the largest of modern dictionaries and encyclopaedias frequently do not give nearly as many examples of usages as does the **Peiwen yunfu**; this advantage more than makes up for its awkward arrangement (mitigated by the 4-corner index published with the Commercial Press edition).

Another (and complementary) eighteenth-century literary phrase dictionary is the **Pianzi leibian** 駢字類編 (1726; Taipei reprint, 8 vols., 1963), access to which has been greatly eased by the publication of an index to the first characters of compounds arranged by stroke order: Zhuang Wei-si 莊為斯 (Wallace S. Johnson Jr.), Index to the **Pianzi leibian (Pianzi leibian yinde** 駢字類編引得; Taipei, 1966).

In the opinion of the editors of the *Imperial Catalogue* (q.v.) there was no phrase or allusion which could not be found in either the **Peiwen yunfu** or in the **Pianzi leibian**. Remember that they were referring to *literary* phrases; broad in coverage though these works were, they certainly do not include a host of socioeconomic, Buddhist, and Taoist phrases or terms from other such special vocabularies.

The first of the modern encyclopaedic phrase dictionaries was the **Ciyuan** 辭源, comp. Lu Er-kui 陸爾奎 et al. (Shanghai, Commercial Press, 1915, and numerous later editions). It includes not only phrases from old Chinese texts but also phrases in use among intellectuals at the end of the nineteenth century, proper names, foreign terms, and the like. It does not always cite sources and the definitions and explanations are often in a difficult hybrid style. Still, it contains many phrases not found in the later production of the rival publishing company, the Zhonghua Shuju's **Cihai,** and for this reason, it was not entirely superseded by that work. The **Cihai** was able to benefit from the pioneering efforts of the **Ciyuan** and is probably more widely used than the latter; it was compiled by Shu Xin-cheng 舒新城 and others and first published in the 1930s: **Cihai** 辭海, 2 vols.

(Shanghai, Zhonghua Shuju, 1936-1937; many later editions in one or two
volumes). Its two major advantages over the **Ciyuan** are that its sources are
usually cited more fully and that it is written in a clearer style. There are, however, phrases which are found in the one but not in the other and vice versa.
There is a guide to the **Cihai** by G.A. Kennedy, *ZH Guide to Sinology: A
Guide to the Encyclopaedia Tz'u-hai* (New Haven, 1953).

There is one outstanding comprehensive combined character and phrase
dictionary, compiled under the direction of the Japanese sinologist Morohashi
Tetsuji 諸橋轍次: *The Great Chinese-Japanese Dictionary* (**Dai kanwa
jiten** 大漢和辞典), 13 vols. (Tokyo, 1955-1960; 2nd printing, 1966-
1968; Taipei and Hong Kong editions also available). The advantage of this
massive encyclopaedic dictionary is that the compilers not only went through
all the major historic Chinese dictionaries and encyclopaedias, but also combed
through a very large number of sources of all periods and from all branches of
Chinese literature; moreover, all sources are cited for each entry. The last
volume contains indexes to the body of the work arranged by readings, stroke
order, etc. If the historian were allowed to choose only one dictionary of
Chinese, it would undoubtedly be this one. It should be noted that the **Dai
kanwa jiten** is encyclopaedic; besides characters and phrases it contains people
(not a strong point) and titles of books, famous paintings, etc. (a strong point),
names of places, and much else besides. Turning first to this huge mine of
information on Chinese language and culture is a time-saving habit to cultivate.

There is what amounts to a Chinese version of the **Dai kanwa jiten** which
has obvious advantages for those with no Japanese: Zhang Qi-yun 張其昀,
ed., *The Encyclopaedic Dictionary of the Chinese Language* (**Zhongwen
da cidian** 中文大辭典), 38 vols., 2 vols. index (Taipei, 1962-1968).

A very handy single volume Chinese-Japanese dictionary, covering all
styles of Chinese and with many illustrations of modern usage, is the *Large
Chinese-Japanese Dictionary* (**Chū-nichi dai jiten** 中日大辞典), compiled at Aichi University (Tokyo, 1968). Not the least of the advantages of this
dictionary is that the *pinyin* readings of *all characters and phrases* are given;
entries are arranged alphabetically by *pinyin* readings.

The best Chinese-Chinese dictionary (especially useful for *bai-hua* 白
話 fiction) is the single volume version of the *Dictionary of the National
Language* (**Guoyu cidian** 國語辭典), 4 vols., rev. (Shanghai, 1941, and

many later editions). It is entitled *Dictionary of the Chinese Language* (**Hanyu cidian** 漢語辞典 ; Shanghai, 1953, and many later editions).

The standard pocket dictionary of characters which has gone through numerous revisions in many millions of copies is the **Xinhua zidian** 新华 字典 (Peking, latest rev. ed., 1971). This dictionary is useful for authoritative readings of the some 8,000 characters contained; for readings of characters not included use the **Guoyu cidian.**

For Japanese characters, use A.N. Nelson's *The Modern Reader's Japanese-English Character Dictionary,* rev. ed. (Rutland, 1966), and for Japanese personal and place names use P.G. O'Neill, *Japanese Names* (New York and London, 1972).

There are also various special purpose dictionaries, most of which are discussed in the appropriate section elsewhere; here the titles only are listed. For biographical and geographical dictionaries see sections 17 and 18 respectively.

Administrative and legal terms

E-tu Zen Sun, *Ch'ing Administrative Terms* (see section 20.4).

Hoshi Ayao 星 斌夫 , **Chūgoku shakai keizaishi goi** 中國社會 經濟史語彙 (see section 16.5.2).

Azumagawa Tokuji 東川德治, **Tenkai** 典海 (Tokyo, 1930).

Buddhist terms

Mochizuki Shinkō 望月信亨, **Bukkyō dai jiten** 佛教大辞典 (see section 30.1).

Soothill and Hodous, *A Dictionary of Chinese Buddhist Terms* (see section 30.1).

Demiéville and Takakusu, *Hōbōgirin* (see section 30.1).

Fiction

Lu Dan-an 陸澹安 , *Collected Explanations of Phrases Found in Chinese Novels* (**Xiaoshuo ciyu huishi** 小说词语汇释 ; Shanghai, 1964; Hong Kong reprint, 1968).

History

Zhou Mu-zhai 周木齋 , *Small Dictionary of Chinese History* (**Zhongguo lishi xiao cidian** 中國歷史小辭典 ; Shanghai, 1934; Hong Kong, 1963; Taipei, 1968).

Mythology and popular religion

    E.T.C. Werner, *A Dictionary of Chinese Mythology* (Shanghai, 1932; Taipei, 1961).

Socioeconomic history

    See under Administrative and legal terms.

Taoist terms

    Dai Yuan-chang 戴源長, **Xianxue cidian** 仙學辭典 (Taipei, 1962).

Weights and measures

    Although they are not dictionaries, the following studies of the different units of weight and measurement are essential for understanding the meaning of these terms in different periods (and in different places) since they changed over time:

        Wu Cheng-lo 吳承洛, *A History of Chinese Weights and Measures* (**Zhongguo duliangheng shi** 中國度量衡史; 1937; 2nd ed., Shanghai, 1957).

        Yang Kuan 楊寬, *Historical Study of the Chinese Foot Measure* (**Zhongguo lidai chidu kao** 中國歷代尺度考; 1938; reprinted Shanghai, 1955, 1957).

        Zeng Wu-xiu 曾武秀, "Outline of the Chinese Foot Measure in Different Periods" (Zhongguo lidai chidu gaishu 中国历代尺度概述), **Lishi yanjiu** (1964), 3: 162-183.

        See also in general L.S. Yang, "Numbers and Units in Chinese Economic History," in his *Studies in Chinese Institutional History* (Cambridge, Mass., 1963), pp. 75-84.

3. How to Find Out What Sources Are Available from a Given Period

    A great deal can be learned about what primary sources are available on a given problem or period by choosing an outstanding secondary work and observing what sources the author has used. Although this is a good habit to cultivate, it still has its obvious drawbacks—for the student may well be accepting unknowingly the author's limitations (or predilections for one type of source over another) and thus hindering his search for primary sources.

Before starting to look for primary sources, it is clearly essential to have developed some understanding of the types of historical writing produced in old China (see sections 14-17) as well as some feel for the many different types of document discussed in sections 19-24, and all the many other technical, literary, or religious genres which have been preserved (sections 25-30). It is also particulary useful to know how a certain type of source would have been classified by traditional historians. They devoted a major effort to bibliography and classification; and knowing where they would have placed a particular type of source, or a work dealing with a specific subject, can often help you locate that source in catalogues of old Chinese books, which still follow the old classification schema (see section 12.2 for a discussion of classification and bibliography).

The best rapid way of finding out what sources are extant from a given period is to consult the *Bibliography of Primary and Secondary Sources for Oriental History* (**Tōyō shiryō shūsei** 東洋史料集成;Tokyo, Heibonsha, 1956), also published as vol. 23 of the *Encyclopedia of World History* (**Sekai rekishi jiten** 世界歷史辭典), 24 vols. (Tokyo, Heibonsha, 1950-1956). Primary sources for each period (archaeological, epigraphical, and documentary, as well as traditional-historical) are listed and briefly discussed. In addition there is a bibliographical essay on the secondary sources for each period. A title index for primary sources and a somewhat unsatisfactory author index for secondary sources makes this work even more convenient to use. It supersedes all previous general introductions to the primary sources of Chinese history, not only because of the broadness of its coverage, but also for the simple reason that it is arranged by period rather than by the more usual arrangement by titles (according to reading or broad bibliographic categories) of earlier works. Once you have found the sources for a given period, however, you will often find fuller descriptions of their contents in some of these earlier works (both Chinese and Japanese), the most important of which are discussed in the next section.

There are a number of guides to primary sources of individual periods, the most comprehensive of which are W. Franke, *An Introduction to the Sources of Ming History* (Kuala Lumpur and Singapore, 1968), and Ma Xian-xing 馬先醒, *Comprehensive Catalogue of Primary and Secondary*

Sources for Han History (**Hanshi cailiao yu Hanshi lunzhu zonghe mulu**
漢史材料與漢史論著綜合目錄 ; Taipei, 1970). Unlike Ma's
work, Franke's has useful section introductions as well as a general introduction; those interested in Ming history should turn to Franke.

For certain purposes it may be necessary to find out in greater detail
than is possible from consulting **Tōyō shiryō shūsei** what printed sources
were in circulation at a given time and who were their authors. This can be
done by looking through the most extensive bibliographies of primary
sources, the *Monographs on Dynastic Bibliography* in the Standard Histories
and their supplements (titles and indexes to these works are given in section
16.5.1), as well as other official and private catalogues when these are
available. A very convenient guide to the Dynastic Bibliographies and also to
other types of bibliography and catalogue is Nagasawa Kikuya 長澤規矩
也 , *Annotated Bibliography of Chinese Books: pt. 1, Library Catalogues
and Bibliographies* (**Shina shoseki kaidai, shomoku shoshi no bu** 支那書籍
解題書目書誌之部 ; Tokyo, 1940, 1952). It introduces 450 library
catalogues under four headings: (1) catalogues in the Standard Histories,
pp. 1-51, (2) catalogues of official collections, pp. 52-92, (3) catalogues of
modern Chinese libraries, pp. 93-151, and (4) catalogues of private collections,
pp. 152-233. There is an index at the front of titles arranged by categories
and also by Japanese syllabary. Containing references to many more hundreds
of library catalogues and bibliographies of all periods than in Nagasawa's
work is Liang Zi-han 梁子涵 , *A Bibliography of Chinese Library
Catalogues* (**Zhongguo lidai shumu zonglu** 中國歷代書目總錄;
Taipei, 1953). Liang's work is valuable as the most comprehensive list of
Chinese bibliographies yet available and it supersedes all such previous works;
it is not, however, an annotated bibliography, having only section prefaces,
and for this reason Nagasawa's book retains its value as an introduction to the
subject. See also Teng and Biggerstaff, pp. 1-82.

Dynastic Bibliographies and the catalogues of library owners, etc., do not
contain references to the very important new types of documentary sources
discovered in the twentieth century such as the oracle bones, the Han
wooden slips, the Dunhuang mss., the Ming-Qing archives, and the discoveries
of modern archaeology (see sections 13 and 24). The **Tōyō shiryō shūsei**
does, however, contain such references.

4. How to Find Rapidly the Contents of Primary Sources

There are several comprehensive works summarizing the contents and editions of printed sources of all periods which can be readily consulted. The only one in English was the pioneering and extremely unreliable work by A. Wylie, *Notes on Chinese Literature* (Shanghai, 1867; 2nd ed., Shanghai, 1922; reprinted New York, 1964), which follows the arrangement of the *Imperial Catalogue (Annotated Catalogue of the Imperial Library*–see below) for the entries under the four divisions of Classics, History, Philosophers, and Belles-Lettres (see section 12.2 for a list of the subdivisions of History and Philosophers).

Wylie's notes themselves were also based on those in the *Imperial Catalogue,* which is by far the largest work of this type to be compiled in traditional China: Ji Yun 紀昀, *Annotated Catalogue of the Imperial Library* (**Siku quanshu zongmu tiyao** 四庫全書總目提要), completed 1782; Dadong Shuju ed., 44 *ce* in 10 vols. (Shanghai, 1926; 1930; Taipei, 1970); Commercial Press punctuated ed., 4 vols. (Shanghai, 1933). This work grew out of the foundation of a definitive Imperial Library (and the incidental weeding out of anti-Manchu literature) during the reign of the Qianlong emperor; starting in 1771, more than 350 scholars worked on the reviewing and annotation of over 10,000 books and manuscripts collected from all over the empire. Of these the texts of some 3,450 works were copied into what was to become the Imperial Library or the "Complete library in four branches of literature" (**Siku quanshu** 四庫全書). The bibliographic annotations and comments (*tiyao* 提要) on the 3,450 works included (*cunshu* 存書), together with the slightly less full notes on the 6,800 works not included (*cunmu* 存目), were compiled into the enormous *Annotated Catalogue of the Imperial Library.* It is the most important of all Chinese annotated catalogues, (1) because of the high quality of the annotations which give information on the nature and style of the work, its table of contents in whole or in part, a brief biographical sketch of the author (on first appearance), and an evaluation of the work, and (2) because it is by far the most comprehensive. There are several indexes to the works in the *Imperial Catalogue,* the most convenient being the *Index to the Catalogue of the Imperial Library and to the Catalogue of Books not Included* (**Siku** quanshu zongmu ji weishou shumu yinde 四庫全書總目及未收書目引得), H-Y Index 7, 2 vols. (Peking, 1932, Taipei, 1966). Although this index is based on the Dadong Shuju (1930) edition, it contains conversion tables making possible its use with other editions. Both authors and titles are indexed. The preface to this index, by the editor-in-chief of the Harvard—Yenching Index series, William Hung, contains a discussion of the editing and compilation of the *Imperial Catalogue* and has been translated into English: W. Hung (Hong Ye 洪業), "Preface to an Index to *Ssu-k'u ch'uan-shu tsung-mu* and *Wei-shou shu-mu,*" *HJAS* 4:47-58 (1939). See also Teng and Biggerstaff, pp. 19-22.

An important supplementary work to the *Imperial Catalogue* is Hu Yu-jin 胡玉縉 and Wang Xin-fu 王欣夫, *Supplement and Corrections to the Imperial Catalogue* (**Siku quanshu zongmu tiyao buzheng** 四庫全书总目提要补正), 2 vols. (Peking, 1964).

Another monumental work correcting mistakes is Yu Jia-xi 余嘉錫, *Critical Studies on the Annotations to the Imperial Catalogue* (**Siku tiyao bianzheng** 四庫提要辨证 ; Peking, 1958). The present edition supersedes the less complete edition of 1937.

Note also Ji Yun's convenient *Simplified Annotated Catalogue of the Imperial Library* (**Siku quanshu jianming mulu** 四庫全书简明目录), completed in 1782, 2 vols. (Shanghai, 1957), which only includes brief summaries of the annotations on the 3,450 works copied into the collection.

In order to find information on different editions of the 3,450 works in the *Simplified Catalogue* (including information on later editions), you should use the excellent bibliographic notes largely prepared by the nineteenth-century scholar Shao Yi-chen 邵懿辰 and posthumously published in 1911 under the title *Marginal Notes to the Simplified Annotated Catalogue of the Imperial Library* (**Zengding siku quanshu jianming mulu biaozhu** 增订四库全书简明目录标注), rev. and enlarged ed. (Shanghai, 1959). This edition has a four-corner and stroke-order index.

Probably easier to handle but ultimately based on the *Imperial Catalogue* are the large number of Japanese introductions to Chinese sources, such as Katsura Isoo (Koson)桂五郎 (湖村), *Annotated Bibliography of*

Chinese Works (**Kanseki kaidai** 漢籍解題), 1st ed. (Tokyo, 1905, and many later editions). Of more use are the similar works compiled by historians, of which the best prewar example was the *Annotated Bibliography of Japanese, Oriental, and Occidental History,* ed. Endō Motoo 遠藤 元男 et al. (**Kokushi Tōyōshi Seiyōshi shiseki kaidai** 国史東洋史西洋史史籍解題 ; Tokyo, Heibonsha, 1936).

It is worth remembering that the **Dai kanwa jiten** includes a very large number of authors and book titles, as do also the Japanese historical encyclopaedias (fewer titles but longer descriptions; see section 2 on **Dai kanwa jiten** and section 1.3 on the encyclopaedias).

Note: The date of a text is usually found at the end of the preface (*xu* 序 , *xu* 敍) or at the end of the colophon (*ba* 跋).

5. Where to Find Primary Sources

During the past 120 years Chinese printed books and manuscripts were dispersed or destroyed on a massive scale; famous Qing collections were burnt, requisitioned, or sold. Central, provincial, and district archives were looted or junked while the great manuscript finds at Dunhuang and elsewhere were acquired by international expeditions. Many Japanese and Western individuals and institutes built up their collections during these chaotic years. The last major movement of books took place in late 1948 and early 1949 when the Kuomintang shipped to Taipei (from the National Central Library, the Institute of History and Philology of Academia Sinica, the National Palace Museum, the National Central Museum, and the archives of the Ministry of Foreign Affairs) huge numbers of rare books plus about 10 per cent of the Qing central archives.

In order to find out if a source is extant and if so, in what library, the student should look through the published library catalogues of the major collections of Chinese books in China, Japan, and the West. (A very real problem encountered throughout Chinese history is the use of more than one title for the same book, then as now, a common sales technique among publishers. If the student has doubts about a title he should check with Du Xin-fu's 杜信孚 thorough *Index of Books with Different Titles* (**Tongshu yiming tongjian** 同書異名通檢; Hong Kong, 1963), in which 4,000 works with their alternative titles are arranged by stroke order.)

5.1 Library catalogues

5.1.1 China

There are many fine libraries in China. Only the four largest are mentioned here:

(a) The Peking Library (Beijing tushuguan 北京图书馆 , formerly the National Library of Peiping, Guoli Beiping tushuguan 國立北平圖書館) is by far the largest with a collection of four and a half million books. See Li Xi-mi 李希泌 and Wang Shu-wei 王树伟, *A Brief Account of the Peking Library* (**Beijing tushuguan** 北京图书馆 ; Peking, 1957). The library possesses probably the finest collection of Chinese rare editions in the world. See *Catalogue of Rare Editions in the Peking Library* (**Beijing tushuguan shanben shumu** 北京图书馆善本书目), 9 vols. (Peking, 1959), which lists 11,000 titles of rare editions collected since 1949. "Rare editions" (*shanben* 善本) usually refers to Song, Yuan, and Ming editions. Note however that the old *Catalogue of Rare Books in the National Library of Peiping* (**Guoli Beiping tushuguan shanben shumu yibian** 國立北平圖書館善本書目乙編), 2 *ce* (Peking, 1935-1937) is devoted exclusively to rare Qing works.

(b) The second largest library in China is the Shanghai Library (Shanghai tushuguan 上海图书馆) with a collection of three and a half million books. (Catalogue of rare editions: **Shanghai tushuguan shanben shumu** 上海图书馆善本书目 ; Shanghai, 1957.) Other important collections in Shanghai are the Shanghai Newspapers and Periodicals Library (Shanghai baokan tushuguan 上海报刊图书馆) and the Shanghai Library of Historical Documents (Shanghai-shi lishi wenxian tushuguan 上海市历史文献图书馆).

(c) The Nanking Library (Nanjing tushuguan 南京图书馆) has a collection of two and a half million volumes including the old Kiangsu Provincial Sinological Library (Jiangsu shengli guoxue tushuguan 江蘇

省立國學圖書館), which published one of the few general catalogues of a major Chinese collection: **Jiangsu shengli guoxue tushuguan zongmu** 江蘇省立國學圖書館總目 , 24 *ce* plus *bubian,* 3 *ce* (Nanking, 1933-1935; 1937; reprinted Taipei, 15 vols., 1970).

(d)   The library of the Academy of Sciences (which is divided among the various institutes of the Academy) contains altogether two and a half million volumes.

There are many other important libraries in China, mainly in the older universities and in some of the provincial capitals. Since many of these were largely built up in the last fifty years, Liang Zi-han's 梁子涵 *A Bibliography of Chinese Library Catalogues,* although compiled in 1953, is still useful as a guide to catalogues of Chinese collections (**Zhongguo lidai shumu zonglu** 中國歷代書目總錄 , Taipei, 1953). For some 2,300 post-1949 catalogues, use *Check List of Library Catalogues* (**Quanguo tushuguan shumu leibian** 全国图书馆书目类编 ; Peking, 1958).

Note the following union catalogues for Chinese libraries: *Combined Catalogues of Chinese Collectanea in 41 Chinese Libraries* (**Zhongguo congshu zonglu** 中国丛书总录), 3 vols. (Shanghai, 1959-1962); Zhu Shi-jia 朱士嘉 , comp., *Enlarged Comprehensive Catalogue of Chinese Local Gazetteers in 41 Libraries* (**Zhongguo difangzhi zonglu, zengding** 中国地方志总录增订 ; Shanghai, 1958; Tokyo, 1968); *Union Catalogue of 19,115 Periodicals in 50 Chinese Libraries* (**Quanguo Zhongwen Qikan lianhe mulu** 全国中文期刊联合目录 ; Peking, 1961).

5.1.2   Taiwan

(a)   National Central Library (Guoli zhongyang tushuguan 國立中央圖書館). Includes portions of the holdings of the former National Central Library of Nanking (founded 1928); the rare editions sent to the U.S.A. from the former National Library of Peiping and the rare edition collection of the former Northeastern University. Catalogue of about 140,000 *ce* of rare editions: **Guoli zhongyang tushuguan shanben shumu** 國立中央圖書館善本書目 , 4 vols., rev. ed. (Taipei, 1967).

(b)   Library of the National Palace Museum (Guoli gugong bowuyuan 國立故宮博物院). Includes 150,000 *ce* of rare editions plus important archival holdings representing between 5 and 10 per cent of the Qing palace records and Grand Council archives. Catalogue of rare editions:

Guoli gugong bowuyaun shanben shumu 國立故宮博物院善本書目 (Taipei, 1968).

(c) Various libraries attached to the Academia Sinica (Nangang, Taipei). The Fu Si-nian Library 傅斯年圖書館 (the former Library of the Institute of History and Philology). Contains important collections of oracle bones; Ming-Qing state papers; Han wooden slips and also the folk songs collected by the Institute in the thirties. Rare edition catalogue: **Guoli zhongyang yanjiu yuan lishi yuyan yanjiusuo shanben shumu** 國立中央研究院歷史語言研究所善本書目 (Taipei, 1968).

Library of the Institute of Modern History. Contains important late Qing archive holdings including the files of the *zongli yamen* and the *waiwubu*.

Note the following union catalogues for Taiwan collections: Wang Bao-xian 王寶先 , comp., "Catalogue of collectanea in Taiwan libraries" (Taiwan ge tushuguan xiancun congshu mulu 臺灣各圖書館現存叢書目錄), **Dalu zazhi,** vol. 28, no. 1; vol. 29, no. 3 (1964); *Union Catalogue of Local Gazetteers in Taiwan Public Collections* (**Taiwan gongcang fangzhi lianhe mulu** 臺灣公藏方志聯合目錄; Taipei, 1960); Chang Pi-de 昌彼得, comp., *Annotated Bibliography of Genealogies in Taiwan Public Collections* (**Taiwan gongcang zupu jieti** 臺灣公藏族譜解題; Taipei, 1969).

5.1.3 Japan

A handy guide to Japanese libraries (which includes addresses, telephone numbers, hours of opening, etc.) is Okada Narō 岡田溫 et al., *A Guide to Japanese Special Collections* (**Nihon bunko meguri** 日本文庫めぐり ; Tokyo, 1964).

For a very full bibliography of some 2,600 published catalogues of Chinese books in Japan, see *Collections of Chinese Books in Japan, a Catalogue of Catalogues of Chinese Books in Public and Private Collections* (**Kanseki kankei mokuroku shūsei. Nihon ni okeru kanseki no shūshū** 漢籍関係目錄集成　日本における漢籍の蒐集 ; Toyo Bunko, Tokyo, 1961).

Tokyo

(a) *Toyo Bunko* 東洋文庫 (Oriental Library)

The Toyo Bunko contains the largest collection of old Chinese books in Japan and also functions as a focus of research on Chinese history.

There is unfortunately no comprehensive published catalogue of the huge holdings of Chinese books (and western books on China) in the Toyo Bunko, although catalogues of sections of the holdings have been published in the series **Tōyō Bunko toshobu sho mokuroku** 東洋文庫圖書部書目録 , vols. 1-38 (1920-1959).

(b) *(Tōkyō daigaku) Tōyō bunka kenkyūjo* (東京大学) 東洋文化研究所 (Institute for Oriental Culture, Tokyo University). The Chinese section has an excellent collection of books with important holdings in socioeconomic history. An up-to-date comprehensive catalogue has been prepared and is about to be published. Meanwhile, note the catalogue of the Institute's Ōki Bunko (rich in Qing legal, economic, and administrative history): **Tōkyō daigaku tōyō bunka kenkyūjo zō, Ōki bunko bunrui mokuroku** 東京大学東洋文化研究所蔵大木文庫分類目録 (Tokyo, 1961). The Institute also possesses the private library of the late Niida Noboru.

Other important libraries in Tokyo (in alphabetical order)

(c) Kunaichō Shoryōbu 宮内庁書陵部 (Imperial Household Library). Published catalogue: **Wa-Kan tosho bunrui mokuroku** 和漢図書分類目録, 2 vols., plus index; plus continuation (1951; 1958; 1968).

(d) Naikaku Bunko 内閣文庫 (Cabinet Library). Published catalogue of Chinese books: **Naikaku bunko kanseki bunrui mokuroku** 内閣文庫漢籍分類目録 (Tokyo, 1956; rev. ed. 1971).

(e) National Diet Library (Kokuritsu kokkai toshokan 国立国家図書館). Work has begun here on a union catalogue of Chinese books in Japan. There is no published catalogue of the Chinese books in the Diet Library but there is a cumulative catalogue.

(f) Seikadō Bunko 靜嘉堂文庫 . Published catalogue of Chinese books: **Seikadō bunko kanseki bunrui mokuroku** 靜嘉堂

文庫漢籍分類目録 (Tokyo, 1930).

(g) Sonkeikaku Bunko 尊經閣文庫 . Published catalogue: **Sonkeikaku bunko kanseki bunrui mokuroku** 尊經閣文庫漢籍 分類目録 (Tokyo, 1934, 1935).

Kyoto

(a) *(Kyōto Daigaku) Jimbun kagaku kenkyūjo* (京都大学) 人文科学研究所 (Research Institute for Humanistic Studies, Kyoto University). The Chinese section contains the major sinological library in the Kansai region. Excellent published catalogue: **Kyoto daigaku jimbun kagaku kenkyūjo kanseki bunrui mokuroku** 京都大学人文 科学研究所漢籍分類目録 , 2 vols. (Kyoto, 1964-1965).

(b) *Tenri University* 天理大学. Situated in Tenri (close to Kyoto), it has an excellent Chinese collection and a distinguished series of published catalogues.

(c) *Hōsa Bunko* 蓬左文庫 . Now housed as a unit in the Nagoya city library. Published catalogue:**Hōsa bunko kanseki mokuroku** 蓬左文 庫漢籍目録 (Nagoya, 1955).

Note the following union catalogues of holdings of Chinese works in important Japanese libraries:

(a) *Catalogue of Extant Ming Gazetteers in Japan* (**Nihon genzon Mindai chihōshi mokuroku** 日本現存明代地方志目録), ed. Yamane Yukio 山根幸夫 (Tokyo, 1971). Holdings of 12 libraries.

(b) *Catalogue of Collected Works of Ming Writers Extant in Japan* (**Nihon genzon Minjin bunshū mokuroku** 日本現存明人文集 目録), ed. Yamane Yukio and Ogawa Takashi 小川尚 (1966). Holdings of 10 libraries. See the similar catalogue for the Yuan (p. 172).

(c) *Catalogue of Whereabouts of Chinese Collectanea* (**Kanseki sōsho shozai mokuroku** 漢籍叢書所在目録; Tokyo, 1966). Holdings of 7 libraries.

(d) *Union Catalogue of Chinese Local Gazetteers in 14 Major Libraries and Research Institutes in Japan* (**Chūgoku chihōshi sōgo mokuroku** 中国 地方志総合目録 ; Tokyo, 1969). Compiled by staff at the National Diet Library, it supersedes all previous catalogues of gazetteers in Japanese libraries. Holdings of 14 libraries.

(e)　*A Union List of Microfilms of Japanese, Chinese, Korean, Manchu, Mongolian, Vietnamese, and Tibetan Books and Manuscripts Preserved in Eight Libraries* (**Tokushu bunko shozō maikurofurirumu rengō mokuroku** 特殊文庫所蔵マイクロフィルム連合目録 ; Tokyo, 1967).

(f)　*Catalogue of Periodicals in Japanese, Chinese, Korean, etc.* (**Nihon-bun Chūgoku-bun Chōsen-bun tō chikuji kankōbutsu mokuroku** 日本文中国文朝鮮文等逐次刊行物目録; Tokyo, 1963). Holdings of 3 libraries.

(g)　*Union Catalogue of Holdings of Chinese Newspapers and Periodicals in Twenty-three Important Japanese Collections* (**Nihon shuyō kenkyū kikan toshokan shozō Chūgokubun shinbun zasshi sōgō mokuroku** 日本主要研究機関図書館所蔵中国文新聞雑誌総合目録 ; Tokyo, 1959).

5.1.4　Europe, America, and the Soviet Union

There are very few up-to-date catalogues of Chinese collections in Europe. Many of the collections are described and the catalogues listed in Y. Hervouet,"Les Bibliothèques d'Europe Occidentale," in *Mélanges publiés par l'École des Hautes Études Chinoises* (Paris, 1957), I, 451-511.

The library cards of the School of Oriental and African Studies, University of London, have been published: *School of Oriental and African Studies, University of London, Library Catalogue*, 28 vols. (Boston, 1963). Same title, *First Supplement*, 1968.

For a full list of American Chinese collections see Tsien Tsuen-hsuin, "East Asian Library Resources in America: A New Survey," *Association for Asian Studies Newsletter* 16.3:1-11 (1971). The six largest collections (in alphabetical order) are:

(a)　Berkeley, published catalogue of library cards: *East Asiatic Library, University of California, Berkeley, Author-Title Catalogue*, 13 vols., *Subject Catalogue*, 5 vols. (Boston, 1968).

(b)　Chicago, University of Chicago.

(c)　Columbia University.

(d)   Harvard; Harvard-Yenching Institute (the leading research library for Chinese history in the U.S.). Published catalogue: K.M. Ch'iu, *A Classified Catalogue of Chinese Books in the Chinese - Japanese Library of the Harvard-Yenching Institute of Harvard University* (1938-1940), now out of date.

(e)   Princeton, Gest Oriental Library.

(f)   Library of Congress, Washington, D.C. Although by far the largest collection of Chinese and Japanese books in the U.S., it is not open stack and not research-oriented. Has cards for the Union Catalogue of Chinese books in the U.S. (which card catalogue it circulates to the University libraries). Published catalogue of rare editions in the Chinese collection: Wang Chung-min, *A Descriptive Catalogue of Rare Chinese Books in the Library of Congress,* 2 vols. (Washington, D.C., 1957). Published catalogue of Local Gazetteers (largest collection in the U.S.): Chu Shih-chia, *A Catalogue of Chinese Local Histories in the Library of Congress* (Washington, D.C., 1942).

The main libraries in the U.S.S.R. are the Lenin State Library (Moscow), the Oriental collections of the Institute of the Peoples of Asia (under Academy of Sciences), Leningrad branch, and the collection of the Sinological Institute, Leningrad University.

Union catalogues of Chinese books and periodicals in the Soviet Union are being prepared.

5.2   Collectanea

After looking through the library catalogues the *congshu* catalogues should be checked. (Chinese works were often preserved in collectanea [*congshu* 叢書], which were collections of independent works published together to prevent their loss or gain them wider circulation.) There are altogether at least 2,800 such collections containing approximately 70,000 individual works. Fortunately there is a very comprehensive and conveniently arranged catalogue of collectanea in 41 major Chinese libraries, compiled at the Shanghai Municipal Library: *Combined Catalogues of Chinese Collectanea*

(**Zhongguo congshu zonglu** 中国业书综录), 3 vols. (Peking, 1959-1962). At an early stage of tracing a work this catalogue should be consulted. Vol. 1 arranges 2,797 collectanea in the four traditional bibliographic categories (*sibu* 四部 -- see section 12.2) with the individual works contained in each collectanea listed. Vol. 2 is arranged by the 70,000 individual works in each collectanea placed in the four categories and further divided into sub-categories. Vol. 3 is an author-title index to vol. 2. The main types of *congshu* (subject, period, region, etc.) are given in the table of contents. For tracing *congshu* in Japan the *Catalogue of Whereabouts of Chinese Collectanea* (**Kanseki sōsho shozai mokuroku** 漢籍叢書所在目録 ; Tokyo, 1966) should be used.

During the 1920s and 1930s many original sources and historical works were collected together and published in huge collectanea. The most important of these were:

(a) **Sibu congkan** 四部叢刊 (3 series containing 468 titles in 3,122 *ce*; Shanghai, Commercial Press, 1919-1937). Many editions photolitho-graphically produced and therefore cutting out type-setting errors found in (b) and (c). The *baina ben* 百衲本 edition of the Standard Histories (see 16.2) was included as a supplement to the series. See K. Lo, *A Guide to the Ssu-pu Ts'ung-k'an* (Kansas, 1965) for a list of the titles in the series,

(b) **Sibu beiyao** 四部備要 (351 titles in 2,500 *ce;* Shanghai, Zhonghua Shuju, 1927-1937; annotated catalogue, 1936; edition in 100 Western-style vols., 1937; Taipei reprint, 1966). Movable type: many type-setting errors as a result. Index available: **Sibu beiyao suoyin** 四部備要索引 (Shanghai, 1937; Taipei, 1971).

(c) **Congshu jicheng** 叢書集成 (4,100 titles in 4,100 *ce* taken from 100 previous *congshu;* Shanghi, Commercial Press, 1935-1939). Mainly in movable type: many type-setting errors as a result. Reprinted from wood-block editions (Taipei, 1965-   ).

(d) **Guoxue jiben congshu** 國學基本叢書 (400 titles; Shanghai, Commercial Press, 1929-1941; 100 titles reprinted, Shanghai during the 1950s). Movable type and punctuated editions of titles considered vital for the study of Chinese culture. (English title: *Basic Sinological Series.*) Despite the type-setting errors in (b) and (c), works in these series are handy to use and were usually taken from good editions. When possible the student should use and quote from works in a major collectanea series, since these are readily accessible.

In order to locate the new types of documentary source discussed in sections 13 and 24, consult the catalogues listed in those sections.

6. How to Locate Places

See section 18.9; also How to find Local Gazetteers (18.6).

7. How to Find Biographical Materials

See section 17.5.

8. How to Convert Dates

There are two main sets of problems concerning dates in Chinese texts. The first concerns the nature and verification of the traditional Chinese lunar and solar calendars and dating systems in use in different periods. This is a complex technical subject, particularly for the pre-Qin period and it belongs properly to the history of Chinese calendrical sciences. The second set of problems, which is the one considered here, concerns the conversion of dates recorded in the different Chinese calendars to the Julian (for pre-1582 dates) and Gregorian calendars (for post-1582 dates).

8.1   Years

Finding the equivalent year in the Julian or Gregorian calendar for years recorded in the most common formula of "number of years since date of accession" of given emperor (or before the Ming, "number of years since the adoption of era name," *nianhao* 年號) requires no special table, because practically all dictionaries contain lists of dynasties, names of emperors, accession dates, and era names. Thus, for example, a glance at such a list will show that Yuan Zhongtong *ernian* 元中統二年 refers to the second year since the adoption of the era name Zhongtong by the Yuan emperoro Shizu (Khubilai khan), i.e. 1261. After the beginning of the Ming only one era name was used for the whole reign. As a result era names become synonymous with reign names. Thus Qing Yongzheng *wunian* 清雍正五年 refers to the fifth year after the adoption of the reign name Yongzheng or in other words the fifth year after the accession of the Yongzheng emperor, i.e. 1727. Note that the year of accession (in this case 1723) counts as the first year.

On "era names" (*nianhao* 年號) see A. F. Wright and E. Fagan, "Era Names and Zeitgeist," *Études Asiatiques* 5:113-121 (1951) and M.C. Wright, "What's in a Reign Name? The Uses of Historical Philology," *JAS* 18.1:103-106 (1958).

If a year is recorded using the equally common method of cyclical characters (*jiazi* 甲子 or *ganzhi* 干支), the dynasty is usually known from the context and the reign name (or era name) is also usually given. No special tables are needed, therefore. Most dictionaries list the cyclical characters in an appendix. Note that events are often referred to by their cyclical dates–e.g. the Xinhai *geming* 辛亥革命, i.e. the 1911 Revolution.

Tables giving the equivalent year in the Julian or Gregorian calendar are especially convenient when dealing with dates in obscure and usurping dynasties of adjacent areas and countries. The most convenient of the many such tables (because it is published as a pocket-sized book) is the *Chronological Table of Oriental History,* comp. Fujishima Tatsurō 藤島達朗 and Nogami Shunjo 野上俊靜 (**Tōhō nempyō** 東方年表 ; Kyoto, 1955 and many later reprints). This table gives (reading across the page)

Gregorian calendar year; cyclical characters for that year; Chinese dynasty, emperor, era name, and year since its adoption (or year since accession), and similar data for the dynasties ruling in the area of modern Korea and Japan. There are twenty rows to a page, each row being one year. Dates covered are 660 B.C. to A.D. 1980. There is an index of era names (reign names) arranged by Japanese readings and an index of emperors arranged chronologically by country.

Especially useful for its clear tables of pre-Qin chronology is *Tables of Chinese History,* comp. Wan Guo-ding 萬国鼎 and checked by Chen Meng-jia 陳梦家 and Wan Si-nian 萬斯年 (**Zhongguo lishi jinian biao** 中国历史纪年表 ; Shanghai, 1954).

Much more comprehensive in its coverage of usurping dynasties, dynasties of adjacent countries, etc. is Mathias Chang, *Synchronismes Chinois: Chronologie complète et concordance avec l'ère chrétienne de toutes les dates concernant l'histoire de l'Extrême Orient (Chine, Japon, Corée, Annam, Mongolie, etc.) (2375 av. J.-C. à 1904 apr. J.-C.), Variétés Sinologiques* no. 24 (Shanghai, 1905; Taipei reprint, 1967). This is a French version of Zhang Huang 張璜 , *Combined Chronological Table of European and Asian Dates* (**Ou Ya jiyuan hebiao** 歐亞紀元合表 ; Shanghai, 1904; reprinted Tokyo, 1968) and is the most commonly used comprehensive concordance of dynastic dates and Gregorian years.

Two works cover the special problems of dynasties, exact dates of accession, and adoption of era names, etc. in greater detail than Zhang: A.C. Moule, *The Rulers of China, 221 B.C. - A.D. 1949* (New York, 1957) and Rong Meng-yuan 荣孟源 , *Table of Chinese History* (**Zhongguo lishi jinian** 中国历史纪年 ; Peking, 1956), Pt. 1, "Tabulated Notes on the Foundation Year of Dynasties and Reigns" (Lidai jianyuan pu 历代建元谱), pp. 1-118.

8.2   Months

Turning now to the conversion of months, which are numbered one to twelve in the lunar calendar, the business of finding the Julian or Gregorian equivalent is a little more complex, for lunar months span different segments of the solar calendar each year. The third lunar month of 1300, for example (Yuan Dade *sinian sanyue* 元大德四年三月), covered the dates March 23 to April 20, but in the following year the third lunar month (Yuan Dade *wunian sanyue* 元大德五年三月) was equivalent to the dates April 10 to May 9. In addition, allowance has to be made for intercalary lunar months. Fortunately reliable conversion tables exist giving Gregorian dates of the lunar months (and also for the 24 traditional Chinese solar divisions of the year, *jieqi* 節氣) for every year throughout Chinese history. Most complete of this kind of concordance and also the easiest to use is Dong Zuo-bin 董作賓, *Chronological Tables of Chinese History* (**Zhongguo nianli zongpu** 中國年曆總譜), 2 vols. (Hong Kong, 1960). Vol. 1 contains very full tables up to 1 B.C. (including much data on the pre-Qin chronologies and on the chronologies of the different kingdoms not found in Zhang) and vol. 2 contains tables from A.D. 1 to 2000. Practically identical in its arrangement of the main tables but lacking the many important appendixes of Dong is the older P. Hoang, *Concordance des Chronologies Néomeniques Chinoise et Europeene,* Variétés Sinologiques no. 29 (Shanghai, 1910).

8.3   Days

Finally, when it comes to converting single days, which are recorded using cyclical characters, two commonly used works are either *A Comparative Daily Calendar for Chinese, Western and Mohammedan History, A.D. 1 to 1940,* comp. Chen Yuan 陳垣 (**Zhong-Xi-Hui shi rili** 中西回史日曆 ; Peking, 1926; 1962) or *Sino-Western Calendar for Two Thousand Years, A.D. 1 to 2000,* comp. Xue Zhong-san 薛仲三 and Ou-Yang-yi 歐陽頤 (**Liangquiannian lai Zhong-Xi li duizhaobiao** 兩千年來中西曆對照表 ; Shanghai, 1940; Peking, 1957; Taipei reprint, 1958). For days falling between the years 1516 and 1941 (and for month and year dates as well), the concordance compiled by Zheng He-sheng 鄭鶴聲 , *Daily Concordance for Modern Sino-Western History* (**Jinshi

Zhong-Xi shi ri duizhaobiao 近世中西史日對照表 ; Shanghai, 1936; Taipei reprint, 1958), is more convenient for use than the larger daily concordances listed above. Less bulky also are the many daily and monthly concordances available for the post-1800 or post-1840 period, e.g. Rong Meng-yuan 荣孟源 , *Chronological Tables for the Years 1830 to 1949* (**Zhongguo lidai shi nianbiao** 中国历代史年表 ; Peking, 1953; Hong Kong reprint, 1962); or *Simplified Chronological Tables for Two Hundred Years,* compiled at the Academy of Sciences Zijinshan observatory (Zhonhhuo Kexueyuan Zijinshan Tianwentai lisuanzu, **Erbainian libiao jianbian** [1821-2020] 二百年历表簡編 ; Peking, 1965), which gives the cyclical characters for the beginning day of each lunar and traditional solar month and their Gregorian calendar equivalents, as well as the day of the week (Sunday, Monday, Tuesday, etc.) of the first day in each month.

Two tables of important events and dates are useful for putting Chinese history in the broader context of Asian and world history at a glance: *An Encyclopaedia of World History,* comp. W.L. Langer et al., 4th ed., rev. and enlarged (London, 1968); and *Chronological Tables of Chinese and World History, 5000 B.C. to A.D. 1918,* comp. Qi Si-he 齐思和 , Liu Qi-ge 刘啟戈 , Nie Chong-qi 聂崇岐, and Jian Bo-zan 翦伯赞 (**Zhong-wai lishi nianbiao, gongyuan qian 5000 nian-gongyuan 1918 nian** 中外历史年表,公元前 5000 年－公元 1918 年 ; Peking, 1958). This is the fullest comprehensive chronological table of important events (900 double-column pages).

Note: Japanese style dating works in a similar manner to the old Chinese system: Lists of emperors' accession dates and era names can be found in most Japanese-English dictionaries, e.g. Nelson, *The Modern Reader's Japanese-English Character Dictionary* (Appendix S).

Korean style dating followed the Chinese until the Japanese occupation at which point the Japanese system was used; in addition the Korean calendar, *tan-ji* 檀紀 , is also used: to convert to Western dates sub-tract 2,333 (e.g., 4305 is 1972).

9. Indexes and Concordances

Old Chinese books were not indexed in detail; hence a great deal of time and effort can be saved by using the large number of concordances and indexes compiled in the twentieth century. By far the most important series of concordances and indexes is the *Harvard-Yenching Institute Sinological Index Series* which was compiled under the general editorship of William Hung in 69 volumes (Yenching University, Peking, 1931-1947); reprinted by Chinese Materials and Research Aids Inc. for Association of Asian Studies Inc., Taipei 1965-1969 (nos. 9, 34, and 35 and Supplements 9 and 21 re-pinted by the Japan Council for East Asian Studies, Toyo Bunko, and No. 40 and Supplement 20 reprinted by the Harvard University Press). The series consists of two separately numbered groups; the first entitled Indices (*yinde* 引得 , 41 works) and the second, Supplements (*yinde tekan* 引得 特刊 , 23 works). The latter include a number of concordances with complete texts as well as other materials. Throughout the present Guide, indexes in this series are referred to as H-Y Index or H-Y Supp.

Another important series of indexes and concordances was published by the Centre Franco-Chinois d'Études Sinologiques under the direction of Nie Chong-qi 聶 崇 岐, 11 vols. (Peking, 1943-1948; Taipei reprint, 1966). It was compiled with the aid of the H-Y Index staff who had been forced to leave Yenching in 1942.

Finally, there are a very large number of indexes and concordances compiled in Japan. These are usually produced by members of a seminar or study group collectively as a working aid (appearing under the senior member's name) and as a result are at times somewhat uneven in quality. As a rule a preliminary mimeographed version is circulated for a number of years before a revised printed edition is produced. Especially notable is the *T'ang Civilization Reference Series,* nine titles to date (Kyoto, 1954-).

Indexes and concordances are listed throughout the present Guide.

For a full annotated bibliography of indexes and concordances see D. L. McMullen, *Concordances and Indexes to Chinese Texts* (London, forthcoming).

10. Secondary Sources

10.1   Comprehensive bibliographies

At an early stage of research it is useful for students to find out what
other historians have written about their chosen topics and related fields.
Thanks to those scholars who have spent a lot of time compiling guides
and bibliographies, this can be done very rapidly.

There are a large number of bibliographies covering a single subject or
a single period or even a single type of historical source; these are not listed
here. The present section is concerned with those bibliographies which
cover the entire sweep of Chinese history.

The most comprehensive and up-to-date of the annual bibliographies
(it carries the publications of the previous year) is the *Annual Bibliography
of Oriental Studies* compiled at the Institute of Humanistic Studies, Kyoto
University. (**Tōyōgaku bunken ruimoku** 東洋學文獻類目;
annual or semi-annual, 1934-1957; thereafter annual, Kyoto).
Secondary works in Chinese, Japanese, Western languages, and Russian are
arranged according to language and further subdivided within each language
group according to subject categories; full author indexes make this bibliography very easy to use. Note that it also includes author's reviews listed
under work reviewed and indexed by the author of the review.

The only other comprehensive annual bibliography covering works in
all languages differs from the **Tōyōgaku bunken ruimoku** in that it is
annotated. It is however not nearly as wide in its coverage and it appears for
each year only after a very considerable time lag (thus the latest volume,
covering research in 1962, appeared in 1969). Despite this drawback, the
annotations are a unique feature of this bibliography, which also includes a
subject index in addition to an author index (*Révue bibliographique de
sinologie,* Paris, 1957-   ). The first year covered was 1955.

10.2   Bibliographies of Chinese secondary sources

Up to the outbreak of the War of Resistance against Japan (1937), learned periodicals proliferated in China. Finding one's way around some 1,300 of them would be next to impossible without the *Index to Chinese Historical Articles,* compiled by members of the Institute of Historical Research of the Academy of Sciences and the History Department of Peking University (Zhongguo kexueyuan lishiyanjiusuo, Beijing daxue lishixi, **Zhongguo shixue lunwen suoyin** 中国史学论文索引), 2 vols. (Peking, 1957). Altogether 30,000 articles which appeared in over 1,300 periodicals between 1900 and 1937 are indexed. The arrangement is by extremely detailed subject categories as well as by period.

Three other bibliographies complete the coverage of Chinese articles on Chinese history down to the mid-1960s. Yu Ping-kuen (Yu Bing-quan) 余 秉權 , *Chinese History: Index to Learned Articles, 1902-1962* (**Zhongguo shixue lunwen yinde** 中國史學論文引得 ; Hong Kong, 1963; Taipei, 1968) indexes 10,325 articles in 355 journals appearing between 1902 and 1962 and written by 3,392 authors. This should be used in conjunction with the same author's expansion. *Chinese History: Index to Learned Articles,* vol. 2, 1905-1964 (Cambridge, Mass., 1970) in which many more journals which had not been included in the first volume were indexed. There is no duplication between the two volumes. The arrangement of both volumes is by total stroke count of authors' names; there is also a Wade-Giles index and a subject index.

For articles written on Chinese history in China between 1949 and 1959 there is a special bibliography which was compiled by members of the History Department of the East China Normal College (Huadong shifan daxue lishixi, **Zhongguo gudai ji zhong shiji shi baokan lunwen ziliao suoyin** 中国古代及中世紀史报刊论文資料索引 ; Shanghai, 1959; reprinted Hong Kong, 1965; Tokyo, 1967). The arrangement is by period. A subsequent volume appeared in 1962 covering Chinese writing on Chinese history (1842-1919) in journals issued between 1949 and 1959 (**Zhongguo jindaishi cankao shumu** 中国近代史参考书 目 ; Shanghai, 1962).

E-tu Zen Sun and J. de Francis, *Bibliography of Chinese Social History: A Selected and Critical List of Chinese Periodical Sources* (New Haven, 1952), covers 176 articles in Chinese on social history appearing mainly during the 1930s and is annotated.

The six bibliographies above only list articles; the best way of locating Chinese historical monographs and books is to look through one of the bibliographic guides listed in section 1.1 or use the **Tōyōgaku bunken ruimoku** or the *Révue bibliographique de sinologie.* See also A. L. Feuerwerker and S. Cheng, *Chinese Communist Studies of Modern Chinese History* (Cambridge, Mass., 1961), in which some 500 books on Chinese history published in China between 1949 and 1959 are discussed under various broad subject headings. ("Modern" includes several works on the Ming.)

Also consult *Modern Chinese Society, 1644-1970: An Analytic Bibliography,* vol. 2, entitled *Publications in Chinese,* ed. G. W. Skinner and W. Hsieh (Stanford, 1973), for a critical, thoroughly arranged, annotated bibliography of Chinese publications covering this period.

10.3   Main Chinese journals and how to locate them

Lishi jiaoxue 历史教学 (1951-1964). Intended for middle school history teachers. Often contains useful short articles.

Lishi yanjiu 历史研究 (1954-1966). This is the most important Chinese historical journal. It has been weighted toward pre-1911 Chinese history.

Qinghua xuebao 清華學報 (1924-1947; new series, 1956—   ). Contains mainly articles by Chinese scholars working in Taiwan and the U.S.A. on all aspects of Chinese culture.

Zhongyang yanjiuyuan lishi yuyan yanjiusuo jikan 中央研究院歷史語言研究所集刊 (Bulletin of the Institute of History and Philology, Academia Sinica, Taipei). Somewhat philological but contains important articles on Chinese history (1928-   ).

Important historical articles are frequently published in university journals. Note also the archaeological journals listed in section 13.1.

A large number of historical journals and journals carrying historical articles appeared in the pre-1949 period, especially in the late 1920s and 1930s. Some of the best have been reprinted. For the titles of the major journals of this period plus a sampling of their contents, see E-tu Zen Sun and J. de Francis (1952); and R. C. Howard, *Index to Learned Chinese Periodicals* (Boston, 1962), which indexes fourteen journals by journal and by subject.

In order to locate Chinese journals in Western libraries, use the following special check-lists:

Union List of Chinese Periodicals in American Libraries (Xerox, Inter Documentation Co., Zug, Switzerland, 1968), which is a printing of the microfilm of the Library of Congress "Union Card File of Oriental Vernacular Series (Chinese)."

Although various projects are under way for producing a union list of Chinese periodicals in European libraries, the only published checklists to date are:

Catalogue des périodiques chinois dans les bibliothèques d'Europe, comp. Y. Hervouet (Paris, 1958), which is selective and out of date.

Chinese Periodicals in British Libraries, Handlist 4 (London, 1972).

Asien and Ozeanen, behandelnde Zeitschriften und ihre Bestande in der Bundesrepublik Deutschland (Hamburg, 1970). Includes holdings of Chinese, Japanese, and Western language periodicals on China.

To locate Chinese journals and periodicals in Japanese collections, use *Union Catalogue of Holdings of Chinese Newspapers and Periodicals in 23 Important Japanese Collections* (**Nihon shuyō kenkyū kikan toshokan shozō Chūgoku-bun shinbun zasshi sōgō mokuroku** 日本主要研究機関図書館所蔵中国文新聞雑誌総合目録; Tokyo, 1959).

For Chinese periodicals and journals in Chinese collections, use *Union Catalogue of 19,115 Periodicals in 50 Chinese Libraries* (**Quanguo Zhongwen qikan lianhe mulu** 全国中文期刊联合目录; Peking, 1961) and note also the catalogue of a very important collection: *Periodical and Newspaper Holdings of the Shanghai Newspaper and Periodical Library* (**Shanghai baokan tushuguan zhongwen qikan mulu** 上海报刊图书馆中文期刊目录), 2 vols.(Shanghai, 1956-1957). Vol. 1, 1888-1949, 8,037 titles; vol. 2, 1949-1956, 1,300 titles.

Journal holdings in Hong Kong (mainly of the Fung Ping Shan Library of the University of Hong Kong) are listed in P. K. Yu, *Chinese History, Index to Learned Articles, 1902-1962* (Hong Kong, 1963).

10.4   Bibliographies of Japanese secondary sources

Almost all Japanese academic writing on Chinese history appears first in journal articles. Authors frequently later assemble their articles and publish them as books (with minimal revisions), the standard form of the title being *Nani nani no kenkyū,* i.e. "Collected researches on such and such" (often mistranslated as "A study of such and such").

Festschrift volumes with contributions by pupils and friends are usually published on a distinguished scholar's retirement or to coincide with his sixtieth (*kanreki kinen* 還曆紀念) or seventieth (*koki kinen* 古稀 紀念) birthday. These frequently contain an appreciation of the scholar as well as a bibliography of his works.

There are two main types of bibliography available to help locate present and past work on a given subject or period; the first is usually in the form of an analytic bibliographic essay and includes the evaluations of the author. This type is called "academic trends" (*gakkai dōkō* 学界動向) or "history of research" *(kenkyūshi* 研究史) and serves to give the context of a given piece of research as well as the present state of the field. The second type is in the form of a straightforward, unannotated bibliography which attempts to list all publications on a given subject or period. This type is called "bibliography of secondary literature" (*bunken mokuroku* 文献目録). In Chinese history the usual arrangement in both types of bibliography is by dynasty, by neighboring peoples, and by special subject. In this section only the most important of these bibliographies of the two types which cover the whole of Chinese history are given. (*Bibliography of Bibliographies of East Asian Studies,* Bibliography no. 3, Center for East Asian Studies [Tokyo, Toyo Bunko, 1964] lists some 822 Japanese bibliographies [to 1963] for all branches of Asian studies, including Chinese history. It is arranged by categories and by countries, and has an index and an appendix of bibliographies of the works of individual scholars.)

Academic-trends style bibliographies

The Development of Historical Studies since the Meiji Period contains bibliographic essays on Chinese history arranged by dynasty and by neighboring peoples (pp. 395-625), and is the standard reference of this kind covering work produced in Japan between c. 1870 and 1926: Rekishi kyōiku kenkyūkai 歴史教育研究会 , ed., **Meiji igo ni okeru rekishigaku no hattatsu** 明治以後における歴史学の発達 (Tokyo, 1933). Originally appeared in **Rekishi Kyōiku**, vol. 7; vol. 9 (1932).

For postwar trends several works are available. Most reliable is the annual summary of the previous year's historical writing which appears in the May issue (no. 5) of **Shigaku zasshi** and has done so since vol. 60, no. 5 (1950). The more radical, problem-oriented journal, **Rekishigaku kenkyū**, also produced a similar annual bibliographic profile of the previous year's research but owing to falling standards stopped the series in 1957. It was published as an annual supplement to the journal for the years 1937-1944 and 1949-1954 by Iwanami and then in the journal itself for the years 1955-1957.

Useful, but necessarily briefer bibliographic essays (having the advantage of being in English translation as well as in Japanese) were prepared for the 11th, 12th, and 13th International Conferences of Historical Sciences (1955, 1960, 1965). Vol. 1 covers Japanese scholarship from 1945 to 1953, vol. 2 from 1953 to 1963, and vol. 3 from 1963 to 1967: English version (with French title): Comité Japonais des Sciences Historiques, ed., *Le Japon au XIe Congrès International des Sciences Historiques à Stockholm* (Stockholm, 1960); Japanese National Committee of Historical Sciences, ed., *Japan at the XIIth International Congress of Historical Sciences in Vienna* (Tokyo, 1966), and *Recent Trends in Japanese Historiography: Bibliographical Essays* (Tokyo, 1970). Japanese version: Kokusai rekishigaku kaigi Nihon kokunai iinkai 国際歴史学会議日本国内委員会, ed., *The Development and Present State of Historical Studies in Japan* **(Nihon ni okeru rekishigaku no hattatsu to genjō** 日本における歴史学の発達と現状; Tokyo, vol. 1, 1959; vol. 2, 1966; vol. 3, 1970).

There is an excellent series of bibliographic essays produced under the auspices of the Society for Socioeconomic History, which includes essays on China: *The Development of Socioeconomic History* (pp. 283-366) summarizes Japanese studies of Chinese socioeconomic history from c. 1870 to 1940; *The Development of Socioeconomic History Since the War* (pp. 111-214) covers 1945 to 1953, while *The Development of Socioeconomic History During the Last Ten Years* (pp. 129-309) covers articles and books written between 1955 and 1965; All three were edited by Shakai keizaishi gakkai 社会経済史学会, and their Japanese titles are: **Shakai keizaishigaku no hattatsu** 社会経済史学の発達 (Tokyo, 1944); **Sengo ni okeru shakaikeizaishigaku no hattatsu** 戦後における社会経済史学の発達, published as a special number of the journal **Shakai keizaishigaku,** vol. 20 (1955); and **Saikin jūnen kan ni okeru shakai keizaishi no hattatsu** 最近十年間における社会経済史の発達, also published as a special number of **Shakai keizaishigaku,** vol. 31, nos. 1-5 (1966).

Bibliography of Primary and Secondary Sources for Oriental History, although not strictly speaking an academic-trends style bibliography, contains annotated bibliographies giving major works in Japanese (to 1953) on all periods of Chinese history: **Tōyō shiryō shūsei** 東洋史料集成(Tokyo, Heibonsha, 1956), also published as vol. 23 of the *Encyclopaedia of World History* (**Sekai rekishi jiten** 世界歴史辞典), 24 vols. (Tokyo, Heibonsha, 1950-1956).

An outstanding, critical annotated bibliography of Japanese works on modern Chinese society should be consulted: *Modern Chinese Society, 1644-1970: An Analytical Bibliography,* vol. 3, *Publications in Japanese,* ed. G. W. Skinner and Shigeaki Tomita (Stanford, 1973).

Many works on individual periods or subjects have bibliographic essays appended.

Unannotated bibliographies

The most comprehensive unannotated bibliography is *Japanese Studies on Asian History: a Catalogue of Articles on Asia [Excluding Japan]* (Tōyōshi kenkyū rombun mokuroku henshū iinkai 東洋史研究論文目録編輯委員会, ed., **Nihon ni okeru Tōyōshi kenkyū rombun**

mokuroku 日本における東洋史研究論文目録,4 vols. (Tokyo,
1964-1967), which lists all articles appearing in no less than 1,885 journals,
periodicals, and collective publications between c. 1880 and 1962. The
arrangement is by journal, all articles in each issue being listed in turn. The
fourth volume is an author index. The very wide coverage of this bibliography
(which also includes an author's reviews) effectively puts out of business
all previous unannotated, general bibliographies of Japanese studies of
Chinese history and more than makes up for the lack of arrangement by
subject categories. The two Harvard-Yenching indexes of Japanese periodicals
(Index series, Supplement 6 and 13, 1933 and 1940 respectively), are
now completely outdated.

A useful bibliography arranged by authors (within broad subject
categories) is *Japanese Studies on Japan and the Far East; a Short
Biographical and Bibliographical Introduction,* compiled by Teng Ssu-yü
with the collaboration of Masuda Kenji and Kaneda Hiromitsu (Hong Kong,
1961). The coverage is mainly of postwar Japanese studies but many younger
scholars were not included and the entries are not complete. There is an
author/subject index.

Both **Shigaku zasshi** and **Tōyōshi kenkyū** list the contents of other
Japanese journals regularly throughout the year and thus provide a
convenient way of keeping up to date with work as it is published (often
in out-of-the-way journals).

An unannotated bibliography on Chinese economic history may be
found in the annual bibliography of books and articles on Chinese economic
history published by the journal **Keizaishi kenkyū**.

The years 1933-1938 are covered annually in the journal from vol. 11
(1934) and then after the war in book form under the title **Keizaishi
nenkan** 経済史年刊 , 3 vols. (Osaka), covering the years 1951-
1955; under the title **Keizaishi bunken** 経済史文献 from 1956 to
1959; and finally under its present title: **Keizaishi bunken kaidai** 経済
史文献解題.

10.5   Main Japanese journals and how to locate them

Acta Asiatica (1960-   ) reprints translations of articles on Chinese
history mainly by well-established, conservative scholars.

Memoirs of the Research Department of the Toyo Bunko (1926-   )
reprints translations of scholarly articles on Chinese historical
geography and Chinese history by senior historians of the Tokyo
school.

Rekishigaku kenkyū 歴史学研究 (1933-   ); establishment
Marxist historical journal.

Rekishi kyōiku 歴史教育 (1926-   ); new series started after the
war; excellent journal devoted to popularizing new departments in
historical studies; frequently organizes issues around a theme.

Shakaikeizai shigaku 社会経済史学 (1931-   ); recently has
tended to carry fewer articles on Chinese history, but important
bibliographical summaries are published in it (see section 10.4).

Shigaku zasshi 史学雑誌 (1889-   ); leading establishment
historical journal in Japan; articles on all periods of history of all
countries. Important annual bibliographic retrospect (see section
10.4).

Tōhō gakuhō 東方学報 (1931-   ); one journal of this name
published in Kyoto, another published in Tokyo (ceased publication
in 1944). Heavily sinological.

Tōyō bunka kenkyūjo kiyō 東洋文化研究所紀要 (1943-
) contains important articles on Chinese history and also on
South and Southeast Asia.

Tōyō gakuhō 東洋学報 (1911-   ); scholarly contributions on
Chinese history before the twentieth century.

Tōyōshi kenkyū 東洋史研究 (1935-   ) carries many important
articles on Chinese history mainly before the twentieth century.

There are a great many other historical journals as well as the journals
of many dozens of history departments, humanities departments, etc., all
of which carry articles on Chinese history. In addition there are specialist
journals (for historical geography, history of law, etc.). As a general rule it

saves time to find out who are the historians who have published important work in a given field and who are those currently publishing in it; in Japan as elsewhere, the activity of publishing articles is not necessarily connected with the communication of new ideas or new approaches.

In order to locate Japanese language periodicals and journals in Western collections, check the standard catalogues of periodicals but note two special check-lists: *Check-list of Japanese Periodicals Held in British University and Research Libraries,* comp. S.M. Mandahl and P. W. Carnell (Sheffield University, 1971); "Union Card File of Oriental Vernacular Series (Japanese)" at the Library of Congress, Washington, D.C.

In order to locate Japanese journals and periodicals in Japanese collections, use: *Catalogue of Periodicals in Japanese, Chinese, Korean, etc.* **(Nihon-bun Chūgoku-bun Chōsen-bun tō chikuji kankōbutsu mokuroku** 日本文中国文朝鮮文等逐次刊行物目録; Tokyo, 1964); holdings of three important libraries are listed.

10.6 Bibliographies of Western secondary sources

The standard bibliography of Western language works (both books and articles) on China up to 1921 was compiled by Henri Cordier, who, although he knew no Chinese, certainly knew the European and treaty-port publications on China extremely well: *Bibliotheca Sinica,* rev. ed., 4 vols. (Paris, 1904-1908; supplementary vol., Paris, 1924; Taiwan reprint, 1966). There is a useful but not entirely reliable *Author Index to the Bibliotheca Sinica of Henri Cordier* (East Asiatic Library, Columbia University, New York, 1953). Two bibliographies bring Cordier down to the 1950s. The first was compiled by Yuan T'ung-li and covers books (not articles): *China in Western Literature: A Continuation of Cordier's Bibliotheca Sinica* (New Haven, 1958), while the second covers articles only and was compiled by J. Lust: *Index Sinicus, A Catalogue of Articles Relating to China in Periodicals and Other Collective Publications, 1920-1955* (Cambridge, 1964). Both are arranged by subject categories and both contain author indexes. Books and articles on China in Western languages appearing between 1941 and 1965 (and therefore bringing Yuan and Lust down to the mid-1960s) are listed in *Cumulative Bibliography of Asian Studies, 1941-1965* (Association of Asian Studies), *Subject Bibliography,* 4 vols., and *Author Bibliography,* 4 vols. (both Boston, 1970). This bibliography is based on the annual *Bibliography of Asian Studies* which appears as a separate issue of the *Journal of Asian Studies,* at the end of each year. *JAS* should be used as a first reference for Western-language works appearing after 1965.

Note also the critical, annotated bibliography: *Modern Chinese Society 1644-1970: An Analytic Bibliography,* vol. 1, *Publications in Western Languages,* ed. G. W. Skinner and E. A. Winckler (Stanford, 1973), for secondary works on the later empire.

For past doctoral dissertations on China see L. H. D. Gordon and F. S. Shulman, eds., *China: A Bibliography of Doctoral Dissertations in Western Languages, 1945-1970* (Seattle, 1972); and for current doctoral dissertations see *Association for Asian Studies Newsletter* (from October 1969); *Society for the Study of Pre-Han China Newsletter; Sung Studies Newsletter;* and *Ch'ing-shih wen-t'i.*

The most comprehensive bibliography of Russian-language publications on China (including Chinese history) is P.E. Skatchkov, *Systematic Bibliography of Books and Journal Articles on China in Russian Published between 1730 and 1957* (**Bibliografia kitaia**), 1st ed. (Moscow, 1930; revised and supplemented, Moscow, 1960). The 19,551 entries are arranged under 25 broad subject categories. An updated version is currently being prepared.

For those without a knowledge of the Russian language, Yuan T'ung-li, *Russian Works on China, 1918-1960, in American Libraries* (New Haven, 1961) is very useful. The section on Chinese history and culture originally appeared as an article in *Monumenta Serica* 18:388-430 (1959).

In order to keep abreast of Soviet publications on Chinese history consult the bibliographic sections of the journal *Narodni Azii i Afriki* (Peoples of Asia and Africa).

The *Annual Bibliography of Oriental Studies* (Kyoto), the *Bibliography of Asian Studies* in the *Journal of Asian Studies,* and the *Révue bibliographique de sinologie* all list recent publications in Russian on Chinese history.

10.7   <u>Main Western journals</u>

To locate Western language journals, check the standard catalogues such as *Union List of Periodicals* (for the U.S.A. and Canada) and *British Union Catalogue of Periodicals.*

AM   *Asia Major* (O.S. 1923-1933; N.S. 1949-   ). Leading British sinological journal.

AO   *Archiv Orientalni* (1929-   ), edited at Prague.

BEFEO   *Bulletin de l'École francaise d'Extrême Orient* (1901-   ). Although it has always concentrated on Indo-China, it not infrequently has important articles on Chinese history.

BMFEA   *Bulletin of the Museum of Far Eastern Antiquities* (1929-   ), edited in Stockholm, contains important articles of Karlgren and his pupils.

BSEI   *Bulletin de la Société d'Études Indochinoises,* edited in Saigon (see comment on *BEFEO*).

BSOAS   *Bulletin of the School of Oriental and African Studies* (1917-   ) carries occasional important articles and reviews on Chinese history.

CSWT   *Ch'ing-shih wen-t'i* (1965-   ), informal communications by those working in Qing history.

HJAS   *Harvard Journal of Asiatic Studies* (1936-   ). The only sinological journal in the U.S. Carries important articles.

JA   *Journal Asiatique* (1922-   ) covers the whole of Asia, but does not carry articles on Chinese history as frequently as it used to.

JAOS   *Journal of the American Oriental Society* (1849-   ) covers the entire "Orient."

JAS   *Journal of Asian Studies* (appeared 1941-1955 under the
(FEQ)   title *Far Eastern Quarterly*) covers North, South, and East Asia; publishes many important articles and also the useful *Bibliography of Asian Studies* (as the final issue of each year).

JESHO   *Journal of the Economic and Social History of the Orient* (1957-   ) is a much needed journal, but unfortunately attempts to cover the entire "Orient."

JRAS *Journal of the Royal Asiatic Society* (1823-   ) has seen better days; divided according to the various branches of the RAS, e.g. North China Branch (1857-1942: *JNCBRAS*): Malayan Branch, Hong Kong Branch, etc. The *JRAS* is still published in London.

MS *Monumenta Serica* (1935-   ). Catholic sinological journal, moved from Peking to Nagoya, then to Los Angeles; jointly edited in Nagoya and Los Angeles.

NAA *Narodni Azii i Afriki* (Peoples of Asia and Africa; 1961-   ), incorporating *PV*.

NdOAG *Deutsche Gesellschaft für Natur- und Völkerkunde Ostasiens,*
(MdOAG) *Nachrichten* (1926-   ); *Mitteilungen* (1873-   ), currently edited at Hamburg.

OE *Oriens Extremus* (1954-   ), edited at Hamburg.

PV *Problemy Vostokovedeniia* (Problems of Oriental Studies; 1959-   ), incorporating *SV*.

S *Sinologica* (1947-   ), edited at Basle.

SSN *Sung Studies Newsletter* (1969-   ), a good way of keeping up to date with new work in this field.

SSPN *Society for the Study of Pre-Han China Newsletter* (1969-), irreg., History Dept., Berkeley, Calif.

SV *Sovetskoe Vostokovedenie* (Soviet Oriental Studies), 20 vols. (Sinological Inst., Moscow, 1940-1959).

TP *T'oung pao* (1890-   ), leading sinological journal in Europe.

ZDMG *Zeitschrift der Deutschen Morgandländischen Gesellschaft* (1845-   ), now published in Wiesbaden.

PART II. TRADITIONAL CHINESE HISTORICAL WRITING AND MAIN CATEGORIES OF PRIMARY SOURCES

11. Introduction

11.1   Characteristics of traditional Chinese historical writing

One of the unique features of Chinese historical studies is that a very large number of the primary sources were works produced in or preserved by a conscious tradition of historical writing and compilation. Instead of working from archives or private documents (as in post-Rankean European historiography), the student of Chinese history is liable to be handling historical works prepared by Chinese historians over the last 2,000 years. In order to be able to assess the qualities and the biases of these works, clearly some knowledge of the aims and methods of the historians and compilers who produced them is essential. Furthermore, in order to be able to start looking for primary sources on the topic of his choice, the student of Chinese history will also need to know how traditional historians organized their materials and classified different types of sources; needless to say, a knowledge of traditional bibliographical classification and historical aims and methods does not imply a slavish adoption of the categories, let alone the methods, of the traditional historians. Traditional bibliographic classification schema are discussed in section 12.2.

What then are the characteristics of traditional Chinese historical writing? (1) Chinese historians were typically Confucian literati, but more significantly, they were frequently also officials, if not keepers of official archives, and they were primarily concerned with the official record. In common with officials in other societies, the final record which they compiled was encoded into bureaucratic (Confucian) categories which were far removed from actual transcripts of conversations or events. From this follow the second, third, and fourth characteristics of traditional historical writing: (2) its many close connections with government and the orthodox ideology, as seen for example in the theory of "legitimate succession" (*zhengtong* 正統) which historians traced in an effort to legitimize new dynasties, and also as seen in the compilation of compendia of historical precedents as a guide to official action; (3) its strong moral didacticism, with the historian's duty being seen as the bestower of "praise and blame" (*baobian* 褒貶), using Confucian moral tenets as the yardstick; (4) its ruthless excision of anything judged in conflict with the above two concerns (thus not only a focus on the elite and its ideology but also a particularly narrow focus on that elite). Additional characteristics of China's traditional historical writing are: (5) its early elevation to the status of an activity differentiated from other branches of writing, to which great importance was attached for two millennia of continuous historical production; (6) its development into many well defined genres and sub-genres; (7) its scholarly attention to such ancillary disciplines as cataloguing, calendrical sciences, historical geography, etc.; (8) its development of an articulated philosophy of history.

The best brief introduction to Chinese traditional historiography in English is E.G. Pulleyblank, "The Historiographical Tradition," in R. Dawson, ed., *The Legacy of China* (Oxford, 1964; paper, 1969), pp. 143-164. See also the essays by A.F. Wright, "On the Uses of Generalization in the Study of Chinese History," in L.Gotschalk, ed., *Generalization in the Writing of History* (Chicago, 1963), pp. 36-58; E. Balazs, "History as a Guide to Bureaucratic Practice," in his *Chinese Civilisation and Bureaucracy* (New Haven and London, 1964), pp. 129-140; and O.B. Van de Sprenkel, "Chronographie et historiographie chinoises," in *Mélanges publiés par l'Institut des Hautes Études Chinoises* (Paris, 1960), II, 407-421. These last two stress the governmental and political nature and concerns of Chinese historical writing. For the connections between history and literature, see J. Prusek, "History and Epics in China and the West," in his *Chinese History and Literature* (Prague, 1970), pp. 17-34. The recent work of Hartwell contains some important generalizations on Chinese historical writing: "Historical Analogism, Public Policy, and Social Science in Eleventh and

Twelfth-Century China," *American Historical Review* 76.3:692-727 (1971). Translations from traditional historians will be found briefly in J. Meskill, *The Pattern of Chinese History* (Boston, 1965), while H. Kahn, *Monarchy in the Emperor's Eyes* (Cambridge, Mass., 1971) contains a perceptive study of official and unoffical historiography of the later empire (pp. 7-75).

The conference volume edited by W.G. Beasley and E.G. Pulleyblank, *Historians of China and Japan* (London, 1961), contains eleven papers on different aspects of Chinese historical writing which together form the best extensive introduction to the subject in a Western language. The somewhat dated monograph of C.S. Gardner, *Chinese Traditional Historiography* (Cambridge, Mass., 1938; rev. ed., 1961) is still a useful overall description; as is Han Yu-shan, *Elements of Chinese Historiography* (Hollywood, 1955), which gives in catalogue form the major genres and terminologies as well as the major works and historians of each period.

The best single-volume account in Chinese (albeit non-colloquial) is chronologically arranged: Jin Yu-fu 金毓黻 , *History of Chinese Historiography* (**Zhongguo shixue shi** 中國史學史 ; Shanghai, 1944; reprinted Shanghai, 1957, 1962; Hong Kong, 1964). By far the most stimulating study in any language is Naitō Torajirō 内藤虎次郎, *History of China's Historiography* (**Shina shigakushi** 支那史學史 ; Tokyo, 1949; 2nd ed., 1953; reprinted as vol. 11 of Naitō's collected works, Tokyo, 1969). It is written in an easy lecture style (it was composed by the author's son from the lecture notes of students) and succeeds better than any other work in placing Chinese historical writing in the social and intellectual context of each period. Zhang Shun-hui 張舜徽, *Introduction to the Major Sources of Chinese History* (**Zhongguo lishi yaoji jieshao** 中国历史要籍介紹 ; Wuhan, 1956) is an excellent starting point especially written for beginners.

11.2   Note on availability of sources from different periods

In common with all other societies, the further back the period in Chinese history, the fewer the sources that have survived. Thus for pre-Qin history (before the third century B.C.) the historian has to work with far fewer sources than are available, for example, for Ming history. The skills required to work in the earlier period, furthermore, are also quite different. They include a knowledge of the special languages of the oracle-bone inscriptions (for Shang history) and of the bronze inscriptions (for Zhou history); the ability to handle the copious findings of the archaeologists; and finally, the skills of a philologist to deal with the corrupt classical texts (with their innumerable commentaries and sub-commentaries) which are the chief literary and historical sources for ancient Chinese history. Westerners, from the eighteenth century on, developed a tradition of "sinology" in which the study of the texts of classical China was seen as the chief desideratum. As a result classical philology (and with it the whole weight of traditional Chinese learning) became the foundation for the study of Chinese history.

There is no reason whatsoever why the student of Chinese history should seek to perpetuate the old sinological tradition which grew out of peculiar historical circumstances in which the display of philological virtuosity was an essential badge of respectability for the classical scholar. Indeed, there are very good reasons why the student of Chinese history should turn to those periods where the sources are plentiful and where the texts of the sources are in reasonably good condition. This does not mean that historians should abandon the study of ancient Chinese history, which was one of the great formative periods of Chinese society, but rather that the emphasis should be changed. Throughout the present Guide, accordingly, the emphasis is placed on the sources for Chinese history from the Qin through to the end of the empire.

After the Han, sources become more plentiful, but for the most part they only survive in excerpted or condensed form. Thus the earlier Standard Histories (see section 16) down to the Tang, contain materials which have long since been lost, and as a result they are vital sources for the period. The reverse however holds true for the post-Song Standard Histories because many of the sources upon which they were based are still extant. This is even more true by the Ming and the Qing, for which periods sources such as the Veritable Records (see section 14), not to speak of many thousands of Local Gazetteers (see section 18.5) and historical, documentary, and literary sources of all kinds, are available in enormous quantitites. This can be seen in the following rough summary:

Standard
Histories;
other secondary works

National Histories and
Veritable Records

Collections of Important Documents
and other compilations of primary materials

Daily Records of central ministries, bureaus, etc.; court
records, imperial audiences, edicts, etc., memorials
from provincial officials

Local official records (land and household registers, routine reports etc.);
writings of private individuals, commemorative writings, private records, etc.

The further back the period in Chinese imperial history, the fewer the
surviving sources from the base of the pyramid. Thus for most earlier periods
of the empire, the lower three levels are only extant insofar as they have
been excerpted or adapted in the highest two levels of compilation and
historical writing (the outstanding exceptions being some of the epigraphical
and new documentary sources discussed in sections 13.3, 13.4, and 24).

Note the minor part played by family and kin, business and other
association records. Although such records from the private sector were
voluminous, few if any have been preserved (with the outstanding exception of the genealogies from the Ming and Qing--see section 17.4),
because as we have seen, Chinese historians throughout most of Chinese
history were officials, if not keepers of official archives, and thus were
primarily concerned with the official record.

11.3   Main categories of Chinese historical sources at a glance:
          Glossary-index to Part II

Ancillary disciplines

Historiography	*shiping*	史評
Classification and bibliography	*mulu*	目錄
Textual criticism	*jiaokan*	校勘

Archaeology and epigraphy

Archaeology	*kaogu*	考古
Epigraphy	*jinshiwen*	金石文
Oracle-bone inscriptions	*jiaguwen*	甲骨文
Bronze inscriptions	*jinwen*	金文
Stone inscriptions	*shike*	石刻

Main forms of historical writing

1. Annals   *bian-nian ti* 編年體
   Annalistic sources   *qijuzhu* 起居注, *shizhengji*
            時政記, *rili* 日歷
   Veritable Records   *shilu* 實錄
2. Topically arranged histories   *jishibenmo ti* 紀事本末體
3. Standard Histories   *zhengshi* 正史, *jizhuan ti*
   First four Standard Histories   *qiansishi* 前四史   紀傳體
   Standard Histories covering 265-618
   Later Standard Histories
   Monographs in the Standard
        Histories   *shu* 書, *zhi* 志
     Dynastic Bibliography   *jingji zhi* 經籍志, *yiwen zhi*
                藝文志
     Financial Administration   *shihuo zhi* 食貨志
     Law   *xingfa zhi* 刑法志
     Official Posts   *zhiguan zhi* 職官志
     Examination System   *xuanju zhi* 選舉志
     Army and Garrisons   *bing zhi* 兵志
     Administrative Geography   *dili zhi* 地理志
4. Biographical writing   *zhuanji* 傳紀
   Commemorative writings   *muzhi* 墓誌, *xingzhuang* 行狀

Historical Biographies   *liezhuan* 列傳
Chronological Biographies   *nianpu* 年譜
Genealogies   *zongpu* 宗譜 , *jiapu* 家譜
Family Instructions   *jiaxun* 家訓 , *jiayue* 家約

Geography

Historical geography   *dili* 地理
Maps   *tu* 圖
Early geographical works   *Yugong* 禹貢 , *Shanhaijing* 山海經

Monographs on Administrative
   Geography   *dili zhi* 地理志
Early comprehensive geographies
Comprehensive Gazetteers of
   the Empire   *yitong zhi* 一統志 , *zongzhi* 總志

Local Gazetteers   *difang zhi* 地方志 , *fangzhi* 方志

Foreign peoples, border areas,   *waiguo* 外國 , *bianjiang* 邊疆
   travels   *lüxing* 旅行
Descriptions of cities
Merchant Manuals
   and route books

Institutional, administrative, and legal documents

Encyclopaedic Histories of
   Institutions   *shitong* 十通
Administrative and penal law
Pre-Tang law
Statutes   *ling* 令
Compendia of Administrative
   Law   *huidian* 會典
Guides and handbooks for
   officials and clerks   *guanzhen gongdu* 官箴公牘
Penal Codes   *lü* 律
Monographs on Law in the
   Standard Histories   *xingfa zhi* 刑法志
Monographs on the Army in
   the Histories   *bing zhi* 兵志

Works on warfare and the
   military   *bing jia* 兵家
Collections of Important
   Documents   *huiyao* 會要
Collections of Edicts   *zhaoling* 詔令
Collections of Memorials   *zouyi* 奏議
Han documents on wooden slips *Hanjian* 漢簡
Dunhuang Mss   *Dunhuang xieben* 敦煌寫本
Ming-Qing archives   *Ming-Qing dang-an ku* 明清檔案庫
Provincial and district archives *difang dang-an ku* 地方檔案庫

Private documents   *siren wenjian* 私人文件

Works on agriculture and technology

Agricultural Treatises   *nongshu* 農書
Works on technology   *gongyi* 工藝
Water control   *shuili* 水利

Encyclopaedias and literature

General Encyclopaedias   *leishu* 類書
Encyclopaedias for Daily Use   *riyong leishu* 日用類書
Literary Anthologies   *zongji* 總集
Collected Works   *wenji* 文集 , *quanji* 全集
Miscellaneous Notes   *biji* 筆記, *suibi* 隨筆

Confucian Classics, philosophical works, Buddhism, and Taoism

Confucian Classics   *jing* 經
Philosophical works of
   Confucians and others   *rujia* 儒家 , *zi* 子
Works of Buddhists   *fojia* 佛家
Works of Taoists   *daojia* 道家

Oral and popular traditions

Folk literature   *suwenxue* 俗文學
Records of Manners and Customs *fengsuji* 風俗記, *fengtuji* 風土記
Modern folklore studies   *minsuxue* 民俗學

Foreign writings

Foreign writings

12. Ancillary Disciplines

12.1 Historiography

The most famous works of historical criticism (*shiping* 史評) in imperial China were by Liu Zhi-ji 劉知幾 (661-721) and by Zhang Xue-cheng 章學誠 (1738-1801). Liu's work, *Generalities on History* (**Shi tung** 史通 , 710) is discussed by E.G. Pulleyblank, in "Chinese Historical Criticism, Liu Chih-chi and Ssu-ma Kuang," in Beasley and Pulleyblank, pp. 135-166. See also W. Hung, "A T'ang Historiographers's Letter of Resignation," *HJAS* 29:5-52 (1969). On Zhang's work, *General Meaning of Historiography* (**Wenshi tongyi** 文史通義 ; 1832), see P. Demiéville, "Chang Hsüeh-ch'eng and his Historiography," in Beasley and Pulleyblank, pp. 167-185. See also D.S. Nivison, *The Life and Thought of Chang Hsüeh-ch'eng (1738-1801)* (Stanford, 1966).

12.2 Traditional classification of primary sources

In order to find sources produced or preserved in the old historiographical tradition it is of course necessary to know where a given type of source would be classified and referred to. As the famous eighteenth-century scholar Wang Ming-sheng 王鳴盛 said of studies in general, "Bibliography is the most important requirement for reading books. Only if bibliography is understood can you pursue your studies; if you don't understand it your studies will be chaotic" (**Shiqishi shangque** 十七史商榷 , q.v., *juan* 22). Historical works and historical sources were classified from the Han dynasty as a separate category in what came to be in the third century A.D. the standard fourfold bibliographic division of Classics, History, Philosophy,

Literature (Belles-Lettres) (*jing* 經, *shi* 史, *zi* 子, *ji* 集). This Guide is mainly (but by no means exclusively) concerned with the primary and secondary sources classified in Chinese catalogues and works on historiography under the division of History (sections 12, 13.2, 14-23, and 26).

Within the division of History many different classifications of sources were used in different periods. In broad outline, however, most were similar to the subdivisions employed by the eighteenth-century editors of the *Imperial Catalogue* which have since that time been accepted as the most authoritative; they are still used in library catalogues of old Chinese books today.

TABLE 1

Subdivisions of the History Division
in the Imperial Catalogue*

1.	Standard Histories (see section 16)	*zhengshi*	正史
2.	Annals (see section 14)	*biannian*	編年
3.	Topically Arranged Histories (see section 15)	*jishibenmo*	紀事本末
4.	"Separate histories" (mainly in Standard History form but not recognized as official)	*bieshi*	別史
5.	Miscellaneous histories	*zashi*	雜史
6.	Edicts and Memorials (see section 23)	*zhaolingzouyi*	詔令奏議
7.	Biographical works (see section 17)	*zhuanji*	傳記
8.	Historical excerpts	*shichao*	史鈔
9.	Records of states not recognized as legitimate	*zaiji*	載記
10.	Works on chronology	*shiling*	時令
11.	Geography (see section 18)	*dili*	地理
12.	Works on evolution of government offices (e.g. sections 19, 20.3)	*zhiguan*	職官

*The above list is based on the table in Pulleyblank (1964), p. 156, which is a summary of the section headings of the History Division in the *Imperial Catalogue* (*juan* 45-90).

13.	Institutional histories (see section 22)	*zhengshu*	政書
14.	Book and epigraphy catalogues (see section 12.2)	*mulu*	目錄
15.	Historical criticism (see section 12.1)	*shiping*	史評

The first and fourth of the Four Division (*sibu* 四部) of the *Imperial Catalogue* (Classics and Belles-Lettres, *jing* 經 and *ji* 集) present comparatively few difficulties as to the nature of their contents (see sections 29 and 27). The third division, Philosophers (*zi* 子), is extremely hetero-geneous. Since it contains many works useful to the historian, the subdivisions are given below:

TABLE 2

Subdivisions of the Philosophers' Division
in the Imperial Catalogue

1.	Confucian writers (see section 29)	*rujia*	儒家
2.	Military experts (see section 21)	*bingjia*	兵家
3.	Legalists (see section 20)	*fajia*	法家
4.	Writers on agriculture (see section 25.1)	*nongjia*	農家
5.	Writers on medicine	*yijia*	醫家
6.	Writers on astronomy and mathematics	*tianwen suanfa*	天文算法
7.	Divination	*shushu*	術數
8.	Arts, painting, calligraphy, etc.	*yishu*	藝術
9.	Treatises on miscellaneous subjects (coins, cooking, etc.)	*pulu*	譜錄
10.	Miscellaneous writers (see section 28)	*zajia*	雜家
11.	General Encyclopaedias (see section 26)	*leishu*	類書
12.	Novels and incidental writing (see section 31)	*xiaoshuo*	小說
13.	Buddhists (see section 30.1)	*shijia*	釋家
14.	Taoists (see section 30.2)	*daojia*	道家

For a discussion of the Imperial Catalogue turn to section 4; on the various problems of locating sources see sections 3, 4, and 5.

References

On the evolution of the four bibliographic divisions (*sibu* 四部) see Tsuen-hsuin Tsien, "A History of Bibliographic Classification in China," *Library Quarterly* 22:307-324 (1952). The various sub-categories of the History division are traced in Zheng He-sheng 鄭鶴聲 , *A Study of the Classifications of the History Division* (**Zhongguo shibu mulu xue** 中國 史部目錄學 ; Shanghai, 1933; 1956). J. Ferguson, "General Survey of Standard Chinese Histories," *Journal of the North China Branch of the Royal Asiatic Society* 57:57-69 (1926) provides a straightforward discussion of the 15-fold classification of the History division in the *Imperial Catalogue,* as does Gardner, pp. 96-105, and Pulleyblank (1964), p. 156.

12.3   Textual criticism *(jiaokan* 校勘 *)*

Textual criticism in China has been focused on the correction and authentification of the various versions and texts of the Confucian Classics. The controversy between the supporters of each version of the different Classics has been a major intellectual debate from the Han dynasty down to the Qing and the early Republic, but the ramifications of this debate need not concern us here. It is sufficient to note that any work on pre-Qin history must take account of traditional textual criticism, since the Classics are of course prime sources for the pre-Qin period. For a brief summary of the debate see I.C.Y. Hsü, tr., *Liang Ch'i-ch'ao: Intellectual Trends in the Ch'ing Period* (Cambridge, Mass., 1959), pp. 85-87; and also B. Karlgren, "The Authenticity of Ancient Chinese Texts," *BMFEA* 2:165-183 (1929).

The advances in textual criticism made by Qing scholars were very great. Although concentrating on the texts of the Classics, they also did much important work on later sources as well. Students should make sure, therefore, especially if working on an earlier text, that they have checked the Qing (and later) scholarship on it. Throughout this Guide every effort has been made to draw attention to the best modern editions and reprints, which are by definition those which take account of, or are based on, the relevant Qing scholarship. On Qing textual criticism see J. Grey, "Historical Writing in Twentieth-Century China: Notes on its Background and Development," in Beasley and Pulleyblank, pp. 186-212. On textual criticism and techniques of collation for the historian, see the introduction by Zhang Shun-hui 張舜徽, *Techniques for the Collation and Study of Sources of Chinese History* (**Zhongguo gudai shiji jiaodu fa** 中国古代 史籍校读法 ; Shanghai, 1962). Zhang also includes a brief section on forged books (pp. 279-291), most of which date from the early empire. The most convenient summary of forged works (to the total of 1,059) is Zhang Xin-cheng 張心澂, *General Study of Forgeries* (**Weishu tongkao** 伪书通考), 2 vols. (Shanghai, 1959).

13. Archaeology and Epigraphy

13.1 Archaeology

Although archaeology falls outside the scope of the present Guide, the student of Chinese history cannot afford to neglect the archaeologists' findings, not only for Prehistoric, Shang, and Zhou China but also, to a lesser extent, for later periods in Chinese history.

The best all-round introduction is the series by T.K. Cheng, *Prehistoric China: Archaeology in China,* vol. 1 (Toronto, 1959); *New Light on Pre-historic China: Archaeology in China,* supplement to vol. 1 (Cambridge and Toronto, 1966); *Shang China: Archaeology in China,* vol. 2 (Cambridge, 1961); and *Chou China: Archaeology in China,* vol. 3 (Toronto, 1963). See also K. C. Chang, *The Archaeology of Ancient China,* rev. and enlarged ed. (New Haven, 1968); and W. Watson, *China Before the Han Dynasty* (London, 1960); also W. Watson, *Cultural Frontiers in Ancient East Asia* (Edinburgh, 1972).

The findings of the 1950s are summed up in *Archaeology in New China* (**Xin Zhongguo kaogu de shouhuo** 新中国考古的收获 ; Peking, 1961), and are also introduced in Hsia Nai, "Archaeology in New China," *Peking Review,* no. 3 (Jan. 18, 1963); *Antiquity* 37:176-184 (1963); as well as in Cheng Te-k'un, "Archaeology in Communist China," in A.L. Feuer-werker, ed., *History in Communist China* (Cambridge, Mass., 1968), pp. 45-55. The findings of the sixties are briefly summed up in Xia Nai, *New Archaeological Finds in China* (Peking, 1972).

Note that the section on archaeology in **Tōyō shiryō shūsei** is particularly useful for listing many of the excavations and reports of sites from Chinese imperial history. Several of the Chinese archaeological journals also carry important articles and illustrations of finds dating from Chinese imperial history, especially **Wenwu cankao ziliao** 文物参考資料, 1950-1958; thereafter **Wenwu** 文物 (1959-1967; 1972-   ) and **Kaogu** 考古 (1959-1967; 1972-   ).

13.2   <u>Epigraphy</u> (*jinshiwen* 金石文)

Epigraphy in China before the twentieth century was devoted mainly to the study of inscriptions on bronze and stone (hence the name *jinshixue* 金石學). As bronze was slowly replaced by iron, fewer and fewer inscriptions were recorded on it; by the Han dynasty stone stele and monuments of various sorts had replaced bronze as a medium for inscriptions. Thus bronze inscriptions or the rubbings taken from them are important sources only for the pre-Han period, while stone inscriptions are important supplementary sources for post-Han history.

In the twentieth century, the traditional study of bronze and stone inscriptions was greatly developed by the discovery of many more in-scriptions (particularly on bronze) and also by the application of new methods and approaches, as well as by the discovery of a whole new type of inscriptional material. These were the inscriptions on oracle bones which predated the bronze inscriptions and which were excavated in very large numbers from the sites of Shang culture. The very extensive archaeological

discoveries in the twentieth century, coupled with the preliminary findings
from the study of the oracle bones and the bronzes, have led to the entire
reconstitution of early Chinese history. All three fields of study have become highly specialized (the languages of the oracle bones and the bronzes
are separate studies in themselves) and this fact coupled with the lack of
other historical sources makes this period by far the most complex and fluid
in the whole of Chinese history.

On the different types of inscriptional materials, see the excellent
introduction by Tsuen-hsuin Tsien, *Written on Bamboo and Silk: The
Beginnings of Chinese Books and Inscriptions* (Chicago, 1962), which deals
with inscriptions on bronze, stone, oracle bones, seals, pottery, and many
other materials.

Problems of early inscriptional sources (including forgery, dating, etc.)
are discussed in N. Bernard, "New Approaches and Research Methods in
chin-shih-hsueh," **Tōyō bunka kenkyūjo kiyō** 19:1-31 (1959). One of the
leading Chinese authorities, Hu Hou-xuan 胡厚宣 , outlines *Problems
of Historical Materials in Research on Ancient China* (**Gudai yanjiu de
shiliao wenti** 古代研究史料的问题 ; Shanghai, 1950) with
special emphasis on the oracle-bone inscriptions. For a reader with
commentary see Huang Gong-zhu 黄公渚 , *Selected Inscriptions of the
Zhou and Qin with Explanations* (**Zhou-Qin jinshiwen xuan pingzhu**
周秦金石文選評注 ; Shanghai, 1935).

For a comprehensive catalogue including all types of inscription, use
Rong Yuan 容媛 , *Catalogue of Epigraphical Collections* (**Jinshi shumu
lu** 金石書目錄 ; Shanghai, 1929; rev. ed., 1936; supplement in
Kaogu tongxun 3:70-80, 1959, reprinted Tokyo, 1963).

13.3   Oracle-bone inscriptions (*jiaguwen* 甲骨文)

Between 100,000 and 150,000 tortoise-shell and bone inscriptions
from the late Shang dynasty (fourteenth to twelfth century B.C.) have been
discovered to date. The discoveries were made mainly in the neighborhood
of Anyang in Honan; hence one of the names of this type of writing, "Yin,

i.e. Shang, capital oracle script" (*yinxu puci* 殷虛卜辭, or *puci* for short). The inscriptions were used for divination; characters were carved on the bones which were then heated, the resulting cracks showing the prognostications. Most of the inscriptions are very short and they are written in a peculiarly difficult script, the full range of which has by no means as yet been deciphered.

As a general introduction see Tsien, pp. 19-37; Cheng Te-k'un (1961); and see also the introduction by Dong Zuo-bin, *Fifty Years of Studies in Oracle Inscriptions* (Tokyo, Toyo Bunko, 1964), a translation of Dong's **Jiaguxue wushi nian** (1955). It includes bibliographies and a chronological biography of Dong, who was a pioneer in this field.

The most important finds have been published in archaeological reports and also by such scholars as Wang Guo-wei, 王國維 Lo Zhen-yu 羅振玉 , Dong Zuo-bin 董作賓 , Guo Mo-ro, Hu Hou-xuan, Rong Geng, Chen Meng-jia, and many others.

There is a very thorough index to published oracle-bone inscriptions in the massive *General Index for Yinxu Oracle Texts,* compiled by Shima Kunio 島邦男 (**Inkyō bokuji sōrui** 殷墟卜辭綜類; Tokyo, 1967). Sixty works containing transcriptions of oracle-bone inscriptions published between 1903 and 1957 were indexed. Single characters or compounds are listed in a radical sequence; context and reference to original work are given.

For a dictionary-type listing of individual characters with explanations of 900 out of a total of 4,672 oracle-bone characters listed, see Sun Hai-bo 孫海波 , *Dictionary of Oracle Bone Script* (**Jiagu wenbian** 甲骨文編), rev. and enlarged ed. (Peking, 1965; originally appeared in 1934).

The interpretation and use of the oracle bones by historians of ancient China was pioneered by Guo Mo-ro 郭沫若 in his *Studies of Ancient Chinese Society* (**Zhongguo gudai shehui yanjiu** 中國古代社會研究; Shanghai, 1930; many later revised editions), pt. 3. To keep abreast of later historical work, see Kaizuka Shigeki's 貝塚茂樹 summary of new studies, *The Development of Historical Studies of Ancient China* (**Chūgoku kodaishigaku no hatten** 中國古代史學の發展; Tokyo, 1946); also the more up-to-date and popular work edited by the same author: *The Ancient Empire of Yin* (**Kodai In-teikoku** 古代殷帝国; Tokyo, 1957, 1967).

Bibliographies

Hu Hou-xuan 胡厚宣 , *A Bibliography of the Study of Shell and Bone Inscriptions, 1899-1949* (**Wushinian jiaguxue lunzhu mu** 五十年甲骨学论著目 ; Shanghai, 1952).

Annual List of Articles and Books Concerning Oracle Bones and Bronze Inscriptions (**Kōkotsugaku** 甲骨学 , annually from 1958). On **Kōkotsugaku** see next entry.

Oracle-bone Journal (**Kōkotsugaku** 甲骨学), ed. Japanese Association for the Study of Oracle Bone Inscriptions (Nihon kōkotsugakkai), annual (Tokyo, 1951-   ). Since 1958 has published an annual bibliography of oracle-bone studies (see entry above).

13.4 Bronze inscriptions (*jinwen* 金文)

A very large number of bronze vessels and objects of all sorts are extant today, but only about six or seven thousand bear inscriptions and of these only a fraction are of interest to the historian. Of the total, about 1,000 date from the Shang; 4,000 from the Zhou and 1,000 from the Qin and Han (Tsien, p. 41). Most of the inscriptions are brief but they are longer than those found on the oracle bones. The longest are found on ritual vessels. Some record the occasion of gifts and bestowals by the monarch (**baobei ciyu xingshi** 寶貝賜與形式), while others record the orders of appointment to office (**ceming xingshi** 策命形式), military campaigns, covenants, treaties, ceremonial events, etc.

For a general description of the bronze inscriptions see Tsien, pp. 38-63, and also W. Watson, *Ancient Chinese Bronzes* (Rutland, 1962), pp. 68-80.

Many of the bronze inscriptions have been published in collections of rubbings or transcriptions by scholars both traditional and modern, but as yet no comprehensive collection exists; the standard index to these collections is still J. Ferguson, *Catalogue of the Recorded Bronzes of Successive Dynasties* (**Lidai zhulu jijin mu** 歷代著錄吉金目 ; Shanghai, 1939).

The standard listing showing modern forms of the characters on bronze inscriptions is Rong Geng 容庚 , *Dictionary of Bronze Inscriptions of the Shang and Zhou* (**Jinwenbian** 金文編 ; 1925; rev. ed., 5 *ce*, Shanghai, 1939; reprinted with corrections, Peking, 1959); and also by Rong Geng, *Dictionary of Bronze Inscriptions of the Qin and Han* (**Jinwenbian xubian** 金文續編), 2 *ce* (Shanghai, 1935).

See also Karlgren's *Grammata Serica Recensa* (Stockholm, 1957; Göteborg, 1964).

For inscriptions on ancient coins, see Wang Yü-ch'üan, *Early Chinese Coinage* (New York, 1951), and Ding Fu-bao 丁福保 , *Encyclopaedia of Ancient Chinese Coins* (**Guqian da cidian** 古錢大辭典 ; Shanghai, 1937; reprinted, Taipei, 1962).

A substantial literature has been published on the vital but difficult question of the dating of the bronzes (partly on stylistic criteria) by scholars such as Karlgren, Guo Mo-ro, Tang Lan 唐蘭 , Chen Meng-jia, and others.

Difficult though the studies of the bronze inscriptions are, no serious history of early China can be written without taking them into account and using them to supplement the literary, archaeological, and other epigraphical sources.

The pioneer in the use of bronze inscriptions as a supplementary source for ancient Chinese history was Guo Mo-ro in his *Studies of Ancient Chinese Society,* pt. 3. For a general discussion see H. G. Creel, "Bronze Inscriptions of the Western Chou Dynasty as Historical Documents," *Journal of the American Oriental Society* 56:335-349 (1936); and also Appendix A of Creel's *The Origins of Statecraft in China,* vol. 1, *The Western Chou Empire* (Chicago and London, 1970), pp. 444-486.

Bibliographies of Secondary Works

Bibliography of Secondary Works on Chinese Bronze Inscriptions, ed. Hiroshima daigaku bungakubu chūgoku tetsugaku kenkyūshitsu 廣島大学文学部中国哲学研究室 (**Kinbun kankei bunken mokuroku** 金文関係文献目録 ; Hiroshima, 1956).
"Annual List of Articles and Books Concerning Oracle Bones and Bronze Inscriptions," in the *Oracle Bone Journal* (**Kokotsugaku**; 1958-   ).

13.5   Stone inscriptions (*shike* 石刻)

Inscriptions on stone have survived from the Han onward in numbers far exceeding any other form of inscriptional materials; they form an important subsidiary source to printed sources for the last two thousand years of Chinese history. Apart from the famous sets of Confucian Classics and the Buddhist Canon carved on stone tablets (whose chief interest lies in correcting the texts of the Classics), many hundreds of thousands of stele of many different types have been transcribed or still survive in their original form. One of the chief uses of the stele was to commemorate individuals (see section 17.1 for a discussion of the different types of grave stele), and hence this type of stele is one of the basic sources for Chinese biographical studies. Most of the stele containing biographical materials have been indexed in the reference tools listed in section 17.5.2. Owing to the early development of the study of inscriptions on stone from the Tang, and systematically from the Song (see R.C. Rudolph, "Preliminary Notes on Sung Archaeology," *JAS* 22:169-177 [1963]), a vast number of the stele inscriptions have survived in transcribed form, either in special collections or in collected works or in Local Gazetteers and other standard historical sources.

Many of the important early collections of stone inscriptions have been published in *Collectanea of Historical Materials on Stone Inscriptions* (**Shike shiliao congshu** 石刻史料叢書), 470 *ce* in 60 cases (Taipei, 1966).

Some idea of the categories of writing recorded on the early stele down to the Yuan may be had from the indispensable index by Yang Dian-xun 楊殿珣, *Index to Inscriptions and Colophons on Stone* (**Shike tiba suoyin** 石刻題跋索引 ; 1941; enlarged ed., Shanghai, 1957), which indexes 137 collections of stone inscriptions from the Zhou to the Yuan and is arranged in the following categories: tomb stele, epitaphs, inscribed classics, inscriptions for statues and pictures, inscribed names, inscribed poems, and miscellaneous inscriptions.

Stele were also used to record boundaries and ownership of fields, guild rules, donors, and details of all kinds of construction, and many other matters of great interest to the student of Chinese social and economic history. Unfortunately such stele did not come within the purview of the literati collectors of stone inscriptions and in the twentieth century too, historians have been slow to use this type of material. There have been some notable exceptions, however; one of the first was the Japanese historian Imahori Seiji 今堀誠二, who based his *Chinese Feudal Society: an Intensive Investigation of Social Groups in a District Town from the Early Qing on* (**Chūgoku hoken shakai no kōzō** 中国封建社会の構造; Tokyo, 1955) partly on interviews and partly on the very large number of transcriptions from temple stele which he made in the town and which are included in an appendix (pp. 701-837). During the 1950s an important selection of transcriptions from similar materials in Kiangsu was published: *Selection of Transcriptions from Stele from Kiangsu in the Ming and Qing* (**Jiangsu Ming-Qing yilai beike ziliao xuanji** 江苏明清以来碑刻资料选辑; Peking, 1959; Tokyo, 1967).

Much greater attention has been paid to monumental inscriptions such as the set of Confucian Classics or the Buddhist inscriptions at Longmen or the examples of calligraphy by famous artists or statesmen. For a general description of these latter types of stone inscriptions see Tsien, pp. 64-89.

There is an excellent reader of Han dynasty stone inscriptions designed for the beginner: Huang Gong-zhu 黄公渚, *Selection of Stele Inscriptions from the two Han with Commentary* (**Liang Han beiwen xuan pingzhu** 两汉碑文选评注; Shanghai, 1935; Hong Kong, 1965).

14. Annalistic Sources and Annals Style

14.1   Introduction

The earliest and one of the most important methods of arranging historical materials throughout Chinese history began as a bare catalogue of court events arranged chronologically: e.g., "on such and such a year/month/day King X of Y went on a hunt." Most of the writing on tortoise shell (*jiaguwen* 甲骨文 , see section 13.3), which predates the first extant historical work by several centuries, contains similar records of single events, but the relations between scapulamancy and the origins of a continuous process of record-keeping are obscure. The court chronicler in early China was an important official charged with astronomical as well as archival functions; he played a key part in the arrangement and timing of royal ancestor worship and sacrifical rites and other ceremonies. He may also have had remonstrance functions, in light of his duties of keeping records of models worthy of emulation and of portents heralding disaster.

In later Chinese history the bare catalogue of events at court was greatly expanded and elaborate composite chronicles of events throughout the empire began to appear, either written privately or under official sponsorship (although always with the major focus on the court and central government).

14.2   Basic annalistic sources and Veritable Records

Throughout Chinese history the basic annalistic sources were produced by officials of the central government; in imperial times these sources had become standardized into the following types: the Diaries of Activity and Repose (*qijuzhu* 起居注) which recorded matters mentioned in official imperial audiences; the Records of Current Government (*shizhengji* 時政記) composed at the ministries; and the Daily Records (*rili* 日曆   )

which were a condensation arranged day by day of the first two. The Daily Records were used in turn as the chief source for the annalistic Veritable Records (*shilu* 實錄), of which there was one for each emperor, as well as for the less detailed National Histories (*guoshi* 國史) which were compiled in some periods for each reign. The final step in this process of progressive distillation of the daily records was the compilation of the Basic Annals section (*benji* 本紀) of the Standard Histories (see section 16).

Only fragments of such court documents as the Diaries of Activity and Repose, the Records of Current Government, and the Daily Records have survived from the Tang and Song and later periods. As for the Veritable Records, a section survives from the Tang (part of the year 805), for which see B. Solomon, *The Veritable Record of the T'ang Emperor Shun-tsung* (Cambridge, Mass., 1956); and from the Song (portions of the years 983 and 996), for which see Huang Han-chao 黃漢超 , "Analysis of the Veritable Records on Song Shen-zong" (Song Shen-zong shilu qianhou gaixiu zhi fenxi 宋神宗實錄前後改修之分析) in **Xinya xuebao** 7.1:363-409 and 7.2:157-195 (1968).

The entire Veritable Records of the Ming and Qing are extant and constitute the single most important source for the last 500 years of Chinese history. Although they are a third-stage distillation of the original records, they still contain an extraordinarily detailed annalistic record, unequaled for any comparable period in any country, and are printed in the staggering total of no less than 7,000 chapters (*juan*). Many edicts, memorials, etc. as well as day-to-day events, are preserved in them.

On the process of the compilation of the Veritable Records, see L.S. Yang, "The Organization of Chinese Official Historiography: Principles and Methods of the Standard Histories from the T'ang through the Ming Dynasty," in Beasley and Pulleyblank, pp. 44-59, reprinted in Yang's *Excursions in Sinology* (Cambridge, Mass., 1969), pp. 96-111. For greater detail, see W. Franke, "The Veritable Records," in *Introduction to the Sources of Ming History* (Kuala Lumpur and Singapore, 1969), pp. 8-23, which supersedes the author's earlier articles on this subject. The best edition of the *Veritable Records of the Ming* (**Ming shilu** 明實錄) is the photographic reprint of the copy formerly in the National Library of Peking and now in Taiwan (183 vols., Taipei, Zhongyang yanjiuyuan lishiyuyan yanjiusuo, 1962-1967, with corrections included in supplementary volumes). The only major modern collection of excerpts from the Veritable Records are Imanishi Shunjū 今西春秋 and Mitamura Taisuke 三田村泰助, eds., *Historical Materials Concerning Manchuria and Mongolia under the Ming Selected From the Veritable Records of the Ming* (**Mindai Mammō shiryō Min jitsuroku shō, Manshūhen** and **Mōkohen** 明代滿蒙史料明實錄抄滿洲篇蒙古篇), 18 vols. (Kyoto University, 1954-1959). There is an itemized index: **Mindai Mammō shiryō, kōmoku sōgō sakuin** 明代滿蒙史料項目總合索引 (Kyoto, 1959).

See also Zhao Ling-yang 趙令揚, *Materials on Southeast Asia from the Veritable Records of the Ming* (**Ming shilu zhong zhi Dongnan Ya shiliao** 明實錄中之東南亞史料), 2 vols. (Hong Kong, 1968); and also the *Selected Excerpts from the Veritable Records of the Ming on the History of Yunnan* (Yunnansheng shaoshu minzu shehui lishi yanjinsuo 雲南省少數民族社会历史研究所 , **Ming shilu youguan Yunnan lishi ziliao zhaiyao** 明实录有关雲南历史资料摘要 ; Kunming, 1959).

The only edition of the *Veritable Records of the Qing* (**Qing shilu** 清實錄) is the sumptuous photographic reproduction **Tai Shin rekichō jitsuroku** 大清歷朝實錄 , 4,485 *juan* in 1,220 *ce* (Tokyo, 1937-1938; complete facsimile reprint, Taipei, 1963-1964). A handy selection of source materials taken from the Veritable Records is *Important Economic Source Materials from the Qing shilu,* edited by the History Department of Nankai University (**Qing shilu jingji ziliao jiyao** 清实录经济资料辑要 ; Peking, 1959), which is arranged by topics. There is a Japanese translation of the private day-to-day records of the Qing imperial house over the years 1607-1636: Kanda Nobuo 神田信夫 , ed., *Old Documents in Manchu* (**Mambun rōtō** 滿文老檔), 4 vols. (Tokyo, 1955-1959).

Another important set of annalistic sources for the Qing is *Records from the Eastern Gate* (**Donghua lu** 東華錄), so called from the fact that the first and subsequent compilers worked in the State History Office (Guoshi guan 國史館), which after 1765 was situated inside the Donghua gate in Peking. Although less full than the Veritable Records (upon which

they were based), the various **Donghua lu** may be used as a quick way of
finding sources in the Veritable Records. The **Shiyichao Donghualu**
十一朝東華錄 covers the years 1644-1874 and the much fuller
Guangxuchao Donghualu 光緒朝東华录 , 5 vols., punctuated ed.
(Peking, 1958) covers the years 1875-1908. The **Xuantong zhengji** 宣統
政记 is a similar source which covers the years 1909-1911.

On the *Veritable Records of the Qing* and other annalistic Qing sources,
see W. Fuchs, *Beiträge zur Mandjurischen Bibliographie und Literatur*
(Tokyo, 1936), pp. 58-71; and K. Biggerstaff, "Some Notes on the *Tung-
hua lu* and the *Shih-lu,*" *HJAS* 4:101-115 (1939). Use J.K. Fairbank,
Ch'ing Documents, An Introductory Syllabus (Cambridge, Mass., 1965),
as a first reference.

14.3   Major works in annals style

The earliest extant example of a historical work in the annalistic style
is the *Spring and Autumn Annals* (**Chunqiu** 春秋), which is the court
chronicle of the state of Lu; events are extremely tersely recorded (the
longest entry is only forty characters) and the years covered are 722-480
B.C. Editorship was traditionally and implausibly ascribed to Confucius.
The third of the three commentaries on the *Spring and Autumn Annals,*
the *Commentary of Zuo* (**Zuo zhuan** 左傳) is much fuller and more
lively than the *Annals* themselves and is a prime source on the social history
of the period.

The most convenient edition of the *Spring and Autumn Annals* and its
three commentaries is included in punctuated form in the first volume of
Combined Concordance to the Spring and Autumn Annals and Commentaries
(**Chunqiu jing zhuan yinde** 春秋經傳引得), H-Y Index Supplement
17, 4 vols. (Peking, 1937; Taipei reprint, 1966).

There is an English translation of the *Spring and Autumn Annals* and
the **Zuozhuan** by J. Legge: *The Chinese Classics* (Hong Kong University
Press reprint, Hong Kong, 1961), vol. 4 in 2 parts. There is also a French

translation by S. Couvreur, *Tch'ouen ts'iou et Tso tschouan,* 3 vols. (Hejian fu, 1914; reprinted Paris, 1951). See also B. Watson, *Early Chinese Literature* (New York and London, 1962), pp. 17-121; P. Van der Loon, "The Ancient Chinese Chronicles and the Growth of Historical Ideals," in Beasley and Pulleyblank, pp. 24-30; B. Karlgren, "On the Authenticity and Nature of the *Tso-chuan,*" *Götesborgs högskolas arsskrift* 32:3-65 (1926; Taipei reprint, 1965); H. Maspero, "La composition et la date du *Tso-chuan,*" *Mélanges chinois et bouddiques* (Brussels, 1931-1932), I, 137-215. Ch'i Ssu-ho, "Professor Hung on the Ch'un Ch'iu," *The Yenching Journal of Social Science* 1.1:49-71 (1938), is a summary of the first half of Hung's important prolegomena to the text printed with the H-Y Index. Note also Karlgren, "Glosses on the Tso-chuan," *BMFEA* 44:1-157 (1969) and 45: 273-295 (1970).

Annalistic writing was to be one of the methods of arrangement adopted by Si-ma Qian in the **Shiji** (in the Basic Annals section) and it remained an integral part of the Standard Histories from that time on (see section 16). Although many annals and chronicles (not to mention Veritable Records, etc.) were written during and after the Han, it was not until the Song that a major step forward took place in this genre with the compilation of the *Comprehensive Mirror for Aid in Government* by Si-ma Guang 司馬光 (**Zizhi tongjian** 資治通鑑, presented in 1084), which magisterially carried the history of China from the end of the fifth century B. C. in continuous chronicle form over the next 1,326 years down to the tenth century A.D. In its catholicity of sources consulted, in its discussion of disputed points as well as in its huge table of contents, it marked an important new level for the chronicle form as well as for general historical methodology; and it was to have an enormous influence on later Chinese historical writing, either directly or through its many abbreviations, continuations, and adaptations.

The most convenient edition of the **Zizhi tongjian** is the punctuated movable-type edition prepared by Wang Chong-wu 王崇武, Nie Chong-qi 聶崇岐, and Gu Jie-gang 顧頡剛, with commentary by Hu San-xing 胡三省, notes on disputed points (*kaoyi* 考異) by Si-ma Guang and text criticism by Zhang Yu 章鈺, 10 vols. (Peking, 1957; Taipei reprint available).

There is an index available compiled by Saeki Tomi 佐伯富 : *Index to the Comprehensive Mirror for Aid in Government* (**Shiji tsūgan sakuin** 資治通鑑索引 ; Kyoto, 1961).

Portions have been translated into English, notably chapters 58-78 (covering the years A.D. 181-265) by R. DeCrespigny, *The last of the Han, being the chronicle of the years 181-220 A.D. as recorded in chapters 58-68 of the Tzu-chih t'ung-chien of Ssu-ma Kuang* (Canberra, 1969); and by A. Fang, *The chronicles of the Three Kingdoms (220-265), chapters 69 to 78 from Tzu-chih t'ung-chien of Ssu-ma Kuang translated with notes,* 2 vols. (Cambridge, Mass., 1952 and 1965). Fang's annotated translation is particularly useful in that the focus is on Si-ma Guang's sources in this period, thus providing a detailed view of his method of compilation.

A, M. M. De Mailla's huge *Histoire Générale de la Chine,* 13 vols. (Paris, 1777-1783; Taipei reprint, 1968) is basically a translation from the Manchu version of Zhu Xi's *Summary of the Comprehensive Mirror for Aid in Government* (**Zizhi tongjian gangmu** 資治通鑑綱目) and its later continuations; it is still the largest general history of China available in a Western language, and has been used by many later textbook writers. There is a partial French translation of one of the continuations of the **Gangmu** by L. C. Delamarre, *Histoire de la dynastie des Ming* (Paris, 1865); this is a translation of the first part of **Zizhi tongjian gangmu sanbian** 資治通鑑綱目三編 (1746), the third continuation of the **Gangmu**.

Although Zhu Xi's *Summary* and its continuations were the most popular historical works among the elite in the Ming and Qing, the very much fuller continuations of the *Comprehensive Mirror* itself are of much greater interest to the modern historian. The most important of the continuations were:

1. Li Tao 李燾 (1114-1183), **Xu Zizhi tongjian changbian** 續資治通鑑長編 , which covers the years 960-1127 (i.e. the N. Song) in great detail.

2. Li Xin-quan 李心傳(1146-1263), **Jianyan yilai xinian yaolu** 建炎以來繫年要錄, which covers the 36 years of Song Gao-zong's reign (first emperor of S. Song, 1127-1163).

3. Bi Yuan 畢沅 (1730-1797) et al., **Xu Zizhi tongjian** 續資治通鑑 , which replaces the other continuations compiled in the Qing and covers the years 960-1370 (published in a uniform edition with the **Zizhi tongjian**, 4 vols. [Peking, 1958]).

For the Ming continuations (of poor quality) and similar Ming annalistic sources, see Franke, pp. 19-44.

On the actual compilation of Si-ma Guang's great work, see E. G. Pulleyblank, "Chinese Historical Criticism: Liu Chih-chi and Ssu-ma Kuang," in Beasley and Pulleyblank, pp. 135-166, as well as the Preface in Crespigny, pp. xi-xxv; see also Zhang Xu 張須 , *Studies on the Comprehensive Mirror* (**Tongjian xue** 通鑑學 ; Shanghai, 1948); and the introductory article by Chen Qian-jun 陈千俊 , "On the Comprehensive Mirror for Aid in Government" (Lun zizhi tongjian 论资治通鉴), in **Lishi yanjiu** 7:27-40 (1957). There is an index to the place names in Hu San-xing's notes (**Shiji tsūgan ko chū chimei sakuin** 資治通鑑胡注地名索引 ; Kyoto, 1967). For an article on Si-ma Guang's work and Zhu Xi's summary, see O. Franke, "Das Tse tschi t'ung kien und das T'ung kien kang-mu, ihr Wesen, ihr Verhältnis zueinander und ihr Quellenwert," *Sitzungsberichte der Preussischen Akademie der Wissenschaften: philosophisch-historischen Klasse* (Berlin, 1930), pp. 103-144.

15. Topically Arranged Histories (*jishi benmo ti* 紀事本末體)

Up to the Song the two main forms of historical writing were Annals (*biannianti* 編年體) and Annals-Biographies (*jizhuanti* 紀傳體), as in the Standard Histories (see section 16). The disadvantages of these two forms was that in order to find out about one person or one event, the reader had either to search through many different entries in the rigid chronological frame of the Annals or to bring together information often scattered in the different parts of the composite Standard Histories. These difficulties were partially resolved when a twelfth-century scholar-official named Yuan Shu 袁樞 (1131-1205) rearranged all the chronological entries in Si-ma Guang's *Comprehensive Mirror for Aid in Government* into 239 topical entries and thus broke out of the strict Annals framework. He called his rearrangement *The Comprehensive Mirror for Aid in Government Topically Arranged* (**Tongjian jishi benmo** 通鑑紀事本末).

Although there were many imitators and Yuan is generally credited with having developed the third major type of Chinese historical writing (the "from-beginning-to-ending-of-events" or "topically arranged" style, *jishi benmo ti* 紀事本末體), for the most part writers in this style only rearranged existing works (as had Yuan); they did not add new materials or interpretations. The single outstanding exception was Gu Ying-tai 谷 應泰 (d. 1689), who wrote his *The Major Events of Ming History* (**Mingchao,** later changed to **Mingshi jishi benmo** 明史紀事本末 ; 1658; Shanghai, 1935-1937; Taipei reprint, 1956), before the annals histories of the Ming had been compiled and thus made an important contribution to Ming history.

Also to be included in the same category are the official histories of campaigns (*fanglüe* 方略), a form of compilation which became particularly popular in the Qing (see section 21.2).

16. The Standard Histories (*zhengshi* 正史)

16.1   Introduction

The first great innovation in historical writing and departure from the annalist style was the work of Si-ma Tan and his son, Si-ma Qian, court astronomers and historians during the second and at the beginning of the first century B.C. The title that their work came to be known by was **Shiji** 史記 , which has been given the English title *Records of the Grand Historian* (following the older title **Taishi gong ji** 太史公記).

Their work is a history of China from the earliest times down to the Han dynasty arranged according to principles which, with certain adaptations, were to set the form for a whole new way of writing history. This form came to be known as Annals-Biography (*jizhuan ti* 紀傳體) after two of its most important parts. It was to be used in each of the Standard Histories, also called Dynastic Histories (*zhengshi* 正史) from the Standard History of the Han onwards.

The two main innovations of Si-ma Qian and his father were the Monographs (*shu* 書 or later *zhi* 志) on the historical evolution of selected institutions such as rituals, the calendar, astronomy, political economy, etc. (see section 16.5), and the Collected Biographies (*liezhuan* 列傳), which are groups of biographies or profiles of both famous and (some) less famous people (as well as foreign peoples) of each age. These two sections of the **Shiji**, together with the older-style Basic Annals (*benji* 本紀) which carried on the court annals tradition, became the three major elements of the Standard History form of historical writing (which might, therefore, be more accurately called Annals-Biographies-Monographs rather than the traditional term, Annals-Biography). The other sections of the *Records of the Grand Historian* (i.e. the Tables, *biao* 表, and the Hereditary Houses, *shijia* 世家) were only incorporated sporadically or not at all in the later Standard Histories.

The most important difference between the Standard Histories from the **Hanshu** onwards and the **Shiji** was that each of the former only covered one dynasty and made no attempt to cover the vast sweep of history embraced by the **Shiji**. Another important difference was that as time went by, the Standard Histories (with some notable exceptions) tended to become more and more standardized as they became the work of large editorial boards of official historians.

The number of Standard Histories has of course varied as new ones were compiled. The first four are often referred to as the Four Histories (**qian sishi** 前四史). By the eighteenth century with the completion of the *Standard History of the Ming* there were altogether 22, and the retrieval of the Old Standard Histories of the Tang and the Five Dynasties brought the total to 24, which became 25 after the official addition of the

New Standard History of the Yuan. Although neither the *Draft History of the Qing* nor the *History of the Qing* have been officially included in the Standard Histories, they are in effect in the old tradition and are included here to bring the total to 26.

Although varying greatly in quality and length, the Standard Histories constitute a monumental *oeuvre,* the importance of which can hardly be exaggerated. They provide remarkably accurate coverage of 2,000 years of Chinese history (seen from the Confucian standpoint, needless to say), and they include historical profiles of the rulers, events, leading personalities, major institutions, administrative boundaries, etc. of each dynasty, as well as a considerable quantity of detailed information on the peoples of East, Central, and Southeast Asia. The value of the earlier Standard Histories is greatly enhanced by the fact that many of the sources upon which they were based have since been lost. For this reason the scissors-and-paste methods of some of their editors should be regarded as an asset.

A huge literature exists on the Standard Histories, especially on the first four, which were regarded as monuments of literary and historical excellence. A fraction of this literature is listed below, together with the various reference tools needed for rapid use of the Histories.

16.2   Editions

The most commonly used uniform edition of all the Histories is the so-called Po-na edition, **Baina ben ershisi shi** 百衲本二十四史 , 820 *ce,* **Sibu congkan** series (q.v.), (Shanghai, 1930-1937; Taiwan reprint, 1965). The title means "hundred patches edition," referring to the fact that each History was taken from the best Song and Yuan edition.

Other commonly used editions of all the Histories are the many reprints of the 1739 Palace edition (**Wuying dian ben** 武英殿本, **Dianben** for short):

1.   Tongwen shuju 同文書局 , Ershisi shi 二十四史 , 711 *ce* (Shanghai, 1894).

2.   Wuzhou shuju 五洲書局 , Ershisi shi 二十四史, 524 *ce* (1869-1878).

3.   Kaiming shudian 開明書店 , Ershiwu shi 二十五史 , 9 vols. (Shanghai, 1935); includes the *New Standard History of the Yuan* but is in much reduced size. Contains important supplementary matter.

4.   Yiwen yinshu guan 藝文印書館 , Ershiwu shi (Taipei, 1956); includes the *New Standard History of the Yuan*. Not nearly as reduced in size as the Kaiming edition and therefore much easier on the eyes.

Editions of individual Histories (some punctuated) are often more convenient to use, textually superior, and are printed with notes and commentaries (see 16.4 below).

Particular sections from all the Histories are sometimes excerpted and published together—e.g., the Monographs on a given subject from each History (see under 16.5 below); thus also the Comments (*lunzan* 論贊), which were placed at the end of each chapter and which were intended to express the personal view of the compilers, have been conveniently published together: Song Xi 宋晞 , *Authors' Comments in the Standard Histories* (Zhengshi lunzan 正史論贊), 5 vols. (Taipei, 1954-1960). So have the sections on foreign peoples in the first fifteen Histories: Jian Bozan 翦伯贊 , ed., *Sections on Foreign Peoples in the Standard Histories* (Lidai ge zu zhuanji huibian 历代各族传记会编), 2 vols. in 3 (Peking, 1958-1959). Whenever possible such excerpted publications should be used, especially those listed under 16.5.2 below.

16.3   Corrections, supplements, and studies

A very large number of corrections and supplements to the Standard Histories were produced by traditional scholars. References to the most important of these are listed at the end of each History in the Kaiming shudian edition. The Kaiming shudian also published six volumes of

corrections and additions to the Monographs and Tables in the Standard
Histories, under the title *Supplements to the Twenty-five Histories* (**Ershiwu
shi bubian** 二十五史補編), 6 vols. (Shanghai, 1936-1937; reprinted
Peking, 1955).

Note that **Tōyō shiryō shūsei** lists the major supplementary works to
the Standard Histories.

During the Qing, the practice of carefully reading and comparing the
Histories gave rise to three brilliant studies which were frequently able to
combine textual acuity with a keen sense of the significance of the historical
topics which they selected for attention. The first of these studies was by
Qian Da-xin 錢大昕 (1728-1804), and was entitled *Critical Notes on the
Twenty-two Standard Histories* (**Nianer shi kaoyi** 廿二史考異 , 1782),
2 vols. (punctuated Shanghai, 1959); the second was by Wang Ming-sheng
王鳴盛 (1722-1798), *A Critical Study of the Seventeen Standard
Histories* (**Shiqi shi shangque** 十七史商榷, 1787), 2 vols. (punctuated
Shanghai, 1958); while the third--and most interesting from the point of
view of analytic insights as opposed to philological expertise--was Zhao Yi
趙翼 , *Critical Studies on the Twenty-two Standard Histories* (**Nianer
shi zhaji** 廿二史劄記, 1799; punctuated ed. Shanghai, 1958). (Zhao's
and Wang's works are indexed in Saeki, 1954 and 1960; see section 28.)

16.3.1 Modern studies of the Standard Histories as a whole

The works on Chinese historiography as a whole (listed in section 11.1)
all have sections on the Standard Histories. Note particularly L. S. Yang,
"The Organization of Chinese Official Historiography: Principles and
Methods of the Standard Histories from the T'ang through the Ming Dynasty,"
in Beasley and Pulleyblank, pp. 44-59; and also L. S. Yang, "A Theory
about the Titles of the Twenty-four Dynastic Histories," in Yang, pp. 87-93.
See also H. Franke, "Some Remarks on the Interpretation of Chinese
Dynastic Histories," *Oriens* 3:113-122 (1950). A factual introduction is
offered in Xu Hao 許浩 , *Introduction to the Twenty-five Standard
Histories* (**Nianwu shi lungang** 廿五史論綱; Shanghai, 1947).

16.3.2 Translations

An indispensable aid for locating translations from the first nineteen Standard Histories (excluding those from the two Standard Histories of the Han and the Records of the Grand Historian) is H.H.Frankel, *Catalogue of Translations from the Chinese Dynastic Histories for the Period 220-960* (Berkeley, 1957), which incidentally brings out very clearly the earlier bias of European sinologists toward translation of those passages dealing with Sino-foreign contacts. Some of the most important translations from the Histories not covered in this Catalogue are listed under 16.4 below. Note especially the translations of Monographs in the Histories which are discussed under 16.5.

16.3.3 Indexes and concordances to the Standard Histories

Indexes and concordances are indispensable in looking up names of people and places, official titles, book titles, and special terms. Apart from the indexes to individual Histories or sections of Histories (which are listed under 16.4 below), there are a number which cover certain sections of all the Histories. Most important of these is the *Biographical Index to the Twenty-five Standard Histories* (**Ershiwu shi renming suoyin** 二 十 五 史 人 名 索 引 ; Shanghai, Kaiming shudian, 1935; Peking, 1956; 1964); also the indexes to the Monographs on Dynastic Bibliography and to the Monographs on Financial Administration, on Law and on Official Posts (see 16.5.1-4).

16.4 Studies and research aids for individual Standard Histories

16.4.1 The first Four Histories

N.B.: The dates of the compiler or author indicate the period in which each History was completed. The Histories down to item no. 18 below were *printed* for the first time in the Song.

1. Si-ma Tan 司 馬 談 (180-110? B.C.) and Si-ma Qian 司馬遷 (145-86? B.C.), *The Records of the Grand Historian* (**Taishi gongji, Shiji**

太史公記, 史記), covering from earliest times to 99 B.C.

Studies

T'ung-tsu Ch'ü, *Han Social Structure* (Seattle, 1972).

B. Watson, *Ssu-ma Ch'ien: Grand Historian of China* (New York and London, 1958).

A.F.P. Hulsewé, "Notes on the Historiography of the Han Period," in Beasley and Pulleyblank, pp. 31-43.

The first fifty chapters of the **Shiji** were translated with an important introduction and supplementary matter by E. Chavannes, *Les mémoires historiques de Se-ma Ts'ien,* 6 vols. (Paris, 1895-1905; reprinted Paris, 1967; extra volume with full index and bibliography of Si-ma Qian, Paris, 1969); B. Watson translated the chapters on the Han in his *Records of the Grand Historian of China,* 2 vols. (New York and London, 1961). The Chavannes extra volume (1969) lists translations from the **Shiji** into Western languages.

See also Zhongguo kexueyuan lishi yanjiuso 中国科学院 历史研究所 , *Bibliography of Editions of Records of the Grand Historian and Secondary Literature* (**Shiji yanjiu de ziliao he lunwen suoyin** 史记研究的资料和论文索引 ; Peking, 1957); also He Zi-jun 何子君 , *Catalogue of Editions of the Shiji* (**Shiji shulu** 史记书录 ; Peking, 1958).

Editions

Zhonghua Shuju (punctuated), **Shiji**, 10 vols. (Peking, 1962; Hong Kong reprint, 1970).

Takigawa Kametarō 瀧川龜太郎 , **Shiki kaichū kōshō** 史記會註考證, 10 vols. (Tokyo, 1932-1934; reprinted with supplementary vols., Tokyo, 1957-1959; Taipei reprint, 1959).

Concordances and indexes

*Combined Indexes to the **Shiji** and the Notes of Bei Yin, Si-ma Zheng, Zhang Shou-jie, and Takigawa Kametarō* (**Shiji ji zhushi zonghe yinde** 史記及注釋綜合引得), H-Y Index 40 (Peking, 1947; reprinted 1966).

Wong Fook-luen 黄福鑾, *Subject Index to the Records of the Grand Historian* (**Shiji suoyin** 史記索引 ; Hong Kong, 1963). This is an index of terms, names, etc., arranged under 24 categories.

2. Ban Gu 班固 (A.D. 32-92) et al., *Standard History of the Former Han* (**Han shu** 漢書 ; **Qian Han shu** 前漢書), covering from 209 B.C. to A.D. 25.

Studies

Hulsewé.

Prolegomena and appendices in H. H. Dubs, *The History of the Former Han Dynasty,* 3 vols. (Baltimore, 1938-1955).

C.B. Sargent, "Subsidized History: Pan Ku and the Historical Records of the Former Han Dynasty," *FEQ* 3:119-143 (1943-1944); also Dubs in reply, "The Reliability of Chinese Histories," *FEQ* 4:23-43 (1946-1947).

O.B. Van Der Sprenkel, *Pan Piao, Pan Ku, and the Han History* (Australian National University, Canberra, 1964).

N.L. Swann, *Pan Chao, Foremost Woman Scholar of China, First Century A.D.* (New York, 1932), chap. 5.

T'ung-tsu Ch'ü.

Editions

M.A.N. Loewe, "Some Recent Editions of the *Ch'ien-Han-Shu,*" *Asia Major* 10.2.162-172 (1963).

Zhonghua Shuju (punctuated), **Han shu**, 8 vols. (Peking, 1962).

Wang Xian-qian 王先謙 , **Han shu buzhu** 漢書補注 (Changsha, 1900; Shanghai, 1940; 1959).

Shi Zhi-mian 施之勉 , **Han shu buzhu bianzheng** 汉书补注 辩证 (Peking, 1961).

Concordances and indexes

Combined Indices to the Standard History of the Han and the Notes of Yan Shi-gu and Wang Xian-qian (**Han shu ji buzhu zonghe yinde** 漢書及補註綜合引得), H-Y Index 36 (Peking, 1940; Taipei, 1966).

Wong Fook-luen 黃福鑾, *Index to Standard History of the Han* (**Han shu suoyin** 漢書索引 ; Hong Kong, 1966); index of names and terms arranged under 25 categories.

3. Fan Ye 范曄 (398-445), *Standard History of the Later Han* (**Hou Han shu** 後漢書), covering the years 25-220.

<u>Studies</u>

H. Bielenstein, "The Restoration of the Han Dynasty, with Prolegomena on the Historiography of the Hou Han Shu," *BMFEA* 21:1-209 (1954); see esp. pp. 20-81.

<u>Editions</u>

Zhonghua Shuju (punctuated), **Hou Han shu**, 8 vols. (Peking, 1963; Hong Kong reprint, 1970).

Wang Xian-qian 王先謙 , **Hou Han shu jijie** 後漢書集解.

<u>Concordances and indexes</u>

Index to Historical Terms in the Standard History of the Later Han (**Gokansho goi shūsei** 後漢書語彙集成), 3 vols. (Kyoto, 1960-1962). Indexes some 15,000 names, place names, official titles, and technical terms.

Combined Indices to the Standard History of the Later Han and the Notes of Li Zhao and Li Xian (**Hou Han shu ji zhushi zonghe yinde** 後漢書及注釋綜合引得), H-Y Index 41 (Peking, 1949; Taipei, 1966).

4. Chen Shou 陳壽 (233-297), *Standard History of the Three Kingdoms* (**San guo zhi** 三國志), covering the years: Wei, 221-265; Shu, 221-264; and Wu, 222-280.

<u>Studies</u>

R. De Crespigny, *The Records of the Three Kingdoms: A Study in the Historiography of the San Kuo Chih* (Canberra, 1970).

Hong Ye, *Prolegomena to H-Y Index 27.*

<u>Editions</u>

Zhonghua Shuju (punctuated), **San guo zhi**, 5 vols. (Peking, 1962).

<u>Index</u>

Combined Indices to the Standard History of the Three Kingdoms and the Notes of Bei Song-zhi (**San guo zhi ji Pei zhushi zonghe yinde** 三國志及裴注釋綜合引得), H-Y Index 27 (Peking, 1938; Taipei, 1966).

<u>16.4.2 The eleven Standard Histories covering the years 265-618</u>

5. Fang Xuan-ling 房玄齡 (578-648) et al., *Standard History of the*

Jin (**Jin shu** 晉書), covers the years 265-419.

6. Shen Yue 沈約 (441-513), *Standard History of the Song* (**Song shu** 宋書), covers the years 420-479.

7. Xiao Zi-xian 蕭子顯 (489-537), *Standard History of the Southern Qi* (**Nan Qi shu** 南齊書), covers the years 479-502. Use Zhonghua Shuju punctuated edition, 3 vols. (Peking, 1971).

8. Yao Cha 姚察 (533-606) and Yao Si-lian 姚思廉 (d. 637), *Standard History of the Liang* (**Liang shu** 梁書), covers the years 502-556.

9. Yao Cha 姚察 (533-606) and Yao Si-lian 姚思廉 (d. 637), *Standard History of the Chen* (**Chen shu** 陳書), covers the years 557-589.

10. Wei Shou 魏收 (506-572), *Standard History of the Wei* (**Wei shu** 魏書), covers the years 386-550.

11. Li De-lin 李德林 (530-590) and Li Bai-yao 李百藥 (565-648), *Standard History of the Northern Qi* (**Bei Qi shu** 北齊書), covers the years 550-577.

12. Ling-hu De-fen 令狐德棻 (583-661), *Standard History of the Zhou* (**Zhou shu** 周書), covers the years 557-581. Use Zhonghua Shuju punctuated edition, 3 vols. (Peking, 1971).

13. Wei Zheng 魏徵 (580-643), et al., *Standard History of the Sui* (**Sui shu** 隋書), covers the years 581-617.

14. Li Yan-shou 李延壽 (c. 629), *Standard History of the Southern Dynasties* (**Nan shi** 南史), covers the years 420-589.

15. Li Yan-shou 李延壽 (c. 629), *Standard History of the Northern Dynasties* (**Bei shi** 北史), covers the years 368-618.

On the above eleven Standard Histories covering the Northern and Southern dynasties as well as the *Standard History of the Sui* (**Suishu** 隋書), see W. Hung, "The Tang *Kuo-shih kuan* before 705," *HJAS* 23:93-107 (1960-1961); L.S. Yang, "The Official History of the Chin Period," in Yang, *Studies in Chinese Institutional History* (Cambridge, Mass., 1963), pp. 119-124; J.R. Ware, "Notes on the History of the *Weishu*," *Journal of the American Oriental Society* 52:33-45 (1932). For translations into Western languages from these Histories, see Frankel, and also the various titles in the translation series *Chinese Dynastic Histories Translations* (Berkeley, 1952-).

82

16.4.3 The Later Histories

16. Liu Xu 劉昫 (887-946) et al., *Old Standard History of the Tang* (**Jiu Tang shu** 舊唐書), covers the years 618-906.

17. Ou-yang Xiu 歐陽修 (1007-1072), Song Qi 宋祁 (998-1061), et al., *New Standard History of the Tang* (**Xin Tang shu** 新唐書), covers the years 618-906.

Studies

For a comparison of the two Tang Histories see R. des Rotours, *Le traité des examens* (Paris, 1932), pp. 56-71. See also J. T. C. Liu, *Ou-yang Hsiu, An Eleventh-Century Neo-Confucianist* (Stanford, 1967). Des Rotours is a translation of the Monograph on the Examination System in the *New Standard History of the Tang*.

H.H. Frankel, "T'ang Literati: A Composite Biography," in Wright and Twitchett, *Confucian Personalities* (Stanford, 1962), pp. 65-83, is a study of the biographical sketches in the "Garden of Letters" section of the *Old Standard History of the Tang*.

Indexes and concordances

Index to the Genealogical Tables of Families of Chief Ministers in the New Standard History of the Tang (**Xin Tangshu ziaxiang shixibiao yinde** 新唐書宰相世系表引得), H-Y Index 16 (Peking, 1934; Taipei, 1966).

Hiraoka Takeo, *Tang Dynasty Administrative Geography* (**Tōdai no gyōsei chiri** 唐代の行政地理), vol. 2 of *T'ang Civilization Reference Series* (Kyoto, 1954), indexes the Monographs on Administrative Geography in both the Standard Histories of the Tang.

18. Xue Ju-zheng 薛居正 (912-981), *The Old Standard History of the Five Dynasties* (**Jiu Wudai shi** 舊五代史), covers the years 907-960.

19. Ou-yang Xiu 歐陽修 (1007-1072), *The New Standard History of the Five Dynasties* (**Xin Wudai shi** 新五代史), covers the years 907-960.

Studies

Wang Gung-wu, "The *Chiu Wu-tai shih* and History-writing during the Five Dynasties," *Asia Major* 6:1-22 (1957-1958). See also Liu.

No indexes or concordances available. Use the Baina (Po-na) or one of the Ershiwu shi editions.

20. *Standard History of the Song* (**Songshi** 宋史), traditionally ascribed to Tuo Tuo 托托 (1313-1355) but in fact by Ou-yang Xuan 歐陽玄 (1274/5-1358), covers the years 960-1279.

<u>Indexes and studies</u>

Chang Fu-jui, *Les Fonctionnaires des Song, Index des Titres* (Paris, 1962). Includes among the works indexed the *Monograph on Officials* (**Songshi zhiguanzhi** 宋史職官志).

Saeki Tomi 佐伯富 , *Index to the Monograph on Officials in the Standard History of the Song* (**Sōshi shokkanshi sakuin** 宋史職官志索引 ; Kyoto, 1963). Arranged by Japanese reading; has stroke-order index. There is a useful introduction by Miyazaki Ichisada 宮崎市定, "Sōdai kansei josetsu: Sōshi shokkanshi o ikani yomubeki ka" 宋代官制序説=宋史職官志を如何に讀むべきか(Introduction to the Song bureaucracy: how should the Monograph on the Civil Service in the Song History be read), pp. 1-63. See also Mei Ching-ying Lee, ed., *Index des noms propres dans les annales principales de l'Histoire des Song* (Paris, 1966).

21. *Standard History of the Liao* (**Liao shi** 遼史), traditionally ascribed to Tuo Tuo 托托 (1313-1355) et al., in fact by Ou-yang Xuan 歐陽玄 (1274/5-1355), covers the years 916-1125.

<u>Studies</u>

Feng Jia-sheng 馮家昇, *Three Studies Correcting Errors in the Liaoshi* (**Liaoshi zhengwu san zhong** 辽史正误三种 ; Shanghai, 1959).

K. A. Wittfogel and Feng Chia-sheng, *History of Chinese Society: Liao (907-1125),* Appendix 4 (Philadelphia, 1949).

<u>Index</u>

Index to the Standard History of the Liao (**Ryōshi sakuin** 遼史索引 ; Kyoto, 1937). Cannot be relied upon for completeness.

22. *Standard History of the Jin* (**Jin shi** 金史), traditionally ascribed to Tuo Tuo 托托 (1313-1355) et al., actually by Ou-yang Xuan 歐陽玄 (1274/5-1355), covers the years 1115-1234.

<u>Studies</u>

Chan Hok-lam, *The Historiography of the Chin Dynasty: Three*

Studies (Wiesbaden, 1970).

Index

Index to Historical Terms in the Standard History of the Jin
(**Jinshi goi shūsei** 金史語彙集成), 3 vols. (Kyoto, 1960-1962). Cannot
be relied upon for completeness.

Editions

Use Baina edition.

23. Song Lian 宋濂 (1310-1381) et al., *Standard History of the
Yuan* (**Yuan shi** 元史), covers the years 1206-1369.

Studies

Yao Shih-ao, "Ein kurzer Beitrag zur Quellenkritik der Reichsannalen
der Kin und Yüan Dynastie," *Asia Major* 9:580-590 (1933).

Index

Index to Historical Terms in the Standard History of the Yuan
(**Genshi goi shūsei** 元史語彙集成), 3 vols. (Kyoto, 1961-1963).
Cannot be relied upon for completeness.

Indexed edition

Use the National Defense College, **Yuan shi**, 4 vols. (Taipei, 1966),
which is punctuated, and also contains a name index and bibliography. Unfortunately this is full of errors.

24. Ke Shao-min 柯紹忞 (1850-1933), *New Standard History of
the Yuan* (**Xin Yuan shi** 新元史), covers the years 1206-1307. Included
in **Ershiwu shi**, various editions.

25. Zhang Ting-yu 張廷玉 (1672-1755) et al., *Standard History of
the Ming* (**Ming shi** 明史), covers the years 1368-1644.

Studies

Li Jin-hua 李晉華 , *A History of the Compilation of the
Standard History of the Ming* (**Mingshi zuanxiu kao** 明史纂修考 ;
Peking, 1933).

Indexed edition

National Defense College, **Ming shi**, 6 vols. (Taipei, 1962).
Punctuated with name index and bibliography. Many errors.

26. Zhao Er-xun 趙爾巽 (1844-1927) et al., *Draft Standard
History of the Qing* (**Qing shi gao** 清史稿), covers the years 1644-1911.

Studies

T. Griggs, "The Ch'ing Shih Kao: A Bibliographical Summary," *HJAS* 18:105-123 (1955).

E. Haenisch, "Das *Ts'ing-shi-kao* und die sonstige chinesische Literatur zur Geschichte der letzten 300 Jahre," *Asia Major* 6.4:403-444 (1930). The Biographies section was included among the materials indexed in H-Y Index 9 (1932).

26a. *History of the Qing* (**Qing shi** 清史), completed in 1962 by a committee in Taiwan; largely based on no. 26 above, covers the years 1644-1911, 8 vols. (Taipei, National Defense College, 1961). Has the advantage of being punctuated. Also has a name index included in vol. 8. Unfortunately it is full of errors. Has been reprinted in **Renshou** edition of Standard Histories with corrections.

16.5   Monographs in the Standard Histories

The best introduction to the Monographs in the Standard Histories is E. Balazs, "History as a Guide to Bureaucratic Practice," in E. Balazs, *Chinese Civilization and Bureaucracy* (New Haven and London, 1964), pp. 129-149. The same paper originally appeared in French in Beasley and Pulleyblank, pp. 78-94. In it Balazs has a useful table showing for each of the Standard Histories the distribution of Monographs among four broad categories. (references to Monographs *not* discussed in this section have been added):

  I. Rites and customs (rites, ceremonial; music and liturgy; sacrifices; insignia and costume)

 II. "Sciences" (astronomy-astrology; calendar; unusual phenomena; cataclysms)

III. Government institutions

    1. Civil administration; military administration (see section 21); selection of officials (examination system); education

    2. Administrative geography (see section 18.4)

    3. Financial administration and political economy

    4. Penal law

IV. <u>Bibliography</u> (catalogues of the imperial library and other important book collections)

See Table 3 on the following page for a detailed inventory of all the Monographs in all the Standard Histories.

Table 3: Monographs in the Standard Histories

Monographs		Histories																										
	1	2	3	4	5	6	7	8	9	10	11	12	13	14	15	16	17	18	19	20	21	22	23	24	25	26	26a
Ritual	x	x	x		x	x	x	x			x				x	x	x	x	x	x	x	x	x	x	x	x	x
Music	x	x	x		x	x	x				x				x	x	x	x	x	x	x	x	x	x	x	x	x
Harmony	x	x	x		x						x				x	x	x	x	x	x	x	x	x	x	x	x	x
Calendar	x	x	x	x	x	x					x				x	x	x	x	x	x	x	x	x	x	x	x	x
Astronomy	x	x	x	x	x	x	x				x				x	x	x	x	x	x	x	x	x	x	x	x	x
Sacrifices	x	x	x																				x				
Rivers and canals	x	x																									
Fiscal administration	x	x			x						x				x	x	x	x	x	x	x	x	x	x	x	x	x
Penal administration		x			x						x				x	x	x	x	x	x	x	x	x	x	x	x	x
Natural omens	x	x			x	x	x								x	x	x	x	x	x	x	x	x	x	x		
Disasters																										x	x
Administrative geo-graphy	x	x			x	x	x				x				x	x	x	x	x	x	x	x	x	x	x	x	x
Bibliographies		x													x	x	x	x	x	x	x	x	x	x	x	x	x
Official posts		x	x		x	x	x				x				x	x	x	x	x	x	x	x	x	x	x	x	x
Sumptuary regulations			x		x	x	x									x	x	x	x	x	x	x	x	x	x		
Auspicious influences						x	x			x																	
Buddhists and Taoists											x																
Imperial guards																	x	x		x	x	x	x	x	x		
Examination system																	x	x		x	x	x	x	x	x	x	x
Army																	x	x		x	x	x	x	x	x	x	x
Border guards																					x						
Communications																										x	x
Foreign relations																										x	x

16.5.1 <u>Dynastic Bibliographies</u> (*yiwen zhi* 藝文志 , *jing-ji zhi* 經籍志)

These are included in six of the Standard Histories. They are essential for tracing what books were in circulation in a given period. These monographs have been printed together in several editions: e.g. *Chinese Dynastic Bibliographies* (**Zhongguo lidai yiwen zhi** 中國歷代藝文志- ; Shanghai, Daguang Shuju 大光書局 , 1936; Taipei, 1955), and they have been indexed (together with Qing supplementary bibliographies) in *Combined Indices to Twenty Dynastic Bibliographies* (**Yiwen zhi ershi zhong zonghe yinde** 藝文志二十種綜合引得), H-Y Index 10, 4 vols. (Peking, 1933; Taipei, 1966). During the 1950s the Commercial Press, Shanghai, brought out a uniform edition of the Dynastic Bibliographies with Qing supplements printed with each. Every volume has a 4-corner index (short titles given below):

*1.　**Han shu yiwen zhi** 漢書藝文志 , 1955.
*2.　**Sui shu jingji zhi** 隋書經籍志, 1955-1957.
*3.　**Tang shu jingji yiwen hezhi** 唐書經籍藝文合志 , 1956.
4.　**Song shi yiwen zhi** 宋史藝文志 , 1957.
5.　**Liao, Jin, Yuan shi yiwen zhi** 遼金元史藝文志 , 1959.
6.　**Ming shi yiwen zhi** 明史藝文志 , 1959.

Works marked with a * give the nearest approximation to a complete summary of the books available at the time of compilation, i.e. the end of the Former Han, the beginning of the Tang, and the mid-Tang respectively.

Further references and advice on how to use the various catalogues and bibliographies of old Chinese books are given in sections 3 and 4.

16.5.2 <u>Monographs on Financial Administration</u> (*shi huozhi* 食貨志)

There are sixteen of these Monographs in the Standard Histories. They constitute the single most important source on the economic institutions (and economy in general) of each period and as a result they have been relatively intensively studied, translated, and indexed.

The texts of the Monographs have been published together several times, e.g. Nakajima Satoshi 中島敏 ed., *Collation of the Palace Edition and the Baina Edition of 13 Monographs on Financial Administration*

(**Taiko jūsanshi shokkashi** 對校十三史食貨志 ; Tokyo, 1965)
which also includes the Monograph in the *Draft Standard History of the Qing.* The Daguang Shuju 大光書局 , *Monographs on Financial Admin-istration of Each Period* (**Zhongguo lidai shihuozhi** 中國歷代食貨志 ; Shanghai, 1936) includes the *Biographies of Wealthy Merchants* from the *Records of the Grand Historian* (**Shi ji huozhi liezhuan** 史記貨殖列傳) but not the Monograph in the **Qing shi gao**. Most complete is the Chengwen edition: **Zhongguo lidai shihuozhi zhengbian** 中國歷代食貨志正編 (Taipei, 1971). Several of the translations noted below conveniently print the original text along with the notes and supplementary matter.

The standard combined index to these Monographs is *Combined Index to the Monographs on Financial Administration in Fifteen Standard Histories* (**Shihuozhi shiwu zhong zonghe yinde** 食貨志十五種綜合引得), H-Y Index 32 (Peking, 1938; Taipei, 1966).

A dictionary which almost serves as a dictionary of special terms in the Monographs on Financial Administration has been compiled by Hoshi Ayao 星斌夫 , *Dictionary of Terms in Chinese Socioeconomic History* (**Chūgoku shakai keizai shi goi** 中國社會經濟史語彙 ; Tokyo, 1966). The brief explanations in this useful work are based on the major Japanese studies and translations of the Monographs on Financial Adminis-tration as well as on 18 other important contributions of Japanese scholars to Chinese socioeconomic history.

The major studies and translations of Monographs on Financial Administration are listed in chronological order below:

R.C. Blue, "The Argumentation of the Shih-huo-chih Chapters of the Han, Wei and Sui Dynastic Histories," *HJAS* 11.1 and 2:1-118 (1948), includes a translation of the prefaces to the *shihuozhi* of the **Shiji, Hanshu, Weishu** and **Suishu.**

N.L. Swann, *Food and Money in Ancient China, the Earliest Economic History of China to A.D. 25, Han Shu 24, with Related Texts, Han Shu 91 and Shih-chi 129* (Princeton, 1950).

L.S. Yang, "Notes on Dr. Swann's *Food and Money in Ancient China,*" *HJAS* 15:507-521 (1952), reprinted in his *Studies in Chinese Institutional History* (Cambridge, Mass., 1963), pp. 85-118.

L.S. Yang, "Notes on the Economic History of the Chin Dynasty," *HJAS* 9:107-185 (1945-1947), reprinted in Yang, pp. 119-197. Includes a translation of the *shihuozhi* of the **Jinshu**, pp. 137-197.

E. Balazs, *Le Traité économique de "Souei-shu,"* *T'oung-pao* 42.3 and 4 (1953).Translation with notes and introduction of **Suishu shihuozhi**.

E. Balazs, "Beiträge zur Wirtschaftsgeschichte der T'ang Zeit, 618-906," *Mitteilungen des Seminars für Orientalische Sprachen* 34:1-92 (1931); 35: 1-73 (1932); 36:1-62 (1933). Analytic study of Tang economy based on the *shihuozhi* of both the **Jiu Tangshu** and the **Xin Tangshu**.

D.C. Twitchett, *Financial Administration under the T'ang Dynasty,* 2nd ed. (Cambridge, 1970). Introductory matter to (unpublished) translation of the Monograph on Financial Administration in the **Jiu Tangshu**.

D.C. Twitchett, "The Derivation of the Text of the *Shih-huo-chih* of the *Chiu T'ang-shu,"* *Journal of Oriental Studies* (Hong Kong) 3:48-62 (1956).

Wada Sei 和田清, *Translation with Notes of Three of the Fourteen Chapters of the* Shihuozhi *of the* **Songshi (Songshi**, 173, 174, 175), **Sōshi shokkashi yakuchū** 宋史食貨志譯註 , vol. 1 (Tokyo, 1960). This massive volume enlisted the aid of many leading experts on the Song economy; their work is in the tradition established by Katō Shigeshi of attempting to produce integral translations of all the Monographs on Financial Administration. In the event only the revised translations of the *Monographs in the Records of the Grand Historian* and in the Standard Histories of the Former Han, the Tang, and the Five Dynasties appeared in Kato's lifetime. The collective annotated translations edited by Wada of the Monographs in the **Songshi** and in the **Mingshi** (see Wada, 1957) are altogether on a much grander scale, however, as the extremely detailed notes succeed in establishing the source for practically every statement in these Monographs which were themselves by far the longest and best compiled of the *shihuozhi*. There are also full indexes.

Sudō Yoshiuki, "The Relationships between the *Shihuozhi* 食貨志 in the **Songchao guoshi** 宋朝国史and the **Songshi**," *Memoirs of the Research Department of the Toyo Bunko* (1961), pp. 63-110.

F. Schurmann, *Economic Structure of the Yuan Dynasty* (Cambridge, Mass., 1956). This is an annotated translation of sections of the Monograph on Fiscal Administration of the **Yuanshi** plus introductions and index.

Wada Sei, ed., *Integral Translation with Notes of the Monograph on Financial Administration in the* **Mingshi** (**Minshi shokkashi yakuchū** 明史 食貨志譯註   ), 2 vols. (Tokyo, 1957). The translation is in *kanbun* while the notes are in current Japanese; the Chinese original is appended and there is an index. See comments under Wada (1960).

Amagai Kensaburō 天海謙三郎 , *Draft Translation of the Population Section of the Monograph on Financial Administration in the* **Qingshi gao** (**Shinshikō shokkashi yakuchūkō kokō** 清史稿食貨志譯註 戶口   ; Dalian, 1943).

Hoshi Ayao 星斌夫 , *Annotated Translation of the Section on Tribute Transportation of the Monograph on Financial Administration in the* **Qingshi gao** (**Shinshikō sōonshi yakuchū** 清史稿漕運志譯註   ; Yamaguchi, 1962).

Note also the Monographs on Rivers and Canals in **Shiji**, **Hanshu**, Song, Jin, Yuan, Ming, and Qing Standard Histories.

16.5.3 Monographs on Penal Law *(xingfa zhi* 刑法志*)*

Most of these 15 Monographs in the Standard Histories have been translated, annotated, or indexed. The texts have been published together: Qiu Han-ping 丘漢平 , ed., *Monographs on Penal Law of each Period* (**Lidai xingfa zhi** 歷代刑法志 ; Changsha, 1938) which includes all the Monographs up to and including **Mingshi** and has added section headings. For the **Qingshi gao** Monograph see: *Monograph on Penal Law from the* **Qingshi gao** (**Qingshi gao xingfa zhi zhujie** 清史稿刑法志註解 ; Peking, 1957).

Studies and translations of the individual Monographs on Penal Law are listed chronologically below:

A.F.P. Hulsewé, *Remnants of Han Law,* vol. 1 (Leiden, 1955). An annotated translation of the first Monograph on Penal Law; the *xingfa zhi* of the **Hanshu.**

Uchida Tomoo 内田智雄, *Annotated Translation of the Monograph on Penal Law in the* **Hanshu** (**Kanjo keihōshi yakuchū** 漢書 刑法志譯註 ; Kyoto, 1958).

92

Uchida Tomoo, *Chinese Monographs on Penal Law from the Standard Histories* (**Chūgoku rekidai keihōshi** 中国歴代刑法志 ; Tokyo, 1964). Annotated translation of the second and third Monographs on Penal Law, those in the **Jinshu** and the **Weishu**. Plus full index.

É. Balazs, *Le traité juridique du "Souei-chou"* (Leiden, 1954). Annotated translation with introduction to the fourth of the Monographs on Penal Law; the *xingfa zhi* in the **Suishu**.

É. Balazs, *Le traité juridique du Tsin-chou* (to appear). Annotated translation of the **Jinshu xingfa zhi.**

K. Bünger, *Quellen zur Rechtsgeschichte der T'ang-zeit,* Monumenta Serica Monograph 9 (Peking, 1946). Annotated translation of the fifth and sixth of the Monographs on Penal Law, those in the **Jiu Tangshu** and **Xin Tangshu.** Also includes the sections on law in **Tang huiyao** (q.v.)

There are no studies on the *xingfa zhi* of the **Jiu wudai shi,** the seventh of the Monographs.

Deng Guang-ming 鄧廣銘 , "Critical study of the Monographs on Penal Law in the Song" (Songdai xingfa zhi kaozheng 宋代刑法志 考證), **Lishi yuyan yanjiusuo jikan,** vol. 20, 2nd part, pp. 123-173 (1949).

There are no outstanding studies of the ninth and tenth of the Monographs, those in the **Liaoshi** and the **Jinshi.**

Otake Fumio 小竹文夫 and Okamoto Yoshiji 岡本敬二, *Annotated Translation of the Monograph on Penal Law in the Standard History of the Yuan with Research Papers* (**Genshi keihōshi no kenkyū yakuchū** 元史刑法志の研究譯注; Tokyo, 1962).

P. Ratchnevsky, *Un Code des Yuan* (Paris, 1937). Annotated translation with long introduction of the first 318 articles of **Yuanshi xingfa zhi.** F. Aubin, "Index d'*Un Code des Yuan* de P. Ratchnevsky," in *Mélanges publiés par l'Institut des Hautes Études Chinoises* 2:423-515 (Paris, 1960).

F. Münzel, *Strafrecht im Alten China nach den Strafrechtskapiteln in den Ming-Annalen* (Wiesbaden, 1968). Annotated translation of the first section of **Mingshi** *xingfa zhi.*

See section 20, <u>Administrative and Penal Law</u>, for much more detailed sources on law than can be found in the Monographs.

16.5.4 <u>Monographs on Official Posts</u> (*baiguan* 百官志 ; *zhiguan* 職官志) and the <u>Examination System</u> (*xuanjuzhi* 選舉志)

Although these are useful as summaries of the organization of the bureaucracy, the more detailed sources are discussed under sections 20, 21, and 22.

An extremely handy work which serves as the best general introduction to the Monographs on Official Posts, etc. in all the Standard Histories and is at the same time useful as a reference for the evolution of all branches of the bureaucracy is Huang Ben-ji 黃本驥, *Tables of Official Posts from the Earliest Times to the Nineteenth Century* (**Lidai zhiguan biao** 歷代職官表), with Introduction and Glossary by Qu Tui-yuan 瞿蛻園 (Shanghai, 1965). Huang produced his original table as a simplified version of the imperially sponsored work of the same title which had been compiled by Ji Yun and others in 1782. Qu Tui-yuan has now added (1) numerous corrections, (2) a four-corner index (with *pinyin* table), (3) an introduction on the evolution of bureaucratic institutions (pp. 1-76), and (4) an excellent annotated glossary of official posts (printed after the table [pp. 1-210] arranged by stroke order and also included in the general index to the table).

For translations of official titles, mainly from these Monographs, but also from the Compendia of Administrative Law (*huidian* 會典), see:

H.H. Dubs and R. de Crespigny, *Official Titles of the Former Han Dynasty, An Index* (Canberra, 1969).

R. Des Rotours, *Le traité des examens* (Paris, 1932). Translated from the *New Standard History of the Tang.*

R. Des Rotours, *Traité des fonctionnaires et traité de l'armée,* 2 vols. (Leiden, 1947-1948). Translated from the *New Standard History of the Tang.*

Chang Fu-jui, *Les Fonctionnaires des Song, Index des Titres* (Paris, 1962).

Saeki Tomi 佐伯富 , *Index to the Monograph on Officials in the Standard History of the Sung* (**Sōshi shokkanshi sakuin** 宋史職官志索引 ; Kyoto, 1963).

F. Aubin, "Index d'*Un Code des Yuan* de P. Ratchnevsky," in *Mélanges publiés par l'Institut des Hautes Études Chinoises* 2:423-515 (Paris, 1960).

C.O. Hucker, "An Index to the Terms and Titles in Government Organization in the Ming Dynasty," in J.L. Bishop, ed., *Studies of Governmental Institutions in Chinese History* (Cambridge, Mass., 1968), pp. 125-152; originally appeared in *HJAS* 23:127-151 (1960-1961).

H.S. Brunnert and V.V. Hagelstrom, *Present-Day Political Organization of China,* revised by N. Th. Kolessoff, tr. A. Beltchenko and E.E. Moran (Shanghai, 1912; Taipei reprint, 1960). Based on *Compendium of Administrative Law of the Qing* (**Da Qing huidian**, q.v.). 大清會典

W.F. Mayers, *The Chinese Government, A Manual of Chinese Titles, Categorically Arranged and Explained with an Index* (Shanghai, 1897; Taipei reprint, 1967), based on *Compendium of Administrative Law of the Qing* (**Da Qing huidian**, q.v.).

Note: E-tu Sun, trans., *Ch'ing Administrative Terms: A Translation of "The Terminology of the Six Boards with Explanatory Notes"* (Cambridge, Mass., 1961).

See section 20 for more detailed sources on administrative law.

17. Biographical Writing

17.1   Commemorative writings

An enormous quantity of biographical writing is extant, particularly from the last thousand years of Chinese history. The greater part of this writing served a ritual or social function, to commemorate, praise, or commend deceased family members or personal friends.

The most important types of commemorative writings were those connected with the ancestral cult. These included the tomb inscriptions (*mubei* 墓碑) which were carved on stele and erected on the tomb (*mubiao* 墓表), or on the avenue leading to it (*shendaobei* 神道碑), or were buried in the grave (*muzhi* 墓誌 ; *kuangming* 壙銘), or deposited in the ancestral temple (*miaozhi* 廟誌). In addition there were the funeral orations (*jiwen* 祭文 , *diaowen* 弔文), eulogies to the dead (*lei* 誄), elegies (*aicu* 哀詞), funerary odes (*zansong* 贊頌), etc.

Biographies were also prepared for family records or the family history (*jiazhuan* 家傳) or to substantiate claims for the subject's inclusion in the Local Gazetteer or even the Standard History, or to make the case for the bestowal of posthumous titles and honors on the subject. Such claims or assessments were put in the standard form of Accounts of Conduct (*xingzhuang* 行狀) and it was upon these that the biographies in historical works were often based.

The classification and models for all these types of writing began to take shape during the Eastern Han, although their origins may be sought in the commemorative writings carved on bronze vessels in Shang and Zhou times. After the Han dynasty the authors of ritual and social biographies began to preserve them in their Collected Works (*wenji* 文集) and they were also included in Literary Anthologies. Special collections of commemorative writings have survived in great numbers from later periods.

Not surprisingly, the ritual and social biographies tend to paint a highly stereotyped picture, since they were intended to laud the virtues and achievements of their subjects rather than to present a well-rounded portrait. Despite this drawback, they provide a huge quantity of basic biographic materials on many thousands of members of central and local elites in all periods of Chinese history from the Han down to the twentieth century. Problems of locating this type of material for a given person are discussed under 17.5 below.

17.2   Historical biographies

Ever since the *Records of the Grand Historian* (see section 16.1), a section of groups of biographies (*liezhuan* 列傳) was included in the Standard Histories and biographies became an accepted form of historical writing. For the most part, historical biographies were based on the various

categories of commemorative and social writings discussed above. Although
they were expected to take a less uniformly eulogistic view of their subject,
they were intended to illustrate some larger moral pattern and were therefore usually arranged in groups to illustrate such themes as chastity of widows,
filial conduct, or loyalty among officials (see Frankel for a study of such
a group of biographies in the *Old Standard History of the Tang*). Nor were
the same standards of historical criticism applied to the biographies as to
other types of historical writing; thus again and again the same clichés (often
drawn from a famous literary model) were used to round out the major stages
of a subject's life, which in the end appears two-dimensional, more ideal than
real. Frequently fiction took over altogether, as has been shown, for example,
not only in the earlier Histories (see Maspero), but also in the later Histories
as well (see Wu Han).

Groups of biographies (*liezhuan* 列傳) account for over half the
space in the Standard Histories (which contain biographical materials on
anything up to 50,000 individuals). Very large numbers of privately compiled
collections of biographies of famous people (of a particular period, region,
or type) are extant. These contain many more biographies than in the
Standard Histories, as do also the Local Gazetteers (see section 18.5), which
usually have a large quantity of grouped biographies. The indexes and
reference aids essential for getting at these historical biographies are listed
under 17.5 below.

17.3   Chronological biographies

From the Song onward, the application of annals style to biographical
materials produced a more rigorous form of biographical writing than the
ritual and social biographies and historical biographies discussed above. This
new form was called Chronological Biography or chronological personal
biography (*nianpu* 年譜). Many trace the subject's life, year by year, in
great detail. *Nianpu* are available for most statesmen, scholars, etc. of the
first rank. See Wang Bao-xian 王寶先 , *Comprehensive Catalogue of
Personal Chronological Biographies* (**Lidai mingren nianpu zongmu** 歷代
名人年譜綜目 ; Taipei, 1956). This includes *nianpu* of 1,200 people

and it is indexed.

Autobiographies, biographical prefaces, and diaries are also important biographical sources and may sometimes be found in a writer's Collected Works.

Readings

There are some excellent introductory studies on the nature and methods of the three types of Chinese biographical writing outlined above, as well as some case studies which discuss the drawbacks of these sources.

See P. Olbricht, "Die Biographie in China," *Saeculum* 8.2/3: 224-235 (1957); D.C. Twitchett, "Chinese Biographical Writing," in Beasley and Pulleyblank, pp. 95-114; D.C. Twitchett, "Problems of Chinese Biography," and A.F. Wright, "Values, Roles and Personalities," in Wright and Twitchett, *Confucian Personalities* (Stanford, 1962), pp. 24-42, 3-23; D.S. Nivison, "Traditional Chinese Biography," *JAS* 21:451-463 (1962); H.H. Frankel, "Objectivität und Parteilichkeit in der offiziellen chinesischen Geschichtsschreibung vom 3 bis 11 Jahrhundert," *Oriens Extremus* 5:133-144 (1958); H. Franke, "Some Remarks on the Interpretation of Chinese Dynastic Histories," *Oriens* 3:113-122 (1950).

For case studies, see H. Maspero, "Le Roman de Sou Ts'in," *Études Asiatiques* 2:127-141 (1925); H. Maspero, "Le Roman historique dans la littérature Chinoise de l'antiquité," *Mélanges Posthumes*, vol. 3 (Paris, 1950); H.H. Frankel, "T'ang Literati: A Composite Biography," in Wright and Twitchett, pp. 65-83; J.T.C. Liu, "Some Classifications of Bureaucrats in Chinese Historiography," in A.F. Wright, ed., *The Confucian Persuasion* (Stanford, 1959), pp. 165-181; Ch'en Shih-hsiang, "An Innovation in Chinese Biographical Writing," *FEQ* 13:49-62 (1953); A.F. Wright, "Biography and Hagiography, Hui-chien's Lives of Eminent Monks," in *Silver Jubilee Volume of the Kimbun Kagaku-Kenkyusyo* (Kyoto, 1954), pp. 383-432; Wu Han 吳晗, "Fictional elements in the *Standard History of the Ming*" (Lishi zhong de xiaoshuo 歷史中的小說), **Wenxue** 2.6:1201-17 (1934); Liu Ts'un-yan, "Men of Letters in the Light of Chinese Historiography," *BMFEA* 37:137-165 (1965).

17.4   Genealogies and Family Instructions

In early Chinese history the descent lines (*xipu* 系譜 , *shibiao* 世表) of royal and aristocratic houses were kept. They were used as the basis for the section of the *Records of the Grand Historian* on Hereditary Houses (*shijia* 世家). From the Han to the Tang the genealogical records (*pudie* 譜牒) of the powerful families (*shizu* 士族) became established as a recognized historical genre. After the revival of clan and family institutions in the Northern Song, the well-to-do began compiling family and clan genealogies (*jiapu* 家譜 and *zupu* 族譜); these have survived in considerable numbers, mainly dating from the Republic and late Qing. Many of the descent lines in these later genealogies are traced back to the Song. See the excellent paper by J.M. Meskill, "The Chinese Genealogy as a Research Source," in M. Freedman, ed., *Family and Kinship in China* (Stanford, 1970); and also the bibliography of genealogies and introduction to this type of source by Taga Akigorō 多賀秋五郎, *An Analytical Study of Genealogical Books*: *Source Materials* (**Sōfu no kenkyū; shiryō-hen**族譜の研究,史料編; Tokyo, Toyo Bunko, 1960). Supplement in Taga's list with Chang Pi-de 昌彼德 , ed., *Annotated Bibliography of Genealogies in Taiwan Public Collections* (**Taiwan gongcang zupu jieti** 臺灣公藏族譜解題; Taipei, 1969). The largest collections of genealogies of China are in the Toyo Bunko in Tokyo and the Chinese collections in Columbia University in New York as well as in Taiwan.

Family Instructions (*jiaxun* 家訓, *jiagui* 家規, *jiayue* 家約 , etc.) are an important source for family and clan education and organization; the first such work extant is **Yanshi jiaxun** 顏氏家訓by Yan Zhi-tui 顏之推(531-591), English tr. by Teng Ssu-yü, *Family Instructions for the Yen Clan* (Leiden, 1968). Family instructions were also commonly printed in genealogies: see Liu [Wang] Hui-chen, *The Traditional Chinese Clan Rules* (New York, 1959); also Liu, "An Analysis of Chinese Clan Rules: Confucian Theories in Action,"in A.F. Wright and D. Nivison, eds., *Confucianism in Action* (Stanford, 1959), pp. 63-96; also D.C. Twitchett, "Documents on the Clan Administration: 1. The Rules of Administration of the Charitable Estate of the Fan Clan," *Asia Major* 8:1-35 (1960).

17.5   How to find biographical materials

17.5.1 Modern biographical dictionaries etc.

For the Qing use A.W. Hummel, ed., *Eminent Chinese of the Ch'ing Period,* 2 vols. (Washington, 1943-1944; Taipei reprint, 1964), which includes biographies of about 800 famous officials, writers, etc. active during the Qing. A similar biographical dictionary in English will appear shortly for the Ming, and there is also a project for a Song biographical dictionary.

The old *A Chinese Biographical Dictionary* by H.A. Giles (1898; 1964) contains biographical sketches of about 2,500 people but is full of inaccuracies and the selection leaves much to be desired.

In the absence of a satisfactory Chinese dictionary of national biography, use Zang Li-he's 臧勵龢 one-volume *Chinese Biographical Dictionary* (**Zhongguo renming da cidian** 中國歷代人名大辭典; Shanghai, 1921 and many later reprints). Zang and his collaborators managed to include brief biographical entries (mainly drawn from the biographies in the Standard Histories) for some 40,000 people. Neither exact dates nor sources are given. The arrangement is by stroke order.

The *Encyclopaedic Dictionary of Chinese Writers* (**Zhongguo wenxuejia da cidian** 中國文學家大辭典 ; Shanghai, 1934; Taipei, 1962; Hong Kong, 1961) contains well-ordered information on about 7,000 literati.

Heibonsha's *Encyclopaedia of Asian History* (**Ajia rekishi jiten**, 1959-1962) contains biographies of famous Chinese and supplies dates and sources. There is also a romanized index of Chinese personal names.

Most Chinese people about whom we have biographical data (i.e. those in the upper strata of society) had several different names. Apart from the regular form of family name (*xing* 姓) and given name (*ming* 名)—e.g., Ma Duan-lin (Ma = *xing;* Duan-lin = ming)—the most common of these alternative names (*yiming* 異名) were "style" (also called "courtesy name"), *zi* 字 ; "nickname" (or "pen name," "literary name"), *hao* 號 ; names derived from studios, gardens, etc. and called "study name" or "studio name," *shiming* 室名 , *biehao* 別號 , and so on. Another important type were the imperially bestowed posthumous name (*shi* 謚, *shihao* 謚號) and titles. Full lists of the many other types of name as well as discussion are supplied in W. Bauer, *Die chinesischen Personenname* (Wiesbaden, 1959).

Zang Li-he contains an appendix of alternative names of the personalities included in the body of his dictionary (**Yiming biao**, pp. 1-34) arranged by stroke number. It often saves time, however, to turn directly to the most comprehensive separate index of alternative names, compiled by Chan Tak-wan 陳德芸 : *An Index to Alternative Names of Personalities Past and Present* (**Gujin renwu bieming suoyin** 古今人物別名索引 ; Canton, 1937; Taipei reprint, 1965). There is a convenient special index for studio names compiled by Chen Nai-qian 陳乃乾 , **Shiming suoyin** 室名索引 (1933), which was reprinted (Peking, 1957) with his **Bieming suoyin** 別名索引 (1936).

Special indexes for looking up emperors' names are given in section 8.1. Names of emperors, in addition to the regular form of family and given name, also included "temple names" (*miaohao* 廟號), e.g. Tang *Tai-zu;* "era name" or reign name" (*nianhao* 年號), e.g., Ming *Wan-li,* Qing *Qian-long.* Especially during the Song, emperors' personal names were made taboo (*hui* 諱   ). The best introduction to such taboo names is Chen Yuan 陳垣   , *Examples of Historical Taboo Names* (**Shihui juli** 史諱舉例; Peking, 1928; 1962). The fullest listing will be found in Zhang Wei-xiang 張惟驤, **Lidai huizipu** 歷代諱字譜 , and **Jiahui kao** 家諱考 (1931).

A quick way of finding someone's dates (Zang Li-he's *Chinese Biographical Dictionary* does not give exact dates) is to look in one of the lists giving the birth and death dates of famous people; the most comprehensive of such lists was compiled by Jiang Liang-fu 姜亮夫 and includes the dates of some 12,000 people: *A Table of Dates and Places of Birth, Dates of Death (with Epitaphs and Biographical Sketches Referenced) of Historical Personalities* (**Lidai renwu nianli beizhuan zongbiao** 歷代人物年里碑傳綜表; Shanghai, 1937; rev. ed., Shanghai, 1959). The table is arranged chronologically and there is also a surname index.

Most available biographical dictionaries heavily reflect the biases of their sources, emphasizing moral, literary, scholarly, and official achievements and drawing a veil of silence over, for example, their subjects' financial dealings and business interests.

17.5.2 Locating historical biographies and other types of biographical materials

First make sure whether a chronological biography is available, using Wang Bao-xian 王寶先 , *Comprehensive Catalogue of Chronological Biographies* (**Lidai mingren nianpu zongmu** 歷代名人年譜綜目﹔ Taipei, 1956), which supersedes previous such catalogues.

Next the largest single repository of historical biographies, the Standard Histories, should be checked. These are readily consulted, thanks to the handy *Biographical Index to the Twenty-five Standard Histories* (**Ershiwu shi renming suoyin** 二十五史人名索引 ﹔Shanghai, Kaiming shudian, 1935; Peking, 1956; 1964). The index was planned as a companion reference to the Kaiming shudian edition of the Standard Histories, and page references are to that edition. Fortunately *juan* numbers are also given so that it does not matter which edition of the Histories is being used. Indispensable as it is as a means of locating those people with biographies in the Biographies and Basic Annals sections of the Histories, this index does not include those people who are mentioned in the Histories but who have no biography, nor does it include references to the same person outside of the biography. This drawback may be overcome to a certain extent by using the indexes to individual Histories (titles given under section 16.4).

Note the special biographical index for the Han: *Index by Rhymes of People not Included in the Biographies Sections of the* **Shiji, Hanshu** *and* **Hou Hanshu** (**Liang Han bulie zhuan renming yunbian** 兩漢不列傳 人名韻編; Peking, 1935).

Another major repository of historical biographies are the Local Gazetteers which began including them for the first time during the Song (see section 18.5). The following indexes to biographies in Local Gazetteers are available:

For the Song, Liao, Jin, and Yuan (960-1368): Zhu Shi-jia 朱士嘉 , *Index to the Biographies in Song and Yuan Local Gazetteers* (**Song Yuan fangzhi zhuanji suoyin** 宋元方志传记索引 ﹔Peking, 1963), which includes 3,949 people in 33 gazetteers. The Japanese Committee for the Song Project's *Song Biographical Index* (**Sōjin denki sakuin** 宋人傳記索引 ﹔Tokyo, 1968), also includes the biographies in Song gazetteers (but not the five Yuan gazetteers).

For the Ming (1368-1644): Yamane Yukio 山根幸夫, *Draft Index of Biographies in Ming Local Gazetteers Extant in Japanese Collections* (**Nihon genzon Mindai chihōshi denki sakuin kō** 日本現存明代地方志傳記索引; Tokyo, 1964); includes references to biographies of some 30,000 people in 299 Ming gazetteers.

There is no comprehensive index to the biographies in Qing gazetteers. Despite the lack of indexes to gazetteer biographies, it is fairly easy to find the biography of a person since it is usually (but not invariably) included in the gazetteer of the county in which the family claimed its domicile.

Far more extensive than the historical biographies in the Standard Histories and Local Gazetteers are the very large numbers of ritual, commemorative, and "unofficial biographies" (*biezhuan* 別傳), i.e. those not included in an official historical work. They are usually contained in the Collected Works (*wenji* 文集) of their authors or in special biographical collections. The great bulk date from the last thousand years of Chinese history and are relatively well indexed. Unfortunately the same is not true of the smaller numbers of such materials dating from before the Song. For this earlier period the student should look first through the Standard Histories (which in the absence of other sources are of greater importance than in later periods), and then check Yang Dian-xun 楊殿珣, *Index to Colophons on Stone* (**Shike tiba suoyin** 石刻題跋索引; 1941; Shanghai, 1957) which indexes 137 collections of epigraphy from the Zhou to the Yuan and includes tomb inscriptions of about 10,000 people. Next the great Literary Anthologies should be checked, many of which include commemorative writings as a category (see section 27). The Collected Works of individual authors also should be checked.

For the Tang, (618-906) note Cen Zhong-mian 岑仲勉 , *Tang Records of Names by Order of Birth* (**Tangren hangdi lu** 唐人行第录; Peking, 1962), which collects the names of many Tang literati with alternate forms and has a finding table by stroke order, as well as H-Y Index 16 (see section 16.4.3, no. 18).

For the Song (960-1279), three excellent indexes are available:

1. *Song Biographical Index* compiled under the direction of Aoyama Sadao 青山定男 by the Japanese Committee for the Song

Project (**Sōjin denki sakuin** 宋人傳記索引 ; Tokyo, 1968). This index has some special features: dates are included where ascertainable (for some 8,000 Chinese who lived during this period) as well as alternate names and the names of paternal ancestors for three generations. The materials indexed included biographies and commemorative writings found in a wide variety of sources including Local Gazetteers, Collected Works, Encyclopaedias, Collections of Epigraphy, etc. There is a romanized index (Wade-Giles) at the end of the work.

2. *Combined Indices to Forty-seven Song Dynasty Biographical Collections* (**Sishiqi zhong Songdai zhuanji zonghe yinde** 四十七種 宋代傳記綜合引得), H-Y Index 34 (Peking, 1939; Taipei reprint, 1966). Altogether 9,024 figures are included. This index is arranged by ordinary names and by alternate names but does not give the other types of information included in the more recent Japanese index. Although there is of course considerable overlap between the two, the Japanese index was designed to include materials not indexed in the H-Y Index. For this reason the two indexes should be used together.

3. *Index to Biographical Materials of Song Figures,* comp. Wang De-yi 王德毅, Chang Pi-de 昌彼得 , and Chen Yuan-min 陳元敏 (**Songren zhuanji ziliao suoyin** 宋人傳記資料索引 ; Taipei, 1972). Planned to supplement both the above indexes as well as correcting errors in them; a feature is the half page or so biographical sketch preceding the list of the references to biographical materials.

For the Liao (907-1125), Jin (1115-1234), and Yuan (1280-1368), see:

1. *Combined Indices to Thirty Liao, Jin, and Yuan Biographical Collections* (**Liao, Jin, Yuan zhuanji sanshi zhong zonghe yinde** 遼金元 傳記三十種綜合引得), H-Y Index 35 (Peking, 1940; Taipei reprint, 1966). To be used with the Song biographical indexes above since these dynasties overlapped.

2. *Index to Biographical Material in Jin and Yuan Literary Works,* comp. I. de Rachewiltz and M. Nakano (Canberra, 1970). Designed to supplement the H-Y Index above. (Only vol. 1 has appeared to date [1972].)

For the Ming (1368-1644), use:

1. *Index to Biographical Materials of Ming Figures* (**Mingren zhuanji ziliao suoyin** 明人傳記資料索引), compiled at the National Central Library, 2 vols. (Taipei, 1966). More than an index to biographic materials, these excellent volumes give short biographical sketches followed by detailed references to the sources.

2. *Combined Indices to Eighty-nine Ming Dynasty Biographical Collections* (**Bashijiu zhong Mingdai zhuanji zonghe yinde** 八十九種 明代傳記綜合引得), 3 vols., H-Y Index 24 (Peking, 1935; Taipei reprint, 1966). Ordinary names in vols. 2 and 3; alternate names in vol. 1; references to biographies of about 30,000 Ming figures.

3. See also Franke, pp. 74-97.

For the Qing (1644-1911), use:

1. *Combined Indices to Thirty-three Qing Dynasty Biographical Collections* (**Sanshisan zhong Qingdai zhuanji zonghe yinde** 三十三種 清代傳記綜合引得), H-Y Index 9 (Peking, 1932; 2nd ed. with corrections, Tokyo, Toyo Bunko, 1960).

2. Chen Nai-qian 陳乃乾 , comp., *Index of Qing Stele Commemorative Writings* (**Qingdai beizhuanwen tongjian** 清代碑傳文 通檢 ; Peking, 1959; pirated edition under the title **Qingren bieji qian zhong beizhuanwen yinde ji beizhuanzhu nianli pu** 清人別集千種 碑傳文引得及碑傳主年里譜 ; Taipei, 1965). This important index completely supersedes the sections on commemorative writings in **Qingdai wenji bianmu fenlei suoyin** (1935). Chen indexed more than twice as many Collected Works (altogether 1,025) and includes references to biographical materials on some 12,000 individuals, including those who died after 1644 or were born before 1911. Dates are included.

3. *Index to the Biographies in the Gazetteer of the Eight Banners* (**Hakki tsūshi retsuden sakuin** 八旗通志列傳索引 ; Tokyo, 1965).

A large number of collections of biographies of special categories of people were compiled: for biographies of famous generals see section 21; for biographies of Buddhist and Taoist monks see sections 30.1 and 30.2; all these special collections cannot be mentioned here. They range from biographies of painters to biographies of mathematicians. Frequently the organizing principle is the inclusion of all famous people living in a certain region or locality; other collections gather the famous men of an age together. The section on Biographies in the *Imperial Catalogue* (subdivision 7 of the History Division) gives some indication of the range of biographical collections available. Note that some of the great literary and philosophical anthologies also included biographical sketches (see sections 27.2 and 29).

17.5.3 <u>Lists of degree holders</u> (*dengke lu* 登科錄)

Examination lists of successful candidates for the *jinshi* 進士 degree were kept from 622 to the end of the Qing. These lists are sometimes useful for checking place of origin, paternal background, and approximate dates of individuals. Similar official registers (*timing lu* 題名錄) or Directories of Officials (*Jinshen quanshu* 搢紳全書) were also kept for other degrees; for candidates of the same year, etc.

None of the Tang lists are extant but an early nineteenth-century scholar managed to piece together references to 3,326 successful candidates: Xu Song 徐松 , **Dengke ji kao** 登科記考 (1838). There is a name index to this work as well as to its short supplement: **Toka-ki kō sakuin ichi, ni** 登科記考索引 一、二 (Kyoto, Jimbun Kagaku Kenkyūjo, 1949).

Lists for only three years of the Song and the Yuan have survived, namely those for 1148, 1256, and 1333. See E.A. Kracke, "Family vs Merit in Chinese Civil Service Examinations under the Empire," *HJAS* 10:103-123 (1947); reprinted in Bishop, pp. 171-194.

From the Ming through the Qing complete lists have survived. See **Ming Qing like jinshi timingbei lu** 明清歷科進士題名碑錄, 4 vols. (Taiwan, 1969), which conveniently prints earlier collections of lists and their supplements. The names of all holders of the *jinshi* degree in the Qing have been indexed in the H-Y Index, Supplement 19 (1941; 1966). On the lists of provincial degree holders as well as the *jinshi* lists, see P.T. Ho, *The Ladder of Success in Imperial China* (New York, 1962).

18. Historical and Administrative Geography

18.1   Introduction

For a convenient description of the main physical regions of China,
see J. Needham, *Science and Civilisation in China,* vol.1, *Introductory
Orientations* (Cambridge, 1954), pp. 55-72. A standard textbook on Chinese
geography is G.B. Cressy, *Land of the 500 Million* (New York, 1955); see
also his earlier *China's Geographic Foundations* (New York, 1934). A
systematic study of changing land-use patterns remains to be written, although
Chi Ch'ao-ting's *Key Economic Areas in Chinese History* (London, 1936;
New York, 1963) is still the single most suggestive work on the importance
of different regions of China in different periods. A well-illustrated popular
work which briefly discusses the main changes in land use patterns is Tuan
Yi-fu's *China* (Chicago, 1969). Finally, of the many geographies of modern
China, note T.R. Tregear, *A Geography of China* (London, 1965) and also
his *An Economic Geography of China* (London, 1970).

A. Herrmann, *An Historical Atlas of China* (new ed., Chicago, Aldine,
1966) is an importantly revised version of Herrmann's *Historical and
Commercial Atlas of China* (Cambridge, Mass., 1935). Much shorter but
extremely good value is the excellent paperback edited by J. Fullard, *China
in Maps* (London, 1968), which includes physical, historical, and modern
land-use maps and should be within the reach of every student. A handy map
of modern China by provinces is **Zhongguo fensheng ditu**   中国分省地
图 (Peking, 1956, and many later reprints); the most accurate and detailed
maps of modern China are in the U.S. Army Map Service Series, the largest
scale being 1:250,000. For Chinese army maps of the Republican period
(1:100,000 and for certain cities, 1:25,000) see the catalogue of the Japanese army reprints available in the National Diet Library and in the Toyo
Bunko: **Chūgoku hondo chizu mokuroku** 中国本土地图目録
(Tokyo, 1967).

18.2   Historical geography

No attempt is made to cover the development of Chinese geography and cartography, which have mainly to be traced through works long since lost.

Works on geography, maps, Local Gazetteers, hydrographical works, descriptions of the coasts and northern border areas, etc. are placed in the History Division of old Chinese catalogues (see section 12.2).

Chinese scholars spent a great deal of time compiling reference tools in all branches of historical studies, not the least in historical geography. Most of these works are not mentioned here since the best of them were used as the basis for the place-name dictionaries and other research aids compiled in the twentieth century (see section 18.9 below).

Two outstanding Qing works on historical geography should, however, be mentioned: Gu Yan-wu, *The Characteristics of Each Province in the Empire* and Gu Zu-yu, *Essentials of Geography for Reading History*. Gu Yan-wu was acknowledged as the founder and Gu Zu-yu was a member of the early Qing group of scholars known as the Zhexi school. This school was characterized by loyalty to the Ming and by its practical studies, one of the objects of which was to find the reasons for the Ming collapse. Members of the group also began work on the first edition of the *Comprehensive Gazetteer of the Qing* and on the Monograph on Financial Administration of the *Standard History of the Ming*. Through these and other geographic and economic studies, they provided the stimulus for the interest in Local Gazetteers which was to make the Qing the most productive period in this field. Both Gu Yan-wu and Gu Zu-yu were also pioneers as historians, in that they used Local Gazetteers very extensively in their own historical and geographical writing.

Gu Yan-wu 顧炎武, *The Characteristics of Each Province in the Empire* (**Tianxia junguo libing shu** 天下郡國利病書 ; written between 1639 and 1662; printed for the first time in 1811; many modern editions, included in **Sibucongkan** 四部叢刊, 3rd series). Emphasizing the effect of topography on political and economic developments, it is the most important study of local conditions throughout China ever to have been written in traditional times. Like his relative Gu Zu-yu, Gu Yan-wu also paid particular attention to strategic considerations (the title means "the strategic advantages and disadvantages of the topography of each province"). Another feature of the work was that it was based on Gu's travels and observations as well as upon his studies of the written record.

Gu Zu-yu 顧祖禹, *Essentials of Geography for Reading History* (**Dushi fangyu jiyao** 讀史方輿紀要; written between the 1630s and 1660s; first printed 1811; many modern editions, including a punctuated 6-volume edition, Peking, 1955). The work is a monumental study of historical-administrative and natural geography with special emphasis on the influence of topography on campaigns, battles, etc. There is an index to Gu's identification of the pre-seventeenth century forms of no less than 30,000 places dealt with in the body of his work: Aoyama Sadao 青山定雄,(**Tokushi hōyu kiyō sakuin) Shina rekidai chimei yōran**(讀史方輿紀要索引)支那歷代地名要覽   (Tokyo, 1933), which also serves as a convenient index to the work itself.

References

On the general history of Chinese geography see J. Needham, "Geography and Cartography," in *Science and Civilisation in China,* vol. III, *Mathematics and the Sciences of the Heavens and the Earth* (1955), pp. 497-590. See also Wang Yong 王庸 , *History of Chinese Geography* (**Zhongguo dilixue shi** 中國地理學史 ; 1938, 1956).

For bibliographies, see Yoshida Tora and Tanaka Naohiko, *Bibliography of Chinese and Japanese Works on Chinese Historical Geography* (**Chūgoku rekishi chiri kenkyū rombun mokuroku** 中國歷史地理研究論文目錄; Tokyo, Tokyo kyōiku daigaku shuppankai, mimeo, 1960); and Wang Yong, *Index to Secondary Works on Chinese Geography* (**Zhongguo dilixue lunwen suoyin** 中國地理學論文索引 ; Peking, 1934; Taipei, 1970).

18.3   Maps

Archaeological discoveries of the twentieth century have so far not
turned up a single trace of the maps and plans which we know from early
Chinese literature were used primarily for military and fiscal purposes and
secondarily for travel and general information. Nor have any of the maps
from the Han through to the early Tang survived, the earliest extant maps
being the two carved on stone in the early twelfth century (they were based
on a late Tang model) known as **Hua-Yi tu** 華夷圖 and **Yuji tu** 禹跡圖
(see Wang). An important step was made in the thirteenth century by Zhu
Si-ben 朱思本 , who produced a new map of the empire (**Yudi tu** 輿地
圖) which, although it has not survived, formed the basis of early Ming
maps which have survived. See W. Fuchs, *The "Mongol Atlas" of China by
Chu Ssu-pen and the Kuang yü-t'u* (Peking, 1946). Fuchs's work includes
photographic reprints of the maps in Lo Hong-xian's 羅洪先 *Maps of the
Broad Earth* (**Guang yu tu** 廣輿圖 ; 1541), the first of the works to be
based on Zhu's "Mongol Atlas." The final stage in the development of
Chinese maps came in the eighteenth century when the Jesuits conducted
trigonometric surveys between 1708 and 1718 (by imperial command) and
drew up a whole series of maps of China and its neighbors which far surpassed
their earlier efforts of the seventeenth century, and which remained the
basis of all maps of China, both in China and abroad, down to the early
twentieth century. See J-B. B. D'Anville, *Nouvelle Atlas de la Chine* (Paris
and the Hague, 1737); W. Fuchs, *Der Jesuiten Atlas der Kanghsi Zeit, seine
Entstehung's-geschichte nebst Namensindices für die Karten der Mandjurei,
Mongolei, Ostturkestand und Tibet mit Wiedergabe der Jesuiten-Karten in
Original-grösse* (Peking, 1943).

Many maps of individual districts and provinces as well as plans of
cities and towns are found in Ming-Qing gazetteers (see section 18.5),
while the Comprehensive Gazetteers of the Empire from the Ming on also
contain maps (see section 18.4). The first extant frontier maps (after the
stone-carved twelfth-century **Hua-Yi tu**), as well as route maps used by
officials and merchants, also date from the Ming (see section 18.8).

References
See Needham (1959) and also Wang Yong 王庸 , *Outlines of the History of Chinese Maps* (**Zhongguo ditu shigang** 中国地图史纲 ; Peking, 1959) which is similar to the same author's *History of Chinese Geographical Works and Maps* (**Zhongguo dili tuji congkao** 中國地理圖籍叢考 ; Shanghai, 1947).

18.4 Administrative geography

18.4.1 Early works

The earliest extant work covering the whole of China, as it then was, is the *Classic of Mountains and Seas* (**Shanhai jing** 山海經), parts of which were written in the Han and Jin and parts also during the Warring States period. The whole work was presumably written as an explanation of a map which has long since been lost. The earliest part is an interesting source for pre-Qin mountain worship, while the remainder describes mountains, rivers, products, etc. in the regions of North China leading out from Loyang. See *Concordance to the Classic of Mountains and Seas* (**Shanhai jing tongjian** 山海經通檢), Centre franco-chinois d'études sinologiques Index 9 (Peking, 1948).

The *Classic of Documents* (**Shangshu** 尚書 , **Shujing** 書經) also contains an early descriptive geographical work, the *Tribute of Yu* (**Yugong** 禹貢) which describes the nine regions of China and their products (see B. Karlgren, tr., *The Book of Documents, BMFEA* 22:1-81 [1950], which includes the Chinese text). The complete text with extensive commentary and explanations is included in Gu Jie-gang 顧頡剛, *Selected Readings from Famous Ancient Chinese Geographical Works* (**Zhongguo gudai dili mingshu xuandu** 中国古代地理名书选读), vol. 1 (Peking, 1957).

Before turning to the Monographs, a third early Chinese geographical work should be mentioned, the *Book of Waterways* (**Shuijing** 水經), a very short third-century work with an extensive and important commentary by Li Dao-yuan 酈道元 (d.527); see the introduction to the *Concordance of Names in the Book of Waterways and Commentary* (**Shuijing zhu yinde**

水經注引得), H-Y Index 17, 2 vols. (Peking, 1934; Taipei reprint, 1966).

18.4.2 The Monographs on Administrative Geography in the Standard Histories

Most early Chinese geographical works from before the Han as well as from the Han to the Tang have been lost. Up to the Tang, therefore, the study of Chinese historical geography (including the study of place names, changing boundaries, local products, and population) has to be based mainly on the above three works, together with the summaries found in the Monographs on Administrative Geography in the Standard Histories of the Former Han, Later Han, Jin, Southern Qi, Wei, and Sui, and the sections on foreign peoples and the Monographs on Rivers and Canals in the **Shiji** and the **Hanshu**.

The Monographs on Administrative Geography (*dili zhi* 地理志, *junguo zhi* 郡國志, *zhoujun* 州郡) reflect much the same origins as were hypothesized for early Chinese maps; they contain information useful for tax gatherers (hearth and head counts; land under cultivation statistics) and administrators (names of administrative units, distances between such units, etc.). After the Tang many more geographical works (including maps) are extant and the Monographs in the Later Standard Histories become only one of many sources for Chinese historical geography. Later sources include the Comprehensive Gazetteers of the Empire which contain similar information to the Monographs (see below), the Local Gazetteers which are filled with much greater detail (see 18.5), the geographical sections of the Encyclopaedic Histories of Institutions (see section 19), not to speak of the many private geographical works, travel books, and scholarly studies which have survived in great numbers.

The *Standard History of the Former Han* (**Hanshu** 漢書) was the first to include a Monograph on Administrative Geography and it is somewhat broader in scope than the Monographs in the other Standard Histories. It includes historical introductions on the regions of China (quoting extensively from the *Tribute of Yu*); population figures (the census of A.D. 2) and the names and numbers of the districts in each province and fief; land under cultivation and brief economic profiles of each region (following **Shiji** 129). See N.L. Swann, "An Analysis of Structure of Treatise on

112

Geography," *Food and Money in Ancient China* (Princeton, 1950), pp. 71-75.

Monographs on Administrative Geography in later Standard Histories followed much the same pattern as that in the **Hanshu** but were more narrowly focused on administrative geography. Although special indexes are only available for the Monographs in the old and New Standard Histories of the Tang (Hiraoka Takeo) and the Standard History of the Song (H.M. Wright, *Geographical Names in Sung China* [Paris, 1956]), the comprehensive indexes to the Standard Histories can be used (see section 16.4). Even without an index it is not difficult to locate places in the Monographs since their arrangement followed standard administrative hierarchies. In order to check changes in place names (often recorded in the Monographs) a modern place-name dictionary such as Zang Li-he, which is in fact based on the Monographs, should be used (see section 18.9).

18.4.3 Early comprehensive geographical works

The earliest comprehensive geographical work covering the whole empire was compiled in the ninth century by Li Ji-fu 李吉甫 , *Maps and Gazetteer of the Provinces and Districts in the Yuan-he Period, 806-814* (**Yuanhe junxian tuzhi** 元和郡縣圖志 ; 814). The maps in this work were lost in the Song, as were also *juan* 19, 20, 23-26 and parts of *juan* 5, 18, and 25, but the work is still an important supplement to the Monographs on Administrative Geography in the Old and New Standard Histories of the Tang. (It is indexed along with these works in Hiraoka Takeo.)

The next extant comprehensive geography was written by Yue Shi 樂史 to explain the geography of China and her neighbors newly unified under the emperor Taizong: *Gazetteer of the World during the Taiping Period, 976-983* (**Taiping huanyu ji** or **zhi** 太平寰宇記.志 ; late tenth century). This was an influential work in that it set the trend toward the inclusion of biographies, literary works, etc. in geographical works, a trend which was taken up in the Local Gazetteers. Yue's gazetteer is largely based on Tang sources and it is therefore an important source for Tang geography (indexed in Wright). Other important comprehensive Song geographies are Wang Cun 王存 , *Gazetteer of the Nine Regions during the Yuan-feng Period, 1078-1086* (**Yuanfeng jiuyu zhi** 元豐九域志 ; 1080), indexed in Wright; Ou-yang Wen 歐陽文 , **Yudi guang ji** 輿地廣記(completed 1119-1125); Wang Xiang-zhi 王象之 , **Yudi jisheng** 輿地紀勝(1227; 32 *juan* missing); Zhu Mu 祝穆 , **Fangyu shenglan** 方輿勝覽 (1239). The importance of these last three is diminished by the ready availability of much fuller sources (including Local Gazetteers). On Tang and Song geographical works see Aoyama Sadao 青山定男 , *Collected Studies on Communications, Gazetteers and Maps of the Tang and Song* (**Tō Sō jidai no kōtsū to chishi chizu no kenkyū** 唐宋時代の交通と地誌 地図の研究 ; Tokyo, 1963).

18.4.4 Comprehensive Gazetteers of the Empire

Only fragments of the enormous *Comprehensive Gazetteer of the Yuan* (**Da Yuan yitong zhi** 大元一統志 , revised version, end of thirteenth century) are extant (35 or so *juan* out of 1000). The title and arrangement of this work were followed however in the Ming and again in the Qing. For the Ming we have the *Comprehensive Gazetteer of the Ming,* comp. Li Xian 李賢 et al. (**Da Ming yitong zhi** 大明一統志 ; 1461; photographic reprint of original palace edition, 10 vols., Taipei, 1965) and for the Qing the following three versions of the *Comprehensive Gazetteer of the Qing:*

1.   Xu Qian-xue 徐乾學 et al., comps., **Da Qing yitong zhi** 大清一統志 completed 1746.

2.   He Shen 和珅 et al., comps., **Da Qing yitong zhi** 大清一統志 , presented in 1784 and printed in 1790.

3.   Mu-zhang-a 穆彰阿 et al., comps., **Da Qing yitong zhi** 大清一統志 completed in 1820 at the end of the Jia-qing period and thus referred to as the **Jiaqing chongxiu da Qing yitong zhi** 嘉慶 重修一統志 , printed in 1842; Commercial Press reprint with this title with an index, Shanghai, 1934; Taipei reprint, 1967.

The Comprehensive Gazetteers of the Empire are easy to use since they, like the Monographs on Administrative Geography in the Standard Histories, are arranged according to well-established administrative hierarchies. The **Jiaqing yitong zhi** was the largest and most accurate of this type of Comprehensive Gazetteer. From it may be gained a detailed picture of the administrative geography of the entire empire at the beginning of the nineteenth century; more detailed information on individual places is of course available in the many thousands of extant Qing Local Gazetteers (upon which ultimately the Comprehensive Gazetteers themselves were based).

18.5   Local Gazetteers

Local Gazetteers (*fangzhi* 方志   ), sometimes also called "local histories"), are called "local" to differentiate them from the various kinds of Comprehensive Gazetteers (*zongzhi* 總志   ) discussed above.

They are usually subdivided into Provincial Gazetteers (*tongzhi* 通志   ), Prefectural Gazetteers (*fuzhi* 府志   ), and District Gazetteers (*xianzhi* 縣志   ). In addition there are a number of gazetteers for market towns, temples, famous mountains, shrines, etc. (*zazhi* 雜志   ).

The Provincial Gazetteers were compiled usually by summarizing the information in the Prefectural Gazetteers which were in turn abridged from previous editions and from the individual District Gazetteers. Altogether about 7,500 Local Gazetteers are extant in a staggering total of 110,000 chapters. They form one of the most important sources for the study of Chinese history in the last thousand years, since they contain copious materials on local administrations, local economies, local cultures, local officials and local worthies. They were usually compiled by members of the local elite and were produced under the sponsorship of the local officials.

By the Qing (the period in which most were compiled), Local Gazetteers contained materials arranged in all or some of the following categories:

1.   Preface and general rules (*fanli* 凡例   ) listing compilers and general editorial policy.

2.   Maps of the district, city plans, etc. (*yutu* 輿圖   , *tukao* 圖考).

3.   Changing borders, tables of changing administrative units included in the district, prefecture, etc. (*jiangyu* 疆輿 , *yange* 沿革).

4.   Main topographical features; rivers, mountains, etc. (*shanchuan* 山川   ).

5. Famous places, ruins, views (*mingsheng* 名勝 , *guji* 古 蹟).

6. Official buildings; walls, yamen (*chengchi* 城池 , *jianzhi* 建置 , *gongshu* 公署); schools (*xuexiao* 學校).

7. Buddhist and Taoist temples (*guansi* 觀寺).

8. Bridges, canals, irrigation works (*qiaoliang* 橋梁 , *hequ* 河渠 , *shuili* 水利); river conservancy (*hefang* 河防).

9. Office holders, from earliest times to time of compilation (*zhiguan* 職官).

10. Examinations (*xuanju* 選舉).

11. Fiscal information: household and head counts (*hukou* 户口), land and other taxes (*fushui* 賦稅).

12. Markets, tolls, and barriers (*shizhen* 市鎮).

13. Local products, local crops (*wuchan* 物產).

14. Local customs and festivals (*fengsu* 風俗).

15. Biographies of local worthies, upright officials, chaste women, etc. (*renwu* 人物, *minghuan* 名宦 , *lienü* 列女).

16. Biographies of exorcists and magicians, Buddhist and Taoist monks (*fangji* 方技 , *shilao* 釋老).

17. Local inscriptions and tombs (*jinshi* 金石 , *lingmu* 陵墓).

18. Bibliographies and examples of the writings of local scholars (*yiwen* 藝文).

19. Chronicle of natural and man-made disasters or omens: flood, drought, hail, snow, locusts; uprisings, soldiers, high prices, low prices, etc. (*zaiyi* 災異 ; *xiangyi* 祥異 ; *bing* 兵).

20. Miscellaneous topics and records (*zalu* 雜錄).

Usually the longest sections were the different categories of Biographies (15-16), followed by the various forms of fiscal information (11-13) and tables of office holders etc. (9-10).

In origin Local Gazetteers derived from the practice of compiling basic information on local conditions, population, and revenue and submitting these together with maps and plans to the central government. At the same time they also derive from the practice, which became widespread in the third century A.D., of collecting biographies of local worthies and their writings. Many elements of the later gazetteers were in earlier periods copied and circulated as separate works (for example the Records of Local Customs (*fengsu zhuan* 風俗傳), Maps and Records of Rivers and Mountains (*shanchuan tuji* 山川圖記). The Local Gazetteer as a work in its own right combining all these elements emerged in the Song (sometimes with the earlier name, *tujing* 圖經). On the earlier types of gazetteer (down to the Yuan), see Zhang Guo-gan's 張國淦 meticulous *Critical Notes on Old Chinese Gazetteers* (**Zhongguo gu fangzhi kao** 中國古方志考 ; Shanghai, 1962), which is an annotated bibliography of well over 2,000 gazetteer-style works compiled to the end of the Yuan, about 99 per cent of which are no longer extant. Titles are arranged by *zongzhi* 總志 and by *fangzhi* 方志 , with the latter grouped by modern provinces. There is a title index by stroke order. See also Aoyama.

Nearly 200 Local Gazetteers are known to have been compiled in the Song (mainly in the Southern Song and therefore for localities in South China), of which only about 30 survive. Yuan scholars are known to have compiled 60, of which only 11 are extant. Thereafter, the number of available Local Gazetteers increases enormously; altogether 900 are extant from the Ming (mainly the late Ming) out of an unknown number compiled, while no less than 5,000 Qing Local Gazetteers are extant. Approximately 650 were compiled during the Republican period.

The stimulus for gazetteer compilation in the Qing came in part from the practical school of geo-military and geo-historical Ming loyalists (the Zhexi group of which Gu Yan-wu and Gu Zu-yu were both members), whose influence was still felt long after the trend in scholarship had turned to critical philological studies. Official orders in 1672 and 1729 that every province compile a gazetteer also greatly stimulated Local Gazetteer production.

A great many Qing scholars, historians, and local officials took part in the compilation of Local Gazetteers and there arose for the first time the phenomenon almost of the professional gazetteer-compiler. These trends were summed up by the historian Zhang Xue-cheng 章學誠 (1738-1801), who was the first to discuss gazetteers as an important branch of historical writing on a par with the national histories. He also suggested that local archives should be kept and that the editing and compilation of the gazetteers should be in the hands of specialists. On Zhang's writing on gazetteers and on the interesting gazetteers written by him, see D.S. Nivison, *The Life and Thought of Chang Hsüeh-ch'eng* (Stanford, 1966), and in greater detail, Zhu Shi-jia, "Chang Hsueh-ch'eng and his Contributions to Local Historiography," Ph.D. thesis (Columbia University, 1950).

18.6   How to find Local Gazetteers

The quickest way of finding out what gazetteers are extant for a particular district, prefecture, or province is to consult the most comprehensive catalogue of gazetteers: Zhu Shi-jia 朱士嘉 , *Enlarged Comprehensive Catalogue of Chinese Local Gazetteers* (**Zhongguo difangzhi zonglu zengding** 中国地方志综录增订 ; Shanghai, 1958; reprinted Tokyo, 1968). In it will be found brief bibliographic notes on some 7,500 Local Gazetteers in 41 major Chinese libraries. Gazetteers are arranged by title and grouped according to mdern provinces. There is a title index as well as an index of some 10,000 author/compilers. Both indexes are arranged by stroke number. The revised edition of Zhu's catalogue contains 1,600 more titles than the original 1935 edition.

The quickest way of finding out what gazetteers are extant from a given period is to consult Zhang Guo-gan for pre-Song titles; the list of titles in Zhu Shi-jia 朱士嘉 , *Index to the Biographies in Song and Yuan Local Gazetteers* (**Song Yuan fangzhi zhuanji suoyin** 宋元方志传记索 引 ; Peking, 1963) for Song and Yuan titles; the list in Franke, pp. 242-309, for Ming titles; and Zhu Shi-jia (1958) for Qing and Republican titles.

Having found the titles and compilers of gazetteers for a given locality or period, next it will be necessary to find out which libraries contain them. Zhu's own catalogue shows which of the major Chinese libraries holds each of the 7,500 gazetteers he lists. Other important library catalogues of Local Gazetteers are :

Europe

Catalogue des monographies locales chinoises dans les bibliothèques d'Europe, comp. Y. Hervouet (Paris, 1957). Lists 1,434 gazetteers in 17 European collections.

U.S.A.

A Catalog of Chinese Local Histories in the Library of Congress, comp. Chu Shih-chia (Washington, 1942).

Other important collections of Local Gazetteers in the U.S.A. are at Columbia University, Harvard University, and the University of Chicago. See *Chinese Local Histories, Reference No. 1* (Chicago, 1970); and *H-Y Classified Catalogue* (1940), vol. 3, pp. 714-812, "Gazetteers."

Japan

Union Catalogue of Chinese Local Gazetteers in Fourteen Major Libraries and Research Institutes in Japan **(Nihon shuyō toshokan kenkyūjo shozō Chūgoku chihōshi sōgō mokuroku** 日本主要図書館研究所所藏中国地方志綜合目録 ; Tokyo, 1969), which supersedes all previous catalogues of Chinese Local Gazetteers in Japanese collections. Arranged by provinces, includes call numbers, and has a Wade-Giles title index.

Taiwan

Union Catalogue of Local Gazetteers in Taiwan Public Collections **(Taiwan gongcang fangzhi lianhe mulu** 臺灣公藏方志聯合目録 ; Taipei, 1957).

Further library catalogues are listed in *Catalogues of Chinese Local Gazetteers,* comp. D. Leslie and J. Davidson (Canberra, 1969).

Even the most recent library catalogues of Local Gazetteers are apt to be out of date (especially for late Qing gazetteers) because of the large gazetteer reprint series being published by several Taipei publishers.

Since gazetteers were usually compiled by committees of local officials and scholars, they are usually referred to by title (sometimes preceded by reign name to distinguish editions) except when the compiler was a well-known writer. The most convenient form of citation for gazetteers is title followed by date of compilation.

Although there are few indexes and concordances to Local Gazetteers, note the indexes to biographies available: Zhu Shi-jia (1963); and Yamane Yukio 山根幸夫 , *Draft Index of People with Biographies in Ming Local Gazetteers (Extant in Japanese Collections)* **(Nihon genzon Mindai chihōshi denki sakuin kō** 日本現存明代地方志傳記索引稿 ; Tokyo, 1964).

In 1934 the Commercial Press reprinted six late Qing Provincial Gazetteers with (4-corner) indexes attached:

1. *P.G. of Metropolitan region* (**Jifu tongzhi** 畿輔通志, 1906).
2. *P.G. of Shantung* (**Shandong tongzhi** 山東通志, 1911).
3. *P.G. of Chekiang* (**Zhejiang tongzhi** 浙江通志, 1736).
4. *P.G. of Hupeh* (**Hubei tongzhi** 湖北通志, 1911).
5. *P.G. of Hunan* (**Hunan tongzhi** 湖南通志, 1885).
6. *P.G. of Hopei* (**Hebei tongzhi** 河北通志, 1884).

On Local Gazetteers, see Fu Zhen-lun 傅振倫, *General Introduction to the Study of Chinese Local Gazetteers* (**Zhongguo fangzhixue tonglun** 中國方志學通論; Shanghai, 1935); and Li Tai-fen 李泰棻, *The Study of Local Gazetteers* (**Fangzhixue** 方志學; Shanghai, 1936), which is the best introduction to gazetteers for historians. Later chapters also touch on problems connected with other sources. See also Earl H. Pritchard, "Traditional Chinese Historiography and Local Histories," in *Uses of History,* ed. H.V. White (Detroit, 1968), pp. 187-219; also Aoyama (1963); and R.H. Myers, "The Usefulness of Local Gazetteers for the Study of Modern Chinese Economic History: Szechwan during the Ch'ing and Republican periods," **Qinghua xuebao**, New Series 6, nos. 1 and 2, pp. 72-102 (1967).

18.7 Miscellaneous geographic works

18.7.1 Foreign peoples and border areas

Works on border areas and foreign peoples are found in many different types of source, including the Standard Histories, where summaries on foreign peoples are found appended to the Biographies section. The summaries from the first fifteen Standard Histories were published together in a punctuated edition in Jian Bo-zan 翦伯贊, ed., *Sections on Foreign Peoples in the Standard Histories* (**Lidai ge zu zhuanji huibian** 历代各族传记会编), 2 vols. in 3 (Peking, 1958-1959). See also Tsunoda Ryusaku, *Japan in the Chinese Dynastic Histories, Later Han through Ming Dynasties* (South Pasadena, 1951) for translations of the sections on Japan; and also H. H. Frankel, *Catalogue of Translations from Chinese Dynastic*

Histories for the Period 200-960 (Berkeley, 1957); many of the translations listed are of the sections on foreign peoples. For a brief discussion of the many different types of source on foreign affairs see Franke, pp. 201-202. There is a full bibliography of primary sources on border areas by Deng Yan-lin 鄧衍林 , *Catalogue of Writings on China's Border Areas* (**Zhongguo bianjiang tuji lu** 中国边疆图籍录 ; Shanghai, 1958). Deng's work is arranged by place and is also indexed; references to maps are included. See also J. Needham, "Descriptions of Southern Regions and Foreign Countries," in Needham, III, 510-514.

Xu Yun-qiao 許雲樵 has compiled a *Bibliography of Sources on Southeast Asia and the Island*s (**Nanhang wenxian xulu changbian** 南洋文獻敘錄長編), **Nanyang yanjiu** 1.1:1-170 (Singapore, 1959).

18.7.2 Travel accounts

The travels of Chinese Buddhist pilgrims to India, mainly in the third to seventh centuries, have frequently been translated; see Needham, "The Buddhist Pilgrims," I, 207-211, for a brief summary. Also see Needham, "A Note on Chinese Explorers," III, 522-525. A popular anthology of English translations from Chinese travel literature was edited by J. Mirsky: *The Great Chinese Travellers* (New York, 1964).

18.7.3 Cities

There are extant many fascinating, detailed, and more informal accounts of cities and city life (usually in the capitals) than can be found in the Local Gazetteers. They were either classified in the geography section of the History Division or among the Miscellaneous Notes in the Philosophers' Division. A few of the most important of these works are listed below:

1.   Yang Xuan-zhi 楊衒之, *Memories of Loyang* (**Loyang qielan ji** 洛陽伽藍記 ; A.D. 530, Shanghai, 1958; Peking, 1963). More than the title suggests; description of Loyang under the Northern Wei.

2.   Hiraoka Takeo 平岡武夫, ed., *Tang Dynasty Loyang and Chang-an* (**Tōdai no Chōan to Rakuyō** 唐代の長安と洛陽), *T'ang Civilization Reference Series,* 3 vols. (Kyoto, 1956). Collects a very large amount of formal and informal writings on the two capitals during the Tang, plus maps, and an index.

3.   Sun Qi 孫棨 , *Anecdotes of the Northern Quarter* (**Bei li zhi** 北里志). French translation by R. Des Rotours, *Courtisanes chinoises à la fin des T'ang* (Paris, 1968). Court Life in Chang-an.

4.   Meng Yuan-lao 孟元老 , *Memories of the Splendors of the Eastern Capital* (**Dong jing menghua lu** 東京夢華錄 ; 1150), punctuated text with notes by Deng Zhi-cheng 鄧之誠 (Peking, 1959). This famous description of Kaifeng under the Northern Song has also been reprinted in a punctuated edition with four descriptions of Hangzhou (Lin-an) in the Southern Song, namely Wu Zi-mu 吳自牧 , *The Past Seems a Dream* (**Meng liang lu** 夢粱錄 ; 1275), indexed in Saeki Tomi 佐伯富 , ed., *Index to Chinese Miscellaneous Notes* (**Chūgoku zuihitsu sakuin** 中国随筆索引 ; Kyoto, 1954); Naide Weng 耐得翁 , *The Wonders of the Capital* (**Du cheng jisheng** 都城紀勝 ; 1253); *Many Marvels of Hangzhou* (**Fan sheng lu** 繁勝錄) by the Old Man of the Western Lake (Xi hu lao ren 西湖老人 ; 1253); and Zhou Mi 周窑 , *Old Stories of Hangzhou* (**Wulin jiushi** 武林舊事 ; 1280), indexed in Saeki. The title of this reprint is **Dong jing menghua lu wu zhong** 東京夢華錄五種 ; Shanghai, 1956. See J. Gernet, *Daily Life in China on the Eve of the Mongol Invasion* (London, 1962); and A.C. Moule, *Qinsai* (Cambridge, 1957).

5.   Zhou Hui 周暉 , *Nanking Trifles* (**Jinling suoshi** 金陵瑣事; 1610), indexed in Saeki.

6.   *Monographs on the Buddhist Temples of Nanking* (**Jinling fansha zhi** 金陵梵刹志 ; 1627).

7.   Yu Huai 余懷 , *Miscellaneous Notes on the Wooden-bridge Section of Nanking* (**Banqiaozaji** 板橋雜記, 1644), tr. H.S. Levy, *A Feast of Mist and Flowers* (Yokohama, 1966).

8.   *Historical Studies of Peking* (**Qinding rixia jiuwen kao** 欽定日下舊聞考 ; 1774).

9.   Li Dou 李斗 , *Records of the Painted Boats of Yangzhou* (**Yangzhou huafang lu** 揚州畫舫錄 ; 1795). Broader than the title suggests. See C.P. MacKerras, *The Rise of the Peking Opera* (Oxford, 1972), ch. 3.

10.   *Miscellaneous Notes on the Capital* (**Dumen zaji** 都門雜記; 1864). Issued under many different titles, it was intended as a guide to the capital for visiting scholars, officials and merchants. See MacKerras, pp. 161 ff.

City maps and plans will be found in the Local Gazetteers (or in archaeological reports for pre-Tang cities). See for example P. Wheatley, *The Pivot of the Four Quarters* (Chicago, 1971); K.C. Chang, *The Archaeology of Ancient China* (New Haven, 1968).

The most detailed city plan known to have survived from the later Empire was of Peking, *Complete Map of the Capital in the Qianlong Period* **(Kenryō keisei zenzu fu kaisetsu sakuin** 乾隆京城全図附解説索引 ; 1940), reprinted from a manuscript copy kept in the Imperial Household archive with notes and an index by Imanishi Shunjū 今西春秋 . Also reprinted by the Palace Museum under the title **Qing neiwufu cang jingcheng quantu** 清内務府藏京城全圖 ; Peking, 1940.

18.8   Merchant manuals and route books

Some twenty to thirty Merchant Manuals and route books are known to have survived from the sixteenth to the late nineteenth century, no doubt reflecting the upsurge of trade at this time. These manuals form a unique and little utilized source for trade routes, market location, business practices, and merchant ethics of the later empire. They usually contain information on trade routes including time taken between stopping points, location of tax barriers and markets and so on, as well as general knowlege for merchants, including information on differences between regional weights and measures, notes on different goods and ethical maxims. The sections of these works on routes were based on official administrative geographical works and they are usually arranged according to the administrative hierarchy. Individual merchants using such works would, or course, have marked up their own copies with marginal notes.

Encyclopaedias for Daily Use of the late Ming and Qing (see section 26.3) also not infrequently contain the same kind of materials as the Merchant Manuals.

For extensive listing and discussion of different editions of these works see E.P. Wilkinson, "Chinese Merchant Manuals and Route Books," *Ch'ing-shih wen-t'i,* vol. 2, no. 1 (November 1972).

The most interesting of these works are listed below:

Ming

1. *Comprehensive Maps and Records of Staging Posts Throughout the Empire* (**Yitong lucheng tuji** 一統路程圖記) by Huang Bian 黃汴 (preface dated 1570). Naikaku bunko, Tokyo.

2. *Land and Water Routes* (**Shuilu lucheng** 水陸路程) by Shang Jun 商濬 (preface dated 1617). Sonkeikaku bunko, Tokyo.

3. *Guide to Merchant Routes* (**Shangcheng yilan** 商程一覽), compiled by Tao Cheng-qing 陶承慶, n.d. Naikaku bunko, Tokyo.

Nos. 1, 2, and 3 are practically identical but no. 3 contains added information on local products, official clothing, jingles, ancient capitals, etc. on the upper half of each page.

Qing

1. *Guide to the Routes of the Empire* ([**Tianxia lucheng**] **Shiwo zhouxing** 天下路程示我周行). The most common of all the merchant route books, with many dozens of copies extant. The earliest edition is dated 1694. Many reprints appeared, often with different compilers or different titles.

2. *Essentials for Scholar-merchants* (**Shishang yaolan** 士商要覽), ed. Tan Yi-zi 澹漪子, early eighteenth century. *Juan* 3 contains important materials on business ethics and methods of trading; see Terada Takanobu 寺田隆信, "On Merchant Manuals of the Ming and Qing" (Min Shin jidai no shogyosho ni tsuite 明清時代の商業書にていて), Tōyōgaku 20:111-126 (1968).

3. *Guide for Traders and Shopkeepers* (**Shang-gu bianlan** 商賈便覽), ed. Wu Zhong-fu 吳中孚 from Feng Gang 鳳岡 (preface date 1792). This manual contains data on all aspects of trading and also uniquely on shopkeeping. Only one copy is known to exist (in the Tōyō bunka kenkyūjo in Tokyo), but two of the works included in the **Shang-gu bianlan** have been reprinted from other copies elsewhere. On the first, see Ju Qing-yuan 鞠清遠, "Collation of **Jianghu bidu**" (Jiaozheng **Jianghu bidu** 校正江湖必讀), Shihuo 5.9:30-42 (1937), and Ju Qing-yuan, "Three early Qing merchant books" (Qing kaiguo qianhou de san bu shangren zhuzuo 清開國前後的三部商人著作), reprinted in

Zhongguo jindaishi luncong, 2nd collection, II, 205-244 (Taipei, 1958).
W. Eberhard has translated in summary form some of the maxims in his
Social Mobility in Traditional China (Leiden, 1962). The second work included in **Shan-gu bianlan** is the **Gongshang qieyao** 工商切要 which is
similar to the instructions for apprentices translated by L.S. Yang in the
appendix to his "Schedules of Work and Rest in Imperial China," in Yang,
Studies in Chinese Institutional History (Cambridge, Mass., 1966), pp. 38-
42.

    4.   *Miscellaneous Notes on the Capital* (see 18.7.3, no. 10).

18.9   How to locate places

Two problems are involved in locating places referred to in historical
sources: place names changed over time and administrative boundaries of
places frequently shifted.

Chinese places often had different names in different periods and most
places of any size usually had a literary name as well as an ordinary name.
Fortunately there are historical place-name dictionaries which list the various
names of a place and the periods in which these names were used as well as
indicating the modern equivalent. The best of these works is Zang Li-he
臧勵龢, *Dictionary of Chinese Place Names* (**Zhongguo gujin diming da
cidian** 中國古今地名大辭典 ; Shanghai, 1931, and many later
reprints). In it are given the location in terms of 1930s provinces and administrative units of the ancient or modern names of some 40,000 towns,
rivers, mountains, etc. The advantage of using Aoyama Sadao's **Shina rekidai
chimei yoran** is that the 30,000 old place names included are arranged conveniently in tabular form opposite their equivalents as of the 1930s.

There is a geographical dictionary in English (based on the *Jiaqing
Comprehensive Gazetteer of the Empire*), which is useful for locating better
known places, rivers, etc. (as of the late nineteenth century): G.M.H. Play-
fair, *The Cities and Towns of China: A Geographical Dictionary* (Hong
Kong, 1879; 2nd ed , Shanghai, 1910; Taipei reprint, 1965). It also gives
coordinates.

Place names in the People's Republic of China are for the most part unchanged since the 1930s below the district (*xian* 県　　) level, but above that level there have been considerable alterations of names; consult *Handbook of Administrative Divisions of the People's Republic of China* (**Zhonghua renmin gongheguo xingzheng quhua shouce** 中华人民共和 国行政区划手册　　; Peking, 1965, etc.)

See also United States Board on Geographic Names, *Mainland China,* 2 vols. (Washington, 1968), which includes 108,000 names, including village names, each identified by finding coordinates and regional code reference. This supersedes previous editions.

Having found out the modern name of an old place (or the old name of a modern place), the next problem is to locate it on the map. The easiest to start with is A. Herrmann, *An Historical Atlas of China* (new ed., Chicago, 1966) which has an index and glossary of characters, but small places (district towns and below) are not included. Yanai Wataru 箭内亘 , comp., *Atlas for the Student of Oriental History* (**Tōyō dokushi chizu** 東洋讀史地図 ; Tokyo, 1912), revised and enlarged by Wada Sei 和田清 (Tokyo, 1941), has one advantage over Herrmann's atlas in that to a greater extent China is shown in its Asian setting.

The most detailed series of empire-wide historical maps is Yang Shou-jing's 楊守敬 somewhat unwieldy *Maps of Changing Places and Boundaries in Different Periods* (**Lidai yudi yange tu** 歷代輿地沿革 圖), 42 *ce* (Shanghai, 1906-1911). The place names of each dynasty are printed in black over a map (in red) of Qing China (based on the *Jiaqing Comprehensive Gazetteer of the Empire).*

The above three maps and atlases are all on an empire-wide scale but it is very likely that the student will want a detailed map of a province, prefecture, or district in a given period. Maps on this scale are available in most Local Gazetteers (see section 18.5). There are usually several editions of a gazetteer for a given place, each edition with the maps of that period.

The problem of changing administrative boundaries is a troublesome one; for example, statistics about a certain province or region in the Tang dynasty are difficult to compare with similar statistics in the Han or Ming dynasty since the boundaries were different in each period. To solve such problems requires a certain amount of time but is easily done. Starting from the district level up, all Local Gazetteers usually contain a "Table of administrative units in different periods" (*yange biao* 沿革表) which shows for example when the area of a former locality (*xiang* 鄉) became upgraded to a district (*xian*縣) and was therefore no longer included in the area of the district to which it had been attached before. Similar tables exist on an empire-wide scale and have been brought together in such works as *Tables of Administrative Units in Different Periods* (**Lidai yange biao** 歷代 沿革表 ; 1814 and modern reprints). Part of the information in these works is of course reproduced in map form, but not accurately, in Herrmann, Yanai and Wada, and Yang.

19. Encyclopaedic Histories of Institutions

The Encyclopaedic Histories of Institutions cover much the same subjects as the Monographs in the Standard Histories (see section 16.5). They were also written for the same purposes, that is, as guides and reference works to the administration and institutions of the past for scholars and officials. In scope, however, they are often wider than the Monographs; furthermore, the authors of the three most famous of them covered much longer periods and left the mark of their own individual views. For these reasons (and also because of the combined index to them) these works are often used as a first reference on Chinese institutional, economic, and social history of all periods.

The work which was to set the model was Du You's 杜佑 *Encyclopaedic History of Institutions* (**Tongdian** 通典 ; 801) which laid greater emphasis on administration as opposed to ritual than had the Monographs in the Standard Histories up to that time.

The two other most famous such works are Zheng Qiao's 鄭樵 *Comprehensive History of Institutions* (**Tongzhi** 通志 ; 1149) and Ma Duan-lin's 馬端臨 *General History of Institutions and Critical Examination of Documents and Studies* (**Wenxian tongkao** 文獻通考 ; 1224).

These three works are usually referred to for short as the *santong* 三通 .

　　Six continuations to them were compiled during the reign of Qian-long in the eighteenth century and they were then published together under the title,*The Nine Encyclopaedic Histories of Institutions* (**Jiutong** 九通). Although lacking the individual editorial touch and broad chronological sweep of the *santong,* these six continuations plus a Ming and a late Qing continuation are useful and well arranged collections of sources for the periods which they cover. The best modern edition was brought out by the Commercial Press under the title *The Ten Tong* (**Shitong** 十通 , 20 vols., Shanghai, 1936; Taipei reprint, 1965). This edition has an index (essential for works with a combined total of over 20,000 triple pages!). The authors, titles and years covered by each of the *tong* are as follows (for a full listing of the different editions etc. see Teng and Biggerstaff, pp. 107-114).

	Authors		
1.	Du You	**Tongdian** (801)	Earliest times to 755; especially important for pre-Tang institutions.
2.	Zheng Qiao	**Tongzhi** (1149)	Most original part, the twenty Monographs (*lüe* 略-) cover from earliest times to the end of the Tang.
3.	Ma Duan-lin	**Wenxian tongkao** (1224)	Earliest times to 1204; especially important for the Song.
4.	Wang Qi 王圻	**Xu Wenxian tongkao** (1586)	Not included in either the **Jiutong** or **Shitong** editions; original edition only. Covers the years 907-1586; especially important for the Ming. Not superseded by no. 9.
5.	Nos. 5 through	**Xu tongdian**	From 756 to end of the Ming.
6.	10 were	**Qing chao tongdian**	From 1644 to 1785.

7.	compiled under	**Xu Tongzhi**	Monographs cover from 907 to 1644.
8.	imperial	**Qing chao tongzhi**	From 1644 to 1785.
9.	sponsorship in the 18th	**Xu Wenxian tongkao**	From 1224 to 1644 (does not supersede no. 4).
10.	century.	**Qing chao wenxian tongkao**	From 1644 to 1785.
11.	Liu Jin-zao 劉錦藻	**Qing chao xu wen-xian tongkao** (1921)	From 1786 to 1911.

The following is a list of the main section headings of the **Wenxian tongkao** which gives some idea of the scope of the subjects covered: (1) land taxes, (2) currency, (3) population, (4) services and corvée, (5) customs and tolls, (6) official markets and purchases, (7) local tribute, (8) national expenditure, (9) examinations and promotions, (10) schools, (11) government posts, (12) imperial sacrifices, (13) minor sacrifices, (14) imperial ancestral temple, (15) other temples and shrines, (16) court rites, (17) posthumous titles, (18) music, (19) army, (20) penal law, (21) bibliography, (22) calligraphy, (23) imperial genealogy, (24) nobility, (25) sun, moon, and five planets, (26) freaks of nature, (27) geography, (28) foreign countries.

Wang Qi's **Xu Wenxian tongkao** (no. 4 above) contains some sections not found in the others, notably on clans and on Taoists and Buddhists; Liu Jin-zao's **Qing chao xu wenxian tongkao** (no. 11 above) contains sections on posts and communications, industry, constitutional government, and foreign affairs.

For detailed tables of section and sub-section headings to seven of the *tong* (including Wang Qi), see *Index to the* **Santong** *and to the Four Continuations of the* **Wenxian tongkao** (Tōyōshi kenkyūkai 東洋史研究会 , **Bunken tsūkō go shu sōmokuroku, fu tsūten, tsūshi** 文献通考五種 總目録附通典通志 ; Kyoto, 1954).

20. Administrative and Penal Law

20.1 Introduction

The most general form of codified administrative law was found in the Statutes (*ling* 令) which were promulgated in most dynasties down to the *Statutes of the Ming* (**Da Ming ling** 大明令; 1368), the first of the Statues to survive complete and also the last to be promulgated. Penal Law was codified in the Codes (*lü* 律) which prescribed the action to be taken and the punishments to be inflicted for all infringements of the laws. The *Tang Code with Commentary* (**Tanglü shuyi** 唐律疏議; 737) is the first Code to survive complete and was the basis for all later Codes in Japan, Korea, and Vietnam, as well as in China itself; see Niida Noboru, "Chinese Legal Institutions of the Sui and T'ang Periods and their Influence on Surrounding East Asian Countries," in *Rapports II, Histoire des Continents,* Comité International des Sciences Historiques (Vienna, 1965), pp. 113-131. The division between the two types of law, penal and administrative (the *lü* and the *ling*) was not hard and fast, although it became much more so after the Tang. Both types of law were altered, expanded, and applied in the light of particular precedents, cases, regulations, etc., the most important types of which are mentioned below.

During the Tang (which marks the first documented watershed in the history of Chinese law and which laid the groundwork for the remainder of Chinese history) there were four main types of codified law. These were the Code (*lü* 律), the Statutes (*ling* 令), the Regulations (*ge* 格), and the Ordinances (*shi* 式). The Code mainly contained penal law while the Statutes contained the most important administrative laws; these were modified or supplemented in the Regulations and their implementation was defined in the Ordinances. From the Tang also dates the practice of compiling comprehensive handbooks of the structure and functions of the bureaucracy, referred to in what follows as Compendia of Administrative Law ultimately modeled on the *Institutes of Zhou* (**Zhouli** 周禮). All these works, to-gether with the Edicts (*chi* 敕, etc.), Precedents or Sub-statutes (*li* 例,

zeli 則例 , *shili* 事例 , etc.) which modified or explained penal and administrative law, are the basic sources for Chinese legal and institutional history. They are also important sources for all the many different areas of Chinese society with which they deal, either in the generalized terms of the Codes, the Statutes, and Compendia of Administrative Law or in the more detailed Commentaries, Precedents, Cases, etc. which frequently illustrate the actual working of the law in concrete terms.

Bibliographies

Sun Zu-ji 孫祖基 , *Bibliographic Study of Works by Legalists* (**Zhongguo lidai fajia zhushu kao** 中國歷代法家著述考 ; Peking, 1934; Taipei, 1970). This bibliography lists all works the author could find references to which had any bearing on: (1) Guanzi, Hanfei, and the other "Legalist" thinkers; (2) works of administrative law arranged by dynasties; (3) all works relating to handling of suspects, including case books; (4) and (5) instructions for investigation officers, coroners, etc.; (6) handbooks for local administrators and their assistants. The great majority of the works cited are no longer extant (with no indication of this by the author) but this bibliography is very useful for finding out what legal works were in existence at a given time. It is also unusual in including categories (5) and (6). See also P. Pelliot, "Notes de bibliographie chinoise, II, Le droit chinois," *BEFEO* 9:123-152; *Short Bibliography of Primary and Secondary Works on the History of Chinese Legal Institutions* (**Zhongguo fazhishi cankao shumu jianjie** 中国法制史参考书目简解 ; Peking, 1957); *Chinese Law Past and Present: A Bibliography of Enactments and Commentaries in English Text* (comp. Lin Fu-shun, New York, 1966).

20.2   Pre-Tang law

The reconstruction of pre-Tang Statutes and administrative law is largely based on the four Monographs on Law and the Five Monographs on Official Posts in the Standard Histories of the pre-Tang period (see the studies, translations, etc. of these works which are listed under 16.5.3).

Fragments of pre-Tang Codes have been retrieved from contemporary and later sources. The first Code is traditionally supposed to have been promulgated at the beginning of the 4th century B.C. (Li Kui, *Canon of Laws* [Fa jing 法經]), but considerable doubt is attached to the later descriptions of this work. See T. Pokora, "The Canon of Laws of Li K'uei: A Double Falsification," *Archiv Orientalni* 27:96-121 (1959). Attempts have been made to reconstruct the early dynastic Codes down to the Tang, using mainly the Monographs on Penal Law in the Standard Histories; see A.F.P. Hulsewé, "Introductory Studies," in his *Remnants of Han Law* (Leiden, 1955), I, 1-307; also Cheng Shu-de 程樹德 *Investigation into the Codes of Nine Dynasties* (Jiu chao lü kao 九朝律考 ; Changsha, 1927; Shanghai, 1935; Peking, 1963)—a notable attempt to piece together fragments of the lost Codes of Han, Wei, Jin, Liang, Chen, N. Wei, N. Qi, Later Zhou, and Sui.

20.3   The Statutes and Compendia of Administrative Law (Tang and post-Tang)

Although the Monographs on Official Posts, Examinations and Law, etc. in the Standard Histories contain useful overviews of administrative law in this period, they are not mentioned in this section again since much more detailed sources are available: Table 2 shows which Histories have which Monographs and sections 16.5.3 and 16.5.4 contain lists of modern studies, indexes, etc. to these Monographs. See also sections 19 and 22 on Encyclopaedic Histories of Institutions and Collections of important Documents for other sources on administrative law and government.

None of the Statutes of the Tang are extant, but no less than 715 of the original 1,546 articles are reconstructed from other Chinese and Japanese sources in a monumental work by Niida Noboru 仁井田陞   , *Collected Vestiges of the Tang Statutes* (Tōryō shūi 唐令拾遺 ; Tokyo, 1933; 1967). Fragmentary remains of the Regulations and Ordinances of the Tang have been preserved in other compilations and in their original form amongst the Mss. discovered at Dunhuang and other sites in northwest China. For an English translation of one of these fragments as well as a useful brief introduction to the different types of Tang administrative law, see D.C. Twitchett, "The Fragment of the T'ang Ordinances of the Department of Waterways Discovered at Tun-Huang," *Asia Major* 6.1:23-79 (1957). On these and other fragments of Tang administrative law found at Dunhuang and elsewhere, see also Niida Noboru, *Collected Papers on Chinese Legal History* (**Chūgoku hōseishi kenkyū** 中国法制史研究; Tokyo, 1964), IV, 229-346.

The earliest extant compendium of Administrative Law was the *Compendium of Administrative Law of the Six Divisions of the Tang Bureaucracy* (**Tang liudian** 唐六典), 738 edition of Konoe Iehiro (1724), together with Tamai Zehaku 玉井是博, "Collation of the **Tang liudian** with the Southern Song print" (Nan Sō hon dai Tō rikuten kokan ki 南宋本大唐六典校勘記), in his *Collected Studies on Chinese Socio-economic History* (**Shina shakai keizaishi kenkyū** 支那社会経済史研究; Tokyo, 1942). The **Tang liudian** is based on all the different types of administrative law as these were applied in all branches of the bureaucracy in the early eighth century.

During the Song the division between penal and administrative law was made even more sharp by separating out the Codes (*lü* 律) and their Commentaries, Sub-statutes, etc. and referring to administrative law under the fourfold division of Edicts, Statutes, Regulations, and Ordinances (*chiling-geshi* 勅令格式). Definitions of these four terms (as in other periods) were not strict and it would be a mistake to suppose that they represent exclusive categories. None of the Song Statutes (which were based on the Tang Statutes) are extant but the *Compendium of Administrative Law of the Qing-yuan Period 1195-1200 (Arranged by Departments)* has been preserved: Xie Shen-fu 謝深甫 et al., comps., **Qingyuan tiaofa shilei** 慶元條法事類; 1202; Tokyo, 1965).

Many of the Edicts, Statutes, Ordinances, Regulations, Sub-statutes, etc. of the Song, as of other periods, were excerpted or quoted in compilations such as the *Collections of Important Documents of the Song* (**Song huiyao** 宋會要, q.v.), etc.

None of the codified administrative law of the Liao or Jin is extant in its original form; however, see Shimada Masao 島田正郎, *Researches on*

Liao Institutions (**Ryōsei no kenkyū** 遼制之研究 ; Tokyo, 1954).

For the Yuan there is the *Compendium of Statutes and Sub-statutes of the Yuan* (**Yuan dianzhang** 元典章 ; 1322); edition of Shen Jia-ben to be used with the corrections and additions supplied in two works of Chen Yuan: **Shen ke Yuan dianzhang jiaobu** 沈刻元典章校補 (Peking, 1931; Taipei, 1967), and **Yuan dianzhang jiaobu shili** 元典章校補事例 (Peking, 1931). A collated, punctuated edition has begun to appear: **Kōteibon Gentenshō keibu dai-issatsu** 校訂本元典章刑部 第一冊; Kyoto, 1964. There is an index to the **Yuan dianzhang**: *Draft Index to the Compendium of Statutes and Sub-statutes of the Yuan* (**Gentenshō sakuin kō** 元典章索引稿), mimeo, 3 vols., Jimbum kagaku kenkyūjo (Kyoto, 1954-1959). For some important studies of the **Yuan dianzhang** see the special issue of **Tōhō gakuhō** (Kyoto), vol. 24 (1954).

See also the detailed but fragmentary *Comprehensive Regulations and Statutes of the Yuan* (**Da Yuan tongzhi tiaoge** 大元通制條格; Taipei reprint of 1930 ed., 2 vols., 1968). Partial index: **Tsūsei jōkaku. Kendai tsūki mokuji sakuin** 通制條格憲臺通記目次索引(Kyoto, mimeo, 1954), and annotated translation: **Tsūsei jōkaku no kenkyū yakuchū dai-issatsu** 通制條格の研究譯注第一冊 (Kyoto, 1964).

Fragments of the less detailed *Compendium for Administering the Empire* (**Jingshi dadian** 經世大典) have also survived.

Although the *Ming Statutes* (**Da Mingling**) 大明令 ; 1368; included in vol. 1 of **Huang Ming zhishu** 皇明制書 ; 1579; Tokyo reprint, 1966) is the first complete extant Statutes, it is much shorter than the previous ones are known to have been and was soon supplemented by such works as the *Statutes of the Central Administration* (**Zhusi zhizhang** 諸司職掌 ; 1393 and 1458), *Regulations for the Censorate* (**Xiangang shilei** 憲綱事類 ; 1371) and other similar works all included in the **Huang Ming zhishu**. These early Statutes and Regulations formed the basis for the important Compendium of Administrative Law, the *Collected Statutes of the Ming* (**Da Ming huidian** 大明會典 ; 1503, presented in 1510 [the 4th year of *Zhengde* 正德] and therefore referred to as the **Zhengde huidian** to distinguish it from the second enlarged edition (1587) which includes Statutes up to 1585 and is referred to as the **Wanli huidian** 萬曆 ;

punctuated reprint of the **Wanli huidian,** 40 vols. [Shanghai, 1936] ; 5 vols. [Taiwan, 1963]).

During the Ming dynasty, many individual branches of the administration printed their rules and regulations in handbooks such as the *Monograph of the Nanking Board of Finance* **(Nanjing hubu zhi** 南京戶部志 ; 1595). For a full list of such works which have survived see W. Franke, *An Introduction to the Sources of Ming History* (Kuala Lumpur and Singapore, 1968), pp. 181-184.

During the Qing dynasty, no Statutes (*ling* 令) were promulgated but the Ming model for issuing very detailed Collected Statutes (*huidian* 會典) was followed. There were five editions of such Compendia of Administrative Law, all of which were entitled *Collected Statutes of the Qing* **(Da Qing huidian** 大清會典). Each carried the important administrative law put in force since the previous edition and each is referred to by the reign name in which it was compiled (although in library catalogues they are entered under the actual title **Da Qing huidian** . . . . .):

1. **Kangxi huidian** 康熙會典, 1690.
2. **Yongzheng huidian** 雍正會典 , 1732.
3. **Qianlong huidian** 乾隆會典 + *zeli* 則例 (sub-statutes), 1764.
4. **Jiaqing huidian** 嘉慶會典 + *shili* 事例 (sub-statutes) + *tu* 圖 (illustrations), 1818.
5. **Guangxu huidian** 光緒會典 + *shili* + *tu,* 1899.

A very large number of works of early Qing administrative law as well as many editions of the Regulations and sub-statutes of individual departments (*buli* 部例 , *zeli* 則例) of the bureaucracy are extant. Many of them are listed in Ma Feng-chen 馬奉琛, *Catalogue of Reference Works for Research on the Qing Administrative System* **(Qingdai xingzheng zhidu yanjiu cankao shumu** 清代行政制度研究參考書目 ; Peking, 1935).

One of the unique features of Qing administrative law is that collections of Provincial Sub-statutes and Cases (*shengli* 省例) relating only to a single province were printed. The largest of these (and the most interesting) is the *Sub-statutes and Leading Cases of Hunan Province* **(Hunan shengli cheng-an** 湖南省例成案 ; Changsha, 1820). The *Sub-statutes of Fukien*

Province (**Fujian shengli** 福建省例; 1873; Taipei reprint, 1967) is also of considerable value. The *Newly Edited Sub-statutes of Kwangtung Province,* comp. Huang En-zheng 黃恩正 has also been reprinted (**Yuedong shengli xinzuan** 粵東省例新纂; 1846), 2 vols. (Taipei, 1968), although it is not as interesting a work as the *Criminal and Civil Cases Decided in the Province of Kwangtung* (**Yuedong chengan chubian** 粵東成案初編; Canton, 1832). On these works see the short article of Niida Noboru in **Ajia rekishi jiten** 4:420-421. See also the further works of this type given in Ma.

In addition to the **Shengli,** provincial yamen from the eighteenth century began printing the official regulations which they received from the central government in works usually called "established regulations" (*dingli* 定例) or "itemized regulations" (*tiaoli* 條例), some of which have survived.

20.4   Guides and handbooks for local officials and clerks

Although not carrying the force of written law, the admonitions and guides to official documents for local officials and underlings (*guanzhen gongdu* 官箴公牘) contain a great deal of interesting supplementary material on the norms and operation of the bureaucracy at the district level.

The tables of contents of fifty-five of these works dating from the Song to the end of the Qing have been indexed in **Kanshin mokuji sōgō sakuin** 官箴目次綜合索引 , mimeo (Kyoto daigaku, Tōyōshi kenkyū-shitsu, 1950). In addition there are indexes to a late twelfth-century and a late seventeeth-century example of this kind of work: **Shokugen satsuyō sakuin** 職源撮要索引 (Kyoto, 1956); **Fukkei zensho goi kai** 福惠全書語彙解 (Kyoto, 1952; 1958).

On these works, see the introduction to the Kyoto index (1950) above by Miyazaki Ichisada: Pt. 5 of Sun Zu-ji; also S. Van der Sprenkel, *Legal Institutions in Manchu China* (London, 1962), pp. 137-150; as well as É. Balazs, "A Handbook of Local Administrative Practice of 1793," in *Political Theory and Administrative Reality in Traditional China* (London, 1965), pp. 50-75, for translations of excerpts and discussion.

Apart from the general guides to local administration, from the Qing there are also extant some practical handbooks containing regulations and procedures for secretarial assistants in charge of financial matters under the local magistrates (qiangu 錢穀) as well as for the secretarial assistants in charge of legal matters (xingming 刑名). Some of these were printed but most circulated in manuscript. The most famous printed financial handbook was Wang You-huai's 王又槐 **Qiangu beiyao** 錢穀備要 (1793), which ran through many editions in the nineteenth century. See also Cai Shen-zhi 蔡申之 , comp., *Informal Materials on Local Government under the Qing Dynasty* (**Qingdai zhouxian gushi** 清代州縣故事 ; Hong Kong, 1968) for examples of excerpts from handbooks of regulations for many varieties of local underling. Ch'ü T'ung-tsu in his *Local Government in China under the Ch'ing* (Cambridge, Mass., 1962) drew heavily on this type of source. H.A. Giles translates Wang You-huai's handbook for coroners: "The Hsi Yuan Lu (洗冤錄) or Instructions to Coroners," *The China Review,* vol. 3 (1924), reprinted in the *Proceedings of the Royal Society of Medicine,* vol. 17 (1924).

The handbook of administrative terms translated by E-tu Zen Sun under the title *Ch'ing Administrative Terms: A Translation of Terminology of the Six Boards with Explanatory Notes* (Cambridge, Mass., 1961) is another example of this type of source and it is also extremely useful for understanding and translating administrative terminology.

20.5   The Penal Codes (Tang and post-Tang)

The *Tang Code with Commentary* (**Gu Tanglü shuyi** 古唐律疏議 ; 737) was the basis of all Chinese Codes down to the Qing. The fundamental modern study of the Tang code of 737 is Niida Noboru 仁井田陞 and Makino Tatsumi   牧野巽 , "Investigation of the date of compilation of the Tang Code With Commentary" (Ko Tōritsusogi seisaku nendai kō 故唐律疏議製作年代考), **Tōhōgakuhō** (Kyoto), 1:70-158, 2:50-226 (1931). See also Dai Yan-hui 戴炎輝, *Comprehensive Introduction to the Tang Code* (**Tanglü tonglun** 唐律通論) and *Discussions on the Tang Code* (**Tanglü ge lun** 唐律各論 ; Taipei, 1964; 1965). There is no translation of the Code into English but see the translation of the Annamite Lê dynasty Code which was modeled closely

137

after it: R. Deloustal, "La Justice dans l'ancien Annam: Le Code des Lê," *BEFEO*, vols. 8-13 (1908-1913), vol. 19 (1919), vol. 22 (1922). See also Niida Noboru, *Researches on Legal Works of the Tang and Song Dynasties* (**Tō-Sō horitsu bunsho no kenkyū** 唐宋法律文書の研究; Tokyo, 1937). There is a concordance available: Zhuang Wei-si 莊葦斯, *Concordance to the Tang Code with Commentary* (**Tanglü shuyi yinde** 唐律疏議引得; Taipei, 1964).

The **Song huiyao gao** 宋會要稿, q.v., *xingfa* 刑法, *ce* 164-171, is an important source for Song legal history, as is also the *Song Repertory of Penal Law* (**Song xingtong** 宋刑統; 963), which was largely based on the *Tang Code*.

Several collections of cases survive from the Song. They were intended to provide examples to assist district magistrates in reaching judicial decisions. The largest has been translated into English: R.H. van Gulik, *T'ang-yin pi-shih, "Parallel Cases from under the pear tree," a 13th century manual of jurisprudence and detention* (Leiden, 1956). The **Tangyin bishi** 棠陰比事 (1211) drew cases from the whole of Chinese history but another extant Song casebook contains judgments and cases dating from the thirteenth century. It has recently been reprinted from a unique copy preserved in Japan: *Collection of Lucid Decisions by Celebrated Judges* (**Minggong shupan qingmingji** 明公書判清明集; 1260-1265; Tokyo, 1966).

None of the Liao or Jin Codes are extant. See Niida Noboru, "A Study of Penal Law of the Jin Dynasty" (Kindai keihō kō 金代刑法考), in Niida (1959), pp. 453-524. The Monograph on Penal Law in the *Standard History of the Yuan,* however, is arranged in the form of a Code and indirectly reflects penal law in the Yuan. See P. Ratchnevsky, *Un Code des Yuan* (Paris, 1937), pp. v-xxiv; Abe Takeo 阿部健夫, "On the relationship between the Monograph on Penal Law in the Standard History of the Yuan and the Yuan Code" (Genshi keihōshi to Genritsu to no kankei ni tsuite 元史刑法志と元律との関係について), **Tōhō gakuhō** 2:251-273 (Kyoto, 1931).

The first version of the *Ming Code* (**Da Ming lü** 大明律; 1373-1374) was largely based on the Tang Code as it had been received down to the Yuan. The third version (1397), however, was completely revised and marks an important break from the 600-year tradition set by the Tang Code. Its title was **Gending Da Ming lü** 更訂大明律 but it is usually referred to as the **Da Ming lü** 大明律 or simply the **Ming lü** 明律 . Like the Tang Code, it was extremely influential in Korea, Japan, and Vietnam. A very large number of editions of the 1397 version are extant; most include the itemized Sub-statutes which after the 1585 edition were made an integral part of the Code. See Franke, pp. 185-187, for an annotated list of 12 editions and also Otake Fumio 小竹文夫 , "Comparison of the *Codes of Tang, Ming, and Qing*" (Tō Min Shin ritsu no hikaku 唐明清律の比較), **Tōyōshigaku ronshū**, vol. 2 (Tokyo, 1954). See also Naito Kenkichi's 内藤乾吉 article comparing the Tang and Ming Codes and discussing the influence of Yuan law, reprinted in his *Collected Studies on Chinese Legal History* (**Chūgoku hōseishi kōshō** 中国法制史考證; Osaka, 1963).

Recently reprinted from a unique manuscript copy are the extremely detailed (5,000 pages) Sub-statutes, Regulations, etc. used in the actual implementation of the Code in the late fifteenth and early sixteenth centuries: Dai Jin 戴金 , comp., **Huang Ming tiaofa shilei zuan** 皇明條法事類纂 , 1531-1533 (?), 2 vols. (Tokyo, 1966). Collections of itemized Sub-statutes (*tiaoli* 條例) have survived in greater numbers from the Qing.

The early version of the *Qing Code* (1646) reached its final form in the expanded *Qing Code with Sub-statutes* (**Da Qing lüli** 大清律例; 1740). For editions and extensive introductions to different aspects of the Qing Code and penal law in the Qing, see D. Bodde and C. Morris, *Law in Imperial China, Exemplified by 190 Ch'ing Cases (Translated from the Hsing-an hui-lan) with Historical, Social, and Judicial Commentaries* (Cambridge, Mass., 1967) and also S. van der Sprenkel, *Legal Institutions in Manchu China: A Sociological Analysis* (London, 1962).

For translations of the *Qing Code* see G.T. Staunton, *Ta Tsing Leu Lee* (1810; Taipei reprint, 1967); and also G. Boulais, *Manuel du Code chinois,* 2 vols., Variétés Sinologiques, No. 55 (Shanghai, 1924; reprinted Taipei, 1957). Although incomplete, it includes translations of the Sub-statutes and also has the Chinese text on each page. For a more complete translation see P.L.F. Philastre, *Le Code annamite, nouvelle traduction complète, comprenant les commentaires officiels du Code, traduits pour la première fois; de nombreuses annotations extraites des commentaires du*

Code chinois . . ., 2 vols. (1875; 2nd ed., 1909; reprinted Taipei, 1967). This is a translation of the 1812 *Annamite Code* which was identical save for a few statutes with the *Qing Code* of 1740.

On the *Qing Code* see Xue Yun-sheng 薛允升 , **Du li cunyi** 讀例存疑 (1905; reprinted, 5 vols., Taipei, 1970).

For translations from the largest Qing casebook, *The Conspectus of Penal Cases* (**Xing-an huilan** 刑案彙覽), see Bodde and Morris. The **Xing-an huilan** (1834; 1886) and its continuation have been reprinted: 16 vols. (Taipei, 1968); and 10 vols. (Taipei, 1970).

21. Army Administration and Warfare

21.1   Army administration

A considerable amount of materials on army administration will be found in the Standard Histories, especially in those with Monographs on Army Administration (*bingzhi* 兵志), Imperial Guards (*yiweizhi* 儀衛志), and Border Guards (*yingweizhi* 營衛志). On army administration, see *New Standard History of the Tang* (tr. R. Des Rotours); also Standard Histories of the Song, Liao, Jin, Yuan, and New Yuan, Ming, Draft Qing, and Qing. On Imperial Guards, see *New Standard History of the Tang;* also Standard Histories of the Song, Liao, Jin and Ming. On Border Guards, see *Standard History of the Liao.*

The Monographs on Law in the **Hanshu** deal with the army and the Han documents on wooden slips (see section 24.2) deal largely with army administration.

The Monographs on Financial Administration in the Standard Histories usually have itemized sections on the various forms of military expenditures which were a major part of state expenditures in most periods of Chinese history.

21.2   Warfare

There is a very large group of writings which in the old catalogues was grouped under the general heading of Military Experts (*bingjia* 兵家), a subdivision of the Philosphers' Division (*zibu* 子部) in the fourfold biblio-graphic arrangement of old Chinese books (see section 12.2). Fortunately there is a modern bibliography of old Chinese writings on war and the military by Lu Da-jie 陸達節 : *A Catalogue of Books on Military Matters of Each Dynasty* (**Lidai bingshu mulu** 歷代兵書目錄 ; Shanghai, 1932; Taipei, 1969). In it 1,304 titles (of which 288 are still extant) are listed by dynasty, with brief notes on each; the works include: (1) collected biographies of famous generals, (2) histories of imperial and other campaigns, (3) tech-niques of warfare (including weapons), (4) strategy and tactics (cavalry and infantry), (5) accounts of sieges (techniques of city defense). See also H. Franke, "Sources on Chinese Military Technology and History," in F.A. Kierman and J. K. Fairbank, eds., *Chinese Ways in Warfare* (Cambridge, Mass., 1973).

Many of the Qing Histories of Imperial Campaigns (*fanglüe* 方略) have been reprinted in a special collectanea: **Zhongguo fanglüe congshu** 中國方略叢書 , 1st and 2nd series (Taipei, 1971).

The most famous work on strategy and tactics (**Sunzi bingfa** 孫子 兵法) has been translated many times; see S.B. Griffith, *Sun Tzu: The Art of War* (Oxford, 1963).

22. Collections of Important Documents (*huiyao* 會要)

Very large quantities of government documents of all sorts were stored, collected, and compiled under each dynasty and some of the resulting printed collections are still extant. Broadest in coverage are the Collections of Important Documents (*huiyao* 會要) of each dynasty. Of these only the *Important Documents of the Tang* (**Tang huiyao** 唐會要), 3 vols.

(Peking, 1955), the *Important Documents of the Five Dynasties* (**Wudai huiyao** 五代會要 ; Shanghai, 1935-1937; Taipei, 1960), and the *Important Documents of the Song* (see below) were compiled during the dynasty itself and, as a consequence, only they contain large amounts of primary materials not found in other sources. The *huiyao* for the other dynasties, although compiled from sources still extant today, have a certain use in that the material they contain is organized systematically and it is, therefore, often easier to find things in them than in the sources from which they were taken (see Teng and Biggerstaff, pp. 115-119, for a list of titles and editions).

See also sections 19, 20 and 16.5 on Encyclopaedic Histories of Institutions, Administrative and Penal Law, and Monographs in the Standard Histories.

Of the three *huiyao* mentioned above, by far the largest is the **Song huiyao** which was compiled throughout the Song dynasty by the specially set up Important Documents Bureau (*huiyao suo* 會要所). It was only retrieved from the *Yongle Encyclopaedia* (q.v.) in the early nineteenth century and printed for the first time in 1936 (**Song huiyao gao** 宋會要稿 , photolithographic reproduction, 200 *ce* [Peking, 1936]; facsimile reproduction, 8 vols. [Peking, 1957]); **Song huiyao jiben** 宋會要輯本 (Taipei, 1964). The materials in the **Song huiyao** were taken from the Daily Records (q.v.), no longer extant, and the Veritable Records (q.v.), no longer extant, as well as the documents of the Six Ministries and records of the Circuit Intendants. See Tang Zhong 湯中 , *Researches on the Collections of Important Documents of the Song* (**Song huiyao yanjiu** 宋會要研究 ; Shanghai, 1931; Taipei reprint, 1966). There is an index to the table of contents: **Sōkaiyō kenkyū biyō (mokuroku)** 宋會要研究 備要(目錄)(Tokyo, 1970). This index indicates subsections and the years covered in each, as well as indicating sources on which each subsection was based; it is usable with any of the editions of the **Song huiyao**.

142

23. Edicts and Memorials (*zhaoling zouyi* 詔令奏議)

23.1 Edicts

Imperial edicts (*zhaoling* 詔令 is the generic term), commonly called *zhi* 制, *chi* 敕or 勅 , *yu* 諭, etc. along with instructions (*jiao* 教), commands (*ling* 令), orders (*gao* 誥), and many other documents originating from the emperor, are valuable sources on practically all subjects. The most important extant collections of such documents are as follows:

Song Min-qiu 宋敏求 , *Collected Edicts of the Tang* (**Tang da zhaoling ji** 唐大詔令集 ; 1070; Shanghai, 1959). Indexed in *T'ang Civilization Reference Series,* Nos. 3 and 7.

Collected Edicts of the Song (compiled in the southern Song: **Song da zhaoling ji** 宋大詔令集 ; Peking, 1962). Contains over 3,800 edicts of the northern Song emperors, many of which are not to be found elsewhere.

Fu Feng-xiang 傅風翔 , *Edicts of the Ming* (**Huang Ming zhaoling** 皇明詔令 ; 1539; Taipei, 1967). Contains edicts of Ming emperors between 1367 and 1539. For four other collections of Ming edicts, see Franke, pp. 199-200.

Sacred Instructions and Edicts of Ten Qing Emperors (**Da Qing shichao shengxun** 大清十朝聖訓; 1880). Most comprehensive collection for Qing; covers the years 1616 to 1874 in 922 *juan.*

Vermilion Endorsements and Edicts of the Yong-zheng Period, 1723-1735 (**[Yongzheng] Zhupi yuzhi** 雍正硃批諭旨 ; 1738; photolithographic reprint, Peking, 1930). Contains several thousand memorials directly dealt with by the emperor and carrying his personal comments, instructions, etc. in red (hence the title).

Edicts of the Yong-zheng Emperor Issued through the Grand Secretariat (**Yongzheng shangyu neige** 雍正上諭內閣; 1741).

Edicts of the Yong-zheng Emperor to do with the Eight Banners (**Shangyu baqi** 上諭八期; 1741).

23.2 Memorials (*zouyi* 奏議)

Memorials (*zouyi* is the generic term) were of many different types
and were called by different names in different periods. Most common
among the various terms used were *zou* 奏, *zouben* 奏本 , *zouzhe* 奏
摺 , *zhe* 摺 or *zhezou* 摺奏 , *shu* 書 , *zhang* 章, *biao* 表 , *qi* 啓 ,
ce 策 , etc. They form one of the basic sources of Chinese history, flowing
in and up to all levels of the bureaucracy on all subjects. Many of the types
of historical writing and documents so far discussed either quote from them
in whole or in part or were based upon them.

For an introduction to the language of Qing memorials and official
documents, use J.K. Fairbank, *Ch'ing Documents: An Introductory Syllabus,*
3rd ed. (Cambridge, Mass., 1965), and see also the other works cited under
section 24.4. A full list of the many terms used for edicts and memorials is
given with brief annotations in E.D. Edwards, "A Classified Guide to the
Thirteen Classes of Chinese Prose," *BSOAS* 12:777-788 (1948).

As in all branches of Chinese historiography, the further back the period,
the fewer such basic sources survive. In earlier periods important memorials
have often survived only in excerpted or adapted form in the Standard
Histories or other compilations; the originals have long since been lost. If
they have survived it is usually in their author's Collected Works (*wenji* 文
集 , see section 27.3). During the Ming it became common practice for
the first time to publish collections of memorials (either of an individual, or
of a given period or on a given subject). This practice was continued in the
Qing. In the twentieth century the Qing central archives were opened and
selections of memorials and other documents began to be edited and published from them. At a conservative estimate something in the order of
4,000,000 Qing memorials have yet to be published (see section 24.4).

There is no easy way of tracing memorials on a particular subject or
by a given author before the Ming. The earliest comprehensive collection of
memorials from all periods was the imperially sponsored *Memorials of
Leading Officials of Each Period* (**Lidai mingchen zouyi** 歷代明臣奏
議 1416), 6 vols. (Taipei, 1964), which excerpted memorials and quotes
from other sources down to the Yuan and arranged them in a somewhat

overcategorized 67 divisions. A table of contents and index of authors are available in the series **Sōdai shakai keizaishi kenkyū hojo shiryō** 宋代社会経済史研究補助史料, no. 4 (Tokyo, 1957).

The surest way of finding memorials by pre-Ming officials is first to check through their biographies (see section 17.5) and then to check through their Collected Works (see section 27.3).

Finding memorials by Ming and Qing officials is much easier; for the Ming see Franke, pp. 119-175, for a long annotated list of approximately 300 collections of Ming memorials (arranged by author, by topic, or by period). To supplement Franke's list the Collected Works of the officials whose memorials are being traced should be checked. See Yamane Yukio 山根幸夫 and Kokawa Hisashi 小川尚 , *Catalogue of Collected Works [by 1,400 Ming authors] Extant in Japanese Collections* (**Nihon genzon Minjin bunshū mokuroku** 日本現存明人文集目録 ; Tokyo, 1966), for titles of Collected Works.

The most important topically arranged collections of memorials for the Qing are the continuations of the huge late Ming work compiled by Chen Zi-long 陳子龍 : *Ming Memorials on Statecraft* (**Huang Ming jingshi wenbian** 皇明經世文編 ; 1638; Taipei reprint, 1964) in which are arranged by topics the memorials of 425 high Ming officials. Altogether sixteen Collections of Memorials on Statecraft (**Jingshi wenbian** 經世文編) were published during the Qing. These collections contain the important memorials of well over 2,000 Qing officials and they have been conveniently indexed by the Seminar on Modern China at the Toyo Bunko (Kindai Chūgoku kenkyūkai iinkai, **Keisei bunhen sōmokuroku** 經世文編總目録 , 3 vols., [Tokyo, 1956]). The first volumes list the subject of each memorial (following the arrangement of the collections) while vol. 3 is an author index (with Wade-Giles finding list).

There is no list comparable to the one in Franke for the Qing; but see Fairbank, I, 39-105, for a list of some major collections of memorials and also the memorial collections published from the Qing archives in the 1930s and later. For a fuller listing of published collections and catalogues of memorials, reports, etc. from the Qing archives, see section 24.4.

The following guides and indexes to the titles of the memorials of high late Qing officials are available:

Chang Chung-li and S. Spector, eds., *Guide to the Memorials of Seven Leading Officials of Nineteenth Century China* (Seattle, 1955) which contains a useful subject index to the contents of the memorials of Zeng Guo-fan, Hu Lin-yi, Zuo Zong-tang, Guo Song-tao, Li Hong-zhang, Zeng Guo-quan, and Zhang Zhi-dong.

The seminar on Modern China, ed., *Index of Memorials by Zuo Zong-tang, Zhang Zhi-dong, Xue Fu-cheng, and Zhang Qian* (**Sa Sōtō, Chō Shidō, Setsu Fukusei, Chō Ken sōgi mokuroku** 左宗棠, 張之洞, 薛福成 張湉奏議目錄; Tokyo, 1955).

The Seminar on Modern China, ed., *Index of Memorials Presented to the Emperor by Sheng Xuan-huai and Yuan Shi-kai* (**Sei Senkai, En Seigai sōgi mokuroku** 盛宣懷, 袁世凱奏議目錄; Tokyo, 1955).

24. New Documentary Sources

24.1 Introduction

China was a society, as we have seen, which had its own well-developed tradition of governmental compilation and historiography and as a result few documents from central or local archives have been preserved in their original form; they were either excerpted in whole or in part in the compilations discussed in the other sections of the present Guide. During the twentieth century, however, important discoveries were made of about 12,000 routine administrative and other documents written on wooden slips and fragments preserved in the sands of the dry Northwest of China (24.2) and of about 30,000 Mss and fragments recorded on paper and also preserved in the dry Northwest, mainly in the caves of the temple library at Dunhuang (24.3). In addition, with the collapse of the Qing government, portions of the central archives became available and many thousands of documents were published from them (24.4). A handful of local archives were also used by historians (24.5), and some private documents, although very few, are also extant (24.6).

24.2 Han Documents on wooden slips

The discovery of wooden slips used in administration and dating mainly from the Han dynasty was made by Folk Bergman in 1930 in the neighborhood of Juyan (Etsingol in modern Gansu province). They are usually referred to as *Hanjian* 漢簡, i.e. *Handai mujian* 漢代木簡, and they mainly concern Han dynasty border and military administration. Altogether about 10,000 were found at Juyan and since 1930 another 2,000 or so have been found at other sites in the area. Most of the slips have been transcribed and photographs of the originals have also been published. See:

M. Loewe, *Records of Han Administration,* 2 vols. (Cambridge, 1967). Vol. I, chap. 1 contains a brief account of the major finds.

Lao Gan 勞榦 et al., *Transcriptions of Han Wooden Slips from Juyan* **(Juyan Hanjian kaoshi zhi bu** 居延漢簡考釋之部; Taipei, 1957).

Lao Gan, *Photographs of Han Wooden Slips from Juyan* **(Juyan Hanjian tuban zhi bu** 居延漢簡圖版之部; Taipei, 1957).

First Collection of Han Wooden Slips from Juyan **(Juyan Hanjian jiabian** 居延汉简甲編; Peking, 1957). Collection of photographs and transcriptions. Not exactly the same as Lao Gan.

H. Maspero, *Les documents chinois de la troisième expédition de Sir Aurel Stein en Asie centrale* (London, 1953).

A.F.P. Hulsewé, "Han-time Documents, a survey of recent research occasioned by the finding of Han-time documents in Central Asia," *T'oung-pao* 45:1-3, 1-50 (1957).

Ōba Osamu, 大庭脩 "Bibliography of research on Han documents on wood" (Kantoku kenkyū bunken mokuroku 簡牘研究文献目錄, **Shizen** 23:44-55 (1961).

24.3 Dunhuang manuscripts

At the end of the nineteenth century and at the beginning of the twentieth a large number of expeditions explored the inner Asian frontiers of China and when they were able, took back what they found to their own countries. At the very beginning of this century Stein (from England) heard about a collection of manuscripts in a temple library at Dunhuang. The collection turned out to be very large and consisted mainly of Chinese manuscripts, the bulk of which were Buddhist sutras and other Buddhist materials. There were also documents in Tibetan, Uighur, and other Central Asian languages. Stein took about 10,000 manuscripts and was soon followed by Pelliot from France, Otani from Japan, Oldenbourg from Russia, and Von Le Coq from Germany. Altogether about 20,000 manuscripts were collected from Dunhuang and neighboring sites and taken out of China; some 10,000 were taken to Peking or found their way into the hands of private collectors.

The majority of the manuscripts date from between the fifth and tenth centuries A.D. and they form by far the most important collection of manuscripts to be found in China before recent times. Apart from being of tremendous value as repositories of Buddhist and Taoist sources, they also contain a considerable amount of popular literature. See the translations made by A. Waley, *Stories and Ballads from Tunhuang* (London, 1960). Preserved on the back of many of the sutras historians also found many documents of local administration of all kinds, including fragments of Ordinances, reports, purchase orders, contracts, and other materials which have led to some of the most detailed researches into Chinese social and economic history of any period. The study of the documents has given rise to a new specialized field known as Dunhuang studies (*Dunhuangxue* 敦煌學). In addition to the written documents, many thousands of Buddhist paintings are preserved on the walls of the temple library.

As a general introduction see Fujieda Akira, "The Tunhuang Manuscripts: A General Description," *Zinbun* 9:1-32 (1966), 10:17-39 (1969); and D.C. Twitchett, "Chinese Social History: The Tun-huang Documents and their Implications," *Past and Present* (1966), pp. 28-53.

A monumental selection of Dunhuang documents bearing on socioeconomic history was published together with important studies in *Researches on Fragmentary Manuscripts on Chinese Socioeconomic History from Dunhuang and Turfan* (**Tonkō Toroban shakai keizai shiryō** 敦煌吐魯番社会経済史料), **Saiiki bunka kenkyū** 西域文化研究

(*Monumenta Serindica*), vols. 2 and 3 (Kyoto, 1959, 1960). Includes a bibliography and summary in English.

Another selection of the documents transcribed according to categories is also of great interest to historians: *Dunhuang Materials* (**Dunhuang ziliao** 敦煌資料), 1st collection (Peking, 1961; Tokyo, 1963).

For many years the Dunhuang manuscripts were almost inaccessible since they were scattered all over the world and no adequate catalogues or collections were published; the situation has been improved greatly now that the following catalogues are available:

Catalogues

1. Most comprehensive to date (but unreliable) is the *Index to General Catalogue of Mss. from Dunhuang* (**Dunhuang yishu zongmu suoyin** 敦煌遺书总目索引 ; Peking, 1962; Tokyo, 1963). Index of titles to the 8,679 manuscripts in the Peking Library; 6,980 manuscripts in the Bibliothèque Nationale (Paris, see Pelliot-Lu below) and manuscripts in nineteen other scattered collections. Note that it does not include the manuscripts in Leningrad whose catalogues appeared after this one (see Menshikov below). Indexes arranged by stroke order.

2. Chen Yuan 陳垣 , comp., *An Analytical List of the Dunhuang Mss. in the National Library of Peking* (**Dunhuang jieyu lu** 敦煌劫餘錄 ; Peking, 1931). Contains fuller bibliographic notes on each manuscript included (condition of text, colophons, dates, seals, etc.) than no. 1 above, but is far less handy to use.

3. L. Giles, comp., *Descriptive Catalogue of the Chinese Manuscripts from Tunhuang in the British Museum* (London, 1957). Sections listing Buddhist texts, Taoist texts, Manichean texts, secular texts, and printed documents in the Stein collection at the British Museum. Annotated and also indexed (proper names and titles).

4. Lu Xiang 陸翔 , tr., "A catalogue of Dunhuang mss. preserved. in the Bibliothèque Nationale" (Bali tushuguan Dunhuang xieben shumu 巴黎圖書館敦煌寫本書目), **Guoli Beiping tushuguan guankan** 7.6:21-72 (1933). This is a translation of Pelliot's accession list to the manuscripts in the Fonds Pelliot, No. 2001-2729; there is no index.

A proper catalogue of the Pelliot Dunhuang manuscripts is being prepared.

5.   L.N. Menshikov, *Chinese Manuscripts from Dunhuang* (Kitajskie rekopisi iz Dun'xuan; Moscow, 1963).

6.   L.N. Menshikov, *Descriptive Catalogue of the Chinese Manuscripts of the Dunhuang Collection of the Institute of the Peoples of Asia* (Opisanie kitajskie rukopisej Dun'xuan skogo fonda Instituta Naradov Azii; Moscow, 1967).

7.   In addition to the above catalogues, the following subject catalogue is particularly useful to students of Chinese socioeconomic history: *Draft Classified Catalogue of Dunhuang Manuscripts Collected by Sir Aurel Stein and of Chinese Manuscripts from Chinese Turkestan Described in Research: Section on Non-Buddhist Material, Ancient Documents* (Sutain Tonkō bunken oyobi kenkyū bunken ni inyō shōkai seraretaru Saiiki shutsudo Kambun bunrui mokuroku shokō: Hibukkyō no bu, kobun shorui スタイン 敦煌文献及乙"研究文献に引用紹介せられたる西域出土 漢文文献分類目録初稿非佛教之部古文書類)vol. 1 compiled by Ikeda On 池田温 and Kikuchi Hideo 菊池英夫 , and vol. 2 by Dohi Yoshikazu 土肥義和 (Tokyo, 1964). In vol. 1, Dunhuang manuscripts from the British Museum (as well as the other major collections) are classified into categories of document (Edicts; the Code; letters of appointment; certificates; passes; memorials relating to Dunhuang and documents relating to Dunhuang administration), further subdivided into nineteen categories and numerous subcategories. Notes supply references to parallel documents in conventionally transmitted sources and to any scholarly writing directly concerned with the document; parallel material from the other Dunhuang manuscript collections is also referred to. At the end of each subject division there is a bibliography of secondary sources covering the topic. An appendix contains bibliographies of books and articles on Dunhuang. There is an index of the manuscripts described.

8.   Vol. 2 follows the same general pattern as vol. 1 and is concerned with the institutional and economic aspects of Buddhism. Its two main subject categories (with numerous subdivisions) are the administration of Buddhist monasteries and their economic organization. There is an index of scholarly articles quoted in the volume as well as an index of the manuscripts described. The main division, categories, and sub-categories are listed in the introduction to the two volumes.

Two catalogues of Taoist works among the Dunhuang manuscripts are available:

9.   Obuchi Ninji 大淵忍爾 , comp., *Catalogue of Taoist Scriptures from Dunhuang* (**Tonkō dōkyō mokuroku** 敦煌道経目録 ; Kyoto, 1960).

10.   Yoshioka Yoshitoyo 吉岡義豊 , comp., *Classified Catalogue of Taoist Texts from Dunhuang in the British Museum* (**Sutain shorai dai ei hakubutsukanzō tonkō bunken bunrui mokuroku-dōkyōbu** スタイン將来 大英博物館蔵敦煌文献分類目録道教之部 ; Tokyo, 1969). In the same series and arranged in the same way as no. 7 above.

Bibliographies

See no. 7 above; also *Monumenta Serindica,* vols. 2 and 3; and *Index of Japanese Research on Dunhuang, 1897-1957* (**Tonkō bunken kenkyū rombun mokuroku** 敦煌文献研究論文目録 ; Tokyo, 1959); also *Bibliography of Central Asian Studies* (**Chuō Ajia kenkyū bunken mokuroku** 中央アジア研究文献目録;Kyoto, 1955).

24.4   Ming/Qing archives

After the fall of the Qing dynasty some four million documents (mainly memorials, reports, rescripts, etc.) which had been stored in the archives of the Grand Council (*junji chu* 軍機處), the Grand Secretariat (*neige* 内 閣), and other central government organs, came into the control of the new government. The overwhelming majority of the documents dated from the Qing but there was a considerable quantity of late Ming materials as well as materials on early Manchu history.

The first action of the new government was to have many hundreds of thousands of the documents placed in sacks and stored out of the way. For ten years they lay neglected and were pilfered (the sacks fetched money and the manuscripts made good firelighters). During the 1920s the Historical Museum (under whose control a portion had come) began selling large quantities of the documents to paper merchants as pulp. Many thousands were bought back from the merchants by a private scholar, Lo Zhen-yu

羅振玉 . The whole matter had reached the proportions of a public scandal which drew the celebrated remark from Lu Xun in an essay on the subject: "Chinese public property really is difficult to keep; if the authorities are incompetent they ruin it but if they are competent they steal it"—Lu Xun 魯迅 , "On the so-called court documents" (Tan suowei 'Danei dangan' 談所謂大內檔案), **Lu Xun quanji** (Peking, 1956), pp. 420-427.

Lu Xun was referring not only to the incompetence of the early Republican officials responsible for the neglect of the documents, but also to the fact that some senior officials had had searches made for Song editions and had appropriated some rare items for themselves, quite apart from authorizing the sale of routine documents as pulp. To give some idea of the extent of the losses during these years, of the original collections of 160,000 Grand Secretariat documents which came into the hands of the Institute of History and Philology of Academia Sinica, some 20,000 had been lost or destroyed by the late 1920s. Figures are not available for the losses of documents held by other organizations.

Partly as a result of the public scandal and partly as a result of the reorganization of the cultural agencies of the government after 1928, the work of cataloguing the documents began for the first time; it was undertaken in the various agencies to which the documents by the late 1920s had become scattered. These were the Document Division of the Palace Museum; the working group on documents of the Institute of History and Philology of Academia Sinica; the Committee for the Organization of Ming-Qing documents at Peking University (which had brought 1,052 sacks and 60 boxes from a private collector in Tientsin) and the library at Qinghua University. Lo Zheng-yu and his son Lo Fu-yi 羅福頤 also sponsored publication and cataloguing of their privately held collection.

No sooner had the work of cataloguing (and to a certain extent publishing) begun than the War of Resistance against Japan broke out and the work was halted. After the war, the Institute of History and Philology took about 120,000 Grand Secretariat documents to Taiwan, while about half a million more, mainly from the Grand Council archives, were appropriated from the Palace Museum holdings. The remaining 3,000,000 or so documents were brought together in the Ming-Qing archives of the National Archives.

Both in the People's Republic and on Taiwan the work of cataloguing and publishing from the documents continued after 1949.

Although these huge archives will not be available for research for many years, some important preliminary catalogues and studies were made of them in the 1930s and in addition a considerable number of selections from the documents were published by the Palace Museum, the Institute of History and Philology, Peking University, and by private scholars. The most important of these publications are given below. Note in particular the catalogues of documents; one can get a fairly good idea of the extent of the archival holdings from them.

24.4.1   Catalogues

1.   *Catalogue of Book Lists and Lists of Documents in the Grand Secretariat Archives* (Neige daku shu-dang jiumu 內閣大庫書檔 舊目 ; Peking, 1933).

2.   *Supplement* to the above (Shanghai, 1936). Based on lists of documents (*dangce* 檔冊) and book lists in the Institute of History and Philology holdings; supplement contains similar materials from Peking University and Palace holdings.

3.   *Catalogue of Book Lists and Lists of Memorials in the Grand Secretariat Archives* (Qing neigeku zhu jiu dang jikan 清內閣庫貯 舊檔輯刊 , 6 *ce;* Peking, 1936). Supplements nos. 1 and 2, since it is based on Palace Museum holdings of Grand Secretariat documents.

4.   *Catalogue of Document Lists and Memorial Bundles in the Grand Council Archives* (Qing junji chu dangan mulu 清軍機處檔案目 錄; Peking, 1933 [?]). Lists year by year the document registers (*dangce* 檔冊) and memorial bundles (*zhebao* 摺包) held by the Palace Museum; total of 7,969 of the former and 3,535 of the latter, containing some 800,000 documents in all. The memorials and other documents in this archive were copies of those passing to and from the emperor. A portion was removed to Taiwan.

5.   *Catalogue of Extant Yellow Books in Chinese in the Archive of the Grand Secretariat* (Neige daku xiancun Qingdai Hanwen huangce mulu 內閣大庫現存清代漢文黃冊目錄   ; Peking, 1936). This

catalogue is particularly important for economic historians, since the Yellow Books (*huangce* 黃册) were those reports on tax returns, construction projects, etc. which were enclosed as attachments with memorials; they contain much fuller materials on these subjects than is found in the memorials themselves. The catalogue lists some 6,000 volumes of these reports, categorizes them, and indicates the nature of their contents.

6. *Union Catalogue of Yellow Books Formerly Stored in the Archive of the Grand Secretariat* (**Qing neige jiucang hanwen huangce lianhe mulu** 清内閣舊藏漢文黃册聯合目錄 ; Peking, 1947).

7. Also important for the same reasons as nos. 5 and 6 is the *Catalogue of Accounts Forwarded to Peking During the Nine Reigns of the Qing Dynasty* (**Qing jiuchao jingsheng baoxiaoce mulu** 清九朝京省報鎖册目錄 ; Peking, 1935) which lists the various accounts of salaries, taxes, household and head counts, grain shipments, granaries, salt administration, prison administration, imperial silk factories, etc. in detail to be included with memorials from the provinces in question (these documents were called *qingce* 青册 or *huangce* 黃册 or generically, *baoxiaoce* 報鎖册). The catalogue is arranged by reigns but only the first two reigns were published. The documents were held by Peking University.

8. Lo Fu-yi 羅福頤 , comp., *Index to Historical Materials in the Grand Secretariat Archives* (**Daku shiliao mulu** 大庫史料目錄), 6 *ce* (Peking, 1934-1935). This is an index of 10,624 of the documents bought by Lo Zhen-yu; it shows dates, names, and subject matter. A continuation was published in **Manshū geppō**, vol. 7 (1942), indexing a further 26,748 documents from the same collection.

9. *Catalogue of Qing Veritable Records Held by the Document Division of the Palace Museum* (**Gugong bowuyuan wenxianguan xiancun Qingdai shilu zongmu** 故宮博物院文獻館現存清代實錄綜目 ; Peking, 1934).

10. *Catalogue of Memorials and Edicts not Included in the Vermilion Endorsements and Edicts of the Yong-zheng period* (**Yongzheng zhupi yuzhi bulu zouzhe zongmu** 雍正硃批諭旨不錄奏摺綜目; Peking, 1930).

24.4.2   Early Manchu history, Veritable Records, etc.

A great many documents and early versions of standard central government annalistic writings (records of Current Government, Diaries of Activity and Repose, etc.—see section 14.2) came to light in the different central Qing archives; some have been published, notably the **Manbun rōtō** 滿文 老檔 (see section 14.2) and the **Qing Taizu gao huangdi shilu, gaoben sanzhong** 清太祖高皇帝寶錄,稿本三種 (Peking, 1933-1934). For a brief introduction to these and other early Qing sources see Xie Guozhen 謝国禎, "Research in Ming-Qing historical materials" (Ming-Qing shiliao yanjiu 明清史料研究), in his *Collection of Notes on Ming-Qing Miscellanous Notes* (**Ming Qing biji tancong** 明清笔记谈丛; Shanghai, 1962), pp. 146-183. See also catalogue no. 9 above.

24.4.3   Selections of published documents from the Qing archives

1.   **Chongzhen cunshi suchao** 崇禎存實疏鈔, 16 *ce* (Shanghai, 1934). Covers years 1628-1644.

2.   **Mingmo nongmin qiyi shiliao** 明末农民起义史料 (Peking, 1952). 220 documents dating from 1627-1648 dealing with the rising of Li Zi-cheng.

3.   **Ming Qing shiliao** 明清史料, 8 collections, 10 *ce* each, first 4 collections published in Shanghai; from 5 on in Taipei. Documents from the Grand Secretariat dating from late Ming and early Qing.

4.   **Ming Qing neige daku shiliao** 明清內閣大庫史料, 2 vols. (Shanghai, 1949). Includes 500 memorials dating from 1623-1644; the remainder from early Qing.

5.   **Mingji shiliao lingshi** 明季史料零拾 (Shanghai, 1934). Six miscellanous Ming documents.

6.   **Ming Qing dangan cunzhen xuanji, chuji** 明清檔案存真選輯初集 (Taipei, 1959). Facsimile of 130 Ming-Qing documents.

7.   **Zhanggu congbian** 掌故叢編, 10 *ce* (Peking, 1928-1929; reprint Taipei, 1963). Mainly early Qing documents from Grand Council archives.

8.   **Wenxian congbian** 文獻叢編, 36 *ce* (Peking, 1930-1936), 7 *ce* (1937—of which the first contains an index to the first 36 *ce*; reprinted Taipei, 1964). This was a continuation of no. 7 above and contains mainly

early Qing documents from the Grand Council archives.

9.   **Shiliao congkan chubian** 史料叢刊初編, 10 *ce* (Shanghai, 1924; Taipei, 1964). Miscellanous early Qing—mainly Grand Secretariat archives.

10.   **Shiliao congbian** 史料叢編, 12 *ce* (Shanghai, 1933-1935). Miscellanous Grand Secretariat, early Qing.

11.   **Shiliao xunkan** 史料旬刊, 40 *ce* (Peking, 1930-1931). Miscellanous Grand Council, early Qing (Taipei, 1964).

12.   **Gugong wenxian** 故宮文獻, quarterly, vols. 1-8 (Taipei, 1970). Early Qing; also contains articles. A continuing facsimile series.

13.   **Qing sanfan shiliao** 清三藩史料, 5 *ce* (Peking, 1932). Materials on the revolt of the three feudatories. Also included in no. 8 (1964).

14.   **Qingdai wenziyu dang** 清代文字獄檔, 12 *ce* (Peking, 1931-1933). Materials on the literary inquisitions which took place in the Qing.

15.   **Gugong erwen shiliao** 故宮俄文史料 (Peking, 1936). Documents in Russian dating from the early seventeenth and eighteenth centuries.

16.   *Memorials of the Suzhuo Textile Commissioner, Li Xu* (**Suzhou zhizao Li Xu zouzhe** 蘇州織造李煦奏摺 (Peking, 1937). Also included in no. 8.

17.   *Hong Cheng-chou's Collected Memorials in Six Ce* (**Hong Cheng-chou zhangzou liuce huiji** 洪承疇章奏六冊彙輯 (Peking, 1937).

18.   *Archival Materials on the Organization of the Imperial Library* (**Banli siku quanshu dangan** 辦理四庫全書檔案), 2 *ce* (Peking, 1934).

Note the collections of memorials and edicts printed from the archives in the collections such as those listed in section 23.1 and 23.2.

The above is by no means an exhaustive list; the large collections (nos. 3, 8, 9, and 12) contain miscellaneous documents as well as materials by a single memorialist or on a single subject. When looking for materials there is no alternative to checking all these collections, since a general index does not exist. Anyone who undertook to prepare such an index or even a general table of contents would be performing a useful service.

A number of important collections of documents have been published on nineteenth and early twentieth-century history: see Fairbank, pp. 97-103, for a list of these collections.

Studies

On the early fortunes of the Ming-Qing archives from the 1911 Revolution down to the 1930s as well as on their contents, see the special issue of **Zhongguo jindai jingjishi yanjiu jikan,** 2.2:166-280 (1934), esp. pp. 239-254, which discuss the importance of some of the materials to the economic historian. A brief note by Fu Zi-ling 傅子凌 and Liu Xiu-yuan 刘秀元 reported in 1959 on "Recent progress in archive work of Ming and Qing documents" (Ming Qing danganguan lishi dangan zhengli gongzuo zai da yaojin zhong 明清档案馆历史档案整理工作在大跃进中), **Lishi yanjiu** 1:95-96 (1959).

The contents of the archives were noted in A. K'ai-ming Ch'iu, "Chinese Historical Documents of the Ch'ing Dynasty, 1644-1911," *Pacific Historical Review* 1:324-336 (1932).

There are several important studies in English on the different types of documents in use in Ming and Qing government. See especially J.K. Fairbank and Teng Ssu-yü, *Ch'ing Administration: Three Studies* (Cambridge, Mass., 1960); S. Wu, "Transmission of Ming Memorials," *T'oung pao* 54:275-287 (1968); S. Wu, "The Memorial Systems of the Ch'ing Dynasty," *HJAS* (1967), pp. 7-75; and S. Wu, *Communication and Imperial Control in China, 1693-1735* (Cambridge, Mass., 1971).

The basic introduction to this type of source is J.K. Fairbank, *Ch'ing Documents: An Introductory Syllabus,* 3rd ed., rev. and enlarged, 2 vols. (Cambridge, Mass., 1965). See also Jian Bo-zan 翦伯赞 , *Historical Materials and Historical Studies* (**Shiliao yu shixue** 史料與史學 ; Shanghai, 1946).

24.5   Provincial and district archives

All district and provincial yamen kept very extensive files and archives containing records of all aspects of official business and copies of official documents. In addition various works of administrative law, regulations, etc. were also kept in the yamen. Some idea of the extent of these archives can be gathered from what is known to have been the huge range of routine reporting and official business conducted by the magistrate's staff and the district clerks; for the general range of activities requiring files, see Ch'ü T'ung-tsu, *Local Government in China Under the Ch'ing* (Cambridge, Mass., 1962), passim. Despite all this documentation, which is known to have been kept in original or in duplicate, no single district or provincial archive has ever been described or is known to have survived intact. Furthermore, the number of historians in the twentieth century who used local archives, or the number of documents which have survived from them, is practically nil.

Some of the only exceptions to the above comments are the statistical series on exchange rates extracted from yamen documents in Ding district and quoted in S.G. Gamble, *Tinghsien* (New York, 1954); also the much more interesting series of documents from the files of Danshui subprefecture and Xinzhu district described in D.C. Buxbaum, "Some Aspects of Civil Procedure and Practice at the Trial Level in Tanshui and Hsinchu from 1789 to 1896," *JAS* 30.2:255-279 (1971). These files contain documents relating to legal cases tried in these yamen and include pleas, documentary evidence, summaries of testimony, warrants, judicial orders, decisions, etc. (ibid., p. 257). Scattered documents from other district archives have survived (Ch'ü makes extensive use of some of the records of transfer of government funds, for example), but on the whole the collection and preservation of local archives never got under way in the disturbed conditions of twentieth-century China: indeed, vast quantities of these materials must have been destroyed in the upheavals of the nineteenth and twentieth centuries. The situation is somewhat mitigated by the fact that long before historians in the West were beginning to emphasize the importance of archival as opposed to literary sources, Chinese historians were still drawing upon a long tradition of handling and quoting from the original documents; thus not a few local documents were preserved in works of summarization higher up the administrative and historiographical hierarchy. Furthermore, there are always the resources of the Provincial and Local Gazetteers, although it should be remembered that these works were never intended to be a summary of the local archives, nor were they intended as practical handbooks on local administrative problems. They were only compiled on the average two or three times a century and their primary purpose was to enshrine the notable people, places, and literary output of a given locality (see section 18.5).

24.6   Private documents

Although the literary output of China's elite has survived in very large quantities and although this includes diaries, letters, notebooks, etc., the only major nonliterary type of private document to have survived are the family and kin genealogies (see section 17.4). Land deeds, accounts, litigation, etc. did not come within the purview of the traditional Chinese historian, and the owners of such documents usually guarded them jealously from prying eyes. For these reasons and also because twentieth-century historians have been slow to collect this type of source, only scattered examples of private documents have been utilized or published. How many are still extant is unknown but a great many must have been destroyed in the upheavals of the nineteenth and twentieth centuries.

A considerable number of private documents were found among (or on the back of) the Dunhuang manuscripts (see section 24.3). The most assiduous collector of private documents of the Ming and Qing has been the historian Fu Yi-ling 傅衣凌, who discovered a chest of land deeds, for example in a Fukien villiage, some of which date back to the Ming dynasty; see his *Rural Society and Economy in the Late Ming and Early Qing* (**Ming Qing nongcun shehui jingji** 明清农村社会经济; Peking, 1961). Other private documents (mainly from the Qing) have been published, summarized, or referred to in various collections of source materials and studies: e.g., in Li Wen-zhi 李文治 and Zhang You-yi 章有益, comps., *Materials on the History of Agriculture in Modern China* (**Zhongguo jindai nongyeshi ziliao** 中国近代农业史资料), 3 vols. (Peking, 1957); and in Jing Su 景甦 and Lo Lun 羅崙, *The Social Nature of Managerial Landlords in Shantung during the Qing* (**Qingdai Shandong jingying dizhu de shehui xingzhi** 清代山東经营地主的社会性质; Shantung,

1959), which brilliantly draws upon original land deeds, wage account books, etc., as well as interviews and data gathered by questionnaire. Note also Zhang De-chang 張德昌, *The Life of a Court Official in the Qing Dynasty, A Study of Personal Income and Expenditure* (**Qingji yige jing-guan de shenghuo** 清季一個京官的生活 ; Hong Kong, 1970), which tabulates the personal expenditures (as recorded in his diaries) of Li Ci-ming 李慈銘 over the years 1854-1894.

Some of the difficulties of persuading people to allow historians to consult their family or business documents are discussed by Zhang Lü-lan 張履鸞 in his "Farm prices in Wujin, Jiangsu" (Jiangsu Wujin wujia zhi yanjiu 江蘇武進物價之研究), **Jinling xuebao** 3.1:157-158 (1933).

25. Works on Agriculture, Technology, and Water Control

25.1   Agricultural Treatises (*nongshu* 農書)

Comprehensive works on all aspects of agriculture as well as specialized works on everything from tea cultivation to horse breeding have been an established genre in China since the Han dynasty. Some quote mainly from previous works; others are based on wide observations; some were officially sponsored (to popularize a new crop or technique, for example); and many were written by private authors (usually retired officials), discussing the agriculture of a single district or locality. Most of the comprehensive Agricultural Treatises contain sections on general principles of agriculture, crop types, the farming year, types of tools (often with illustrations), and side occupations. Taken as a whole, the *nongshu* are an important source for the history of Chinese agriculture and agricultural techniques, and taken singly some of them are also important sources for the organization of agriculture in specific places at specific times.

The single indispensable reference on all types of Agricultural Treatises for all periods is Wang Yu-hu's 王毓瑚 revised *Annotated Catalogue of*

Chinese Agricultural Treatises (**Zhongguo nongxue shulu** 中国农学书录; Shanghai, 1964), which arranges all known Agricultural Treatises (whether lost or extant) according to broad categories with bibliographic notes and summaries of the contents of each.

Important Comprehensive Agricultural Treatises

Although not *nongshu*, both the **Guanzi** 管子 and **Lüshi chunqiu** 呂氏春秋 contain important chapters on agriculture. On the former, see *Economic Dialogues in Ancient China; Selections from the Kuan-Tzu*, tr. T'an Po-fu and Wen Kung-wen, ed. L.A. Maverick (Carbondale, 1954); and on the latter see R. Wilhelm, *Frühling und Herbst des Lü Bu We* (Jena, 1928).

1. Second half of first century B.C.: **Fan Sheng-zhi shu** 氾勝之書. See Shih Sheng-han, *On "Fan Sheng-chih shu"* (Peking, 1959).

2. Latter half of second century A.D.: *Monthly Ordinances for the Four Classes* (**Simin yueling** 四民月令).

3. Sixth century: Jia Si-xie 賈思勰, *Techniques Essential for the Common People* (**Qimin yaoshu** 齊民要術). The first complete extant Comprehensive Agricultural Treatise. See Shih Sheng-han, *A Preliminary Survey of the Book "Ch'i Min Yao Shu": An Agricultural Encyclopaedia of the 6th Century* (Peking, 1958; 1962). See also Amano Motonosuke, "Dry Farming and the *Ch'i-min yao-shu*," in *Silver Jubilee Volume of the Zimbun-Kagaku Kenkyūsyo* (1954), pp. 451-466.

4. Eleventh century: Chen Fu 陳旉 , comp., *Agricultural Treatise* (**Nongshu** 農書).

5. Late thirteenth century: *Essentials of Agriculture and Sericulture* (**Nongcan jiyao** 農桑輯要 ; 1286). Comprehensive; imperially sponsored.

6. Late thirteenth century: *Essentials of Agriculture, Sericulture, Clothing and Food* (**Nongcan yishi cuoyao** 農桑衣食撮要), compiled by a Uighur official, Lu Ming-shan 魯明善 . Important because written as an actual handbook for magistrates in their role as agricultural instructors.

7. Early fourteenth century: Wang Zhen 王禎 , comp., *Agricultural Treatise* (**Nongshu** 農書 ; 1313). Important because full of author's observations and well illustrated.

8. First half of seventeenth century: Song Ying-xing 宋應星 , comp., *The Creations of Nature and Man* (**Tiangong kaiwu** 天工開物 ;

1637). The most important comprehensive treatise on all branches of industry; contains sections on agriculture and agricultural tools, mainly reflecting conditions in Kiangsi, Song's native province. For a translation, see E-tu Zen Sun and Sun Shiou-chuan, *T'ien-kung k'ai-wu* (Pennsylvania, 1966). See also the collection of studies edited by Yabuuchi Kiyoshi, **Tenko kaibutsu no kenkyū** 天工開物の研究 (Tokyo, 1953); Chinese tr. by Zhang Xiong and Wu Jie under the title **Tiangong kaiwu yanjiu lunwenji** (Peking, 1959).

9.   First half of the seventeenth century: Xu Guang-qi 徐光啟 comp., *Comprehensive Treatise on Agriculture* (**Nongzheng quanshu** 農政全書 ; 1639). Important because it summed up the state of the art; highly popular in Tokugawa Japan. Contains translations of European works on hydraulics.

10.   Mid-seventeenth century: Zhang Lü-xiang 張履祥, comp., *Enlarged Version of Agricultural Treatise of 1643* (**Bu nongshu** 補農書 ; 1658). Important because it contains advice on how to run a single estate in Tongxiang, Chekiang. See Chen Heng-li 陳恆力 and Wang Da 王达 , *Studies on the Bunongshu* (**Bunongshu yanjiu** 补农书研究), rev. and enlarged ed. (Peking, 1961).

11.   Mid-eighteenth century: *Comprehensive Study of the Farming Year* (**Shoushi tongkao** 授時通考 ; imperially sponsored, 1747). Mainly culled from previous works.

12.   Mid-eighteenth century: *Pictures of Ploughing and Weaving* (**Gengzhi tu** 耕織圖). Imperially sponsored, included here because of the study by O. Franke, *Keng Tschi T'u: Ackerbau und Seidegewinnung in China, ein kaiserliches Lehr und Mahn-Buch* (Hamburg, 1913).

For a short article on the Agricultural Treatises by the leading Japanese authority on the history of Chinese agriculture, Amano Motonosuke 天野 元之助 , see **Ajia rekishi jiten** 7:300-302. In this article Amano briefly lists the most important works, including those of the nineteenth century.

Note that practically all the Agricultural Treatises of any importance were reprinted in China in the 1950s in carefully edited, punctuated editions.

25.2 <u>Technology</u>

Chinese primary sources on all aspects of technology and science are discussed throughout the volumes of J. Needham's work in process, *Science and Civilisation in China:*

Vol. 1.   *Introductory Orientations* (Cambridge, Eng., 1954).

Vol. 2.   *History of Scientific Thought* (Cambridge, Eng., 1956).

Vol. 3.   *Mathematics and the Sciences of the Heavens and the Earth* (Cambridge, Eng., 1959).

Vol. 4,   Pt. 1. *Physics* (Cambridge, Eng., 1962).

Vol. 4,   Pt. 2. *Mechanical Engineering* (Cambridge, Eng., 1965).

Vol. 4,   Pt. 3. *Civil Engineering* (Cambridge, Eng., 1971).

Note especially "Bibliographical Notes (d) Chinese Traditions of Inventors," I, 51-54; "Survey of the Principal Landmarks in Chinese Mathematical Literature," III, 18-53; "Astronomy (2) The Principal Chinese Sources," III, 186-209; "Mineralogy (d) Mineralogical Literature and Its Scope," III, 643-647; "Traditions of the Artisanate," vol. IV, pt. 2, pp. 42-50; "The Nature of Chinese Engineering Literature," vol. IV, pt. 2, pp. 166-173; "Building Science in Chinese Literature," vol. IV, pt. 3, pp. 80-89.

The most comprehensive traditional work on industrial and agrarian arts was Song Ying-xing's 宋應星 *The Creations of Nature and Man* **(Tiangong kaiwu** 天工開物; 1637) which has been translated into English by E-tu Zen Sun and Sun Shiou-chuan. See also the collection of studies edited by Yabuuchi Kiyoshi, which were translated into Chinese by Zhang Xiong and Wu Jie.

Chapters cover the growing of grains; the preparation of grains; clothing materials; salt technology; sugar technology; ceramics; bronze casting; ships and carts; iron metallurgy; calcination of stones, vegetable oils, and fats; paper making; metallurgy of silver, lead, tin, copper and zinc; military technology; vermilion and ink; yeasts; pearls and gems. Under each section the principal processes are discussed and illustrated. Notice that the author concluded his preface by warning: "An ambitious scholar will undoubtedly toss this book onto his desk and give it no further thought: it is a work that is in no way concerned with the art of advancement in officialdom" (Sun and Sun, p. xiv).

25.3   Water control (*shuili* 水利)

Primary sources are catalogued in Mao Nai-wen's 茅乃文 *Catalogue of Works on Chinese Hydrography and Water Control* (**Zhongguo hequ shuili gongcheng shumu** 中國河渠水利工程書目 ; Peking, 1935). Mao also published an annotated catalogue but in a less accessible form: "Notes on Chinese works on river works and canals" (Zhongguo hequ shu tiyao 中國河渠書提要), **Shuili**, vol. 11 (1936), vol. 12 (1937), vol. 13 (1938). See also Needham, vol. IV, pt. 3, "The literature on Civil Engineering and Water Conservancy," pp. 323-329; and note also his "Hydrographic books and Descriptions of the Coast" (Needham, III, 514-517).

The Monographs on Financial Administration, on Rivers and Canals, and on Administrative Geography in the Standard Histories contain important materials on irrigation and water control (see section 16.5).

26. Encyclopaedias

26.1   Introduction

Many different kinds of "encyclopaedia" (*leishu* 類書) were compiled in China and for many different purposes. Typically the General Encyclopaedias consisted of large numbers of quotations from primary sources on a broad range of subjects arranged under twenty or thirty major divisions and many hundreds of subdivisions. Some were compiled for the emperor as source books of moral and political precedent to assist him and his officials in government; others were intended as elementary primers or as the sum total of necessary knowlege for passing the examinations. Others again were more literary and lexicographical and served as aids to literary composition, as vast repositories of well-turned phrases either general in application or devoted to specific models, such as letter writing or document drafting. By the later Empire the tendency to include all existing human knowledge led to the compilation of monumental imperially-sponsored *leishu* in which whole works, rather than excerpts, were copied. Also in the later Empire with the spreading of written knowledge to strata outside the literati, popular Encyclopaedias for Daily Use (*riyong leishu* 日用類書) began to be compiled, summarizing practical information for townsfolk and others not primarily concerned with mastering the Confucian heritage.

The *leishu* are extremely important for the historian for a number of reasons. In the first place, works which have long since been lost have often been preserved in whole or in part in the great literati *leishu* (especially in the ten most important ones listed below). Secondly, the *leishu* not only provide a unique view of how Confucian education and knowledge were actually received, but they also provide a useful shortcut to materials on any given, traditionally-defined subject. Thirdly, the popular *leishu* contain important materials on culture and attitudes of strata below the Confucian elite. Besides these general reasons, there are specific reasons why particular categories of *leishu* are still useful as works of reference. Thus the Encyclopaedic Histories of Institutions provide easily accessible sources on all branches of the government, while some of the great encyclopaedias compiled as aids to literary composition are still essential for placing characters or phrases in the contexts in which they were used at different periods.

The Encyclopaedic Histories of Institutions are discussed in section 19 while the Encyclopaedias of Phrases are discussed in section 2. The present section briefly introduces the main general *leishu* and also refers to the popular Encyclopaedias for Daily Use.

26.2   General Encyclopaedias (a selection of ten of the most important literati *leishu*)

1.   Yu Shi-nan 虞世南 (558-638), *Excerpts from Books in the Northern Hall* (**Beitang shuchao** 北堂書鈔), 2 vols. (Taipei, 1962). Divided into nineteen sections and many subsections. Deals mainly with government, with quotations from many pre-Sui works long since lost; sources indicated.

2.   Ou-yang Xun 歐陽詢 (557-641), *Collection of Literature Arranged by Categories* (**Yiwen leiqu** 艺文类聚), 2 vols. (Shangahi, 1965).

Divided into 47 sections and many subsections. Covers all subjects and contains many quotations from works long since lost; sources cited.

3.   Xu Jian 徐堅 (659-729), *Writings for Elementary Instruction* (**Chuxue ji** 初學記), 3 vols. (Peking, 1962). Background knowledge for beginning students. Divided into 23 main categories and 313 sub-categories. Largely drawn from pre-Tang sources.

4.   Li Fang 李昉 (925-996), *Imperially Reviewed Encyclopaedia of the Taiping Era* (**Taiping yulan** 太平御覽), 4 vols. (Peking, 1960). Divided into 54 main sections and 5,000 subsections. Quotations from over 2,000 sources, 70 of which have since been lost. Important for Tang and Five Dynasty history. Index available: H-Y Index 23 (Peking, 1935; Taipei, 1966). See J.W. Haeger, "The Significance of Confusion: The Origins of the *T'ai-p'ing yu-lan*," *Journal of the American Oriental Society* 88.3:401-410 (1968).

5.   Li Fang, *Wide Gleanings Made in the Taiping Era* (**Taiping guangji** 太平廣記). Fictional sources considered improper for inclusion in no. 4 above. Contains quotations from 485 titles, 240 of which have since been lost. Important sociological and mythological materials. H-Y Index to titles: H-Y 15.

6.   Wang Qin-ruo 王欽若, *Outstanding Models from the Storehouse of Literature* (**Cefu yuangui** 册府元龜; completed in 1013), 12 vols. (Peking, 1960). Divided into 31 main sections and 1,104 subsections, covers from earliest times to the end of the Five Dynasties (960). Sources mainly drawn from the Standard Histories and the Classics but often from editions since lost. Particularly important for Tang and Five Dynasty history. Index to the names, titles, and technical terms in the sections on foreign countries and diplomatic affairs available: **Sappu genki hoshi-bu gaishin-bu sakuin** 册府元龜奉使部外臣部索引 (Tokyo, 1938). There is a Wade-Giles index appended.

7.   Wang Ying-lin 王應麟 (1223-1296), *Ocean of Jade* (**Yuhai** 玉海). Clumsily arranged but contains much important material for Song history, including quotations from the lost *Song Veritable Records*, National Histories and Daily Records, etc.

8.   *Yongle Encyclopaedia* (**Yongle dadian** 永樂大典; completed in 1408 in 22,900 *juan;* approx. 800 *juan* extant today). Whole works were

copied in by rhyme in this gigantic imperially-sponsored attempt to save for posterity the sum total of all written knowledge. A total of 2,169 scholars worked on the project. During the eighteenth and nineteenth centuries (before the two original copies were burnt), approximately 300 works which did not exist elsewhere were copied from it. Some 700 of the extant *juan* have been gathered together and photolithographically reprinted: **Yongle dadian,** 202 fascicles (Peking, 1959-1960). See L. Giles, "A Note on the *Yong-lo ta-tien,*" *New China Review* 2:137-153 (1920).

9.   Zhang Ying 張英 , *Exemplary Models Arranged by Categories* **(Yuanjian leihan** 淵鑑類函; completed 1701), 8 vols. (Taipei, 1967). The second most comprehensive extant *leishu* after no. 10 below; contains quotations from works from earliest times down to 1556.

10.   Chen Meng-lei 陳夢雷 et al., presented by Jiang Ting-xi 蔣廷錫 , *Synthesis of Books and Illustrations Past and Present,* also called *The Imperial Encyclopaedia* (**[Qinding] gujin tushu jicheng** 欽定古今圖書集成), 10,000 *juan,* plus table of contents, 40 *juan* (Peking, 1725; poor quality ed., Shanghai, 1885-1888; facsimile reproduction of 1725 edition, Shanghai, 1934; Taipei rearranged ed., 1965).

This huge work (the original edition numbered 852,408 pages) is by far the largest of the *leishu.* It is divided into six main categories, 32 sections, and 6,109 subsections (see Table 4 on following page). Under each of the 6,109 subsections are gathered sources from the earliest time to the seventeenth century arranged under the following eight headings: (1) orthodox writings, especially the Classics; (2) other Confucian writings; (3) biographies; (4) literary works; (5) felicitous phrases and sentences; (6) historical works; (7) indirect reports; (8) anecdotes and myths. There is an excellent index to the translated titles of the subsections which provides the most convenient way of looking up something in this vast work: L. Giles, *Index to the Chinese Encyclopaedia* (London, 1911; Taipei reprint, 1966).

The **Tushu jicheng** (as it is sometimes called for short) has frequently been used not only as a short cut to primary sources but also as the only route to primary sources. To use it this way is to become circumscribed by the biases of the Confucian eighteenth-century editors. On the *leishu* in general see W. Bauer, "The Encyclopaedia in China," *Cahiers d'histoire mondiale* 20:665-691 (1966); also Teng and Biggerstaff, pp. 83-96. Zhang

TABLE 4

The Imperial Encyclopaedia: Categories and Section Headings

Section (*dian* 典)		Number of subsections (*bu* 部)	Number of *juan*
	Category I. Celestial Matters (*lixiang* 曆象)		
I	The Heavens (*qianxiang* 乾象)	21	100
II	The Year (*suigong* 歲功)	43	116
III	Astronomy and Mathematics (*lifa* 曆法)	6	140
IV	Strange Phenomena (*shuzheng* 庶徵)	50	188
	Category II. Geography (*fangyu* 方輿)		
V	The Earth (*kunyu* 坤輿)	21	140
VI	Political Divisions of China (*zhifang* 職方)	223	1544
VII	Mountains and Rivers of China (*shanchuan* 山川)	401	320
VIII	Foreign Countries (*bianyi* 邊裔)	542	140
	Category III. Human Relationships (*minglun* 明倫)		
IX	The Emperor (*huangji* 皇極)	31	300
X	The Imperial Household (*gongwei* 宮闈)	15	140
XI	The Government Service (*guanchang* 官常)	65	800
XII	Family Relationships (*jiafan* 家範)	31	116
XIII	Social Intercourse (*jiaoyi* 交誼)	37	120
XIV	Clan and Family Names (*shizu* 氏族)	2694	640
XV	Man and his Attributes (*renshi* 人事)	97	112
XVI	Womankind (*guiyuan* 閨媛)	17	376
	Category IV. Arts and Sciences (*bowu* 博物)		
XVII	Arts, Occupations, and Professions (*yishu* 藝術)	43	824
XVIII	Religion (*shenyi* 神異)	70	320
XIX	The Animal Kingdom (*qinchong* 禽蟲)	317	192
XX	The Vegetable Kingdom (*caomu* 草木)	700	320
	Category V. Confucianism and Literature (*lixue* 理學)		
XXI	Canonical and other Literature (*jingji* 經籍)	66	500
XXII	The Conduct of Life (*xuexing* 學行)	96	300
XXIII	Branches of Literature (*wenxue* 文學)	49	260
XXIV	Characters and Writing (*zixue* 字學)	24	160

TABLE 4 continued

Section (*dian* 典)	Number of subsections (*bu* 部)	Number of *juan*
Category VI. Political Economy (*jingji* 經濟)		
XXV The Examination System (*xuanju* 選舉)	29	136
XXVI The Official Career (*quanheng* 銓衡)	12	120
XXVII Foods and Other Articles of Commerce (*shihuo* 食貨)	83	360
XXVIII Ceremonies (*liyi* 禮儀)	70	348
XXIX Music (*yuelü* 樂律)	46	136
XXX Military Administration (*rongzheng* 戎政)	30	300
XXXI Law and Punishment (*xiangxing* 祥刑)	26	180
XXXII Industries and Manufactured Articles (*kaogong* 考工)	154	252
Totals	6109	10000

Source: Giles, Appendix 2.

Ti-hua 張滌华 , *On the Different Types of leishu* (**Leishu liubie** 类书流別), rev. ed. (Shanghai, 1958) contains the important primary sources on the compilation of *leishu* as well as an exhaustive list of over 400 lost and extant *leishu* from all periods.

26.3 Encyclopaedias for Daily Use

From the Song and increasingly from the Yuan and the Ming, encyclopaedias were compiled for a more popular audience than the emperor, the officials, and the literati. The arrangement of such works as **Shilin guangji** 事林廣記, **Santai wanyong zhengzong** 三臺萬用正宗 , and **Wanbao quanshu** 萬寶全書 , which were issued in innumerable editions by the pulp publishers of Fukien and Kiangnan, followed the literati *leishu*. There were sections on Heaven, Earth, and Man but the contents of these sections were concerned with current practical matters (e.g. advice to merchants and trade routes) rather than with literary and historical models from the past. Many also contained sections on popular superstitions with instructions, for example, on how to select lucky days. Most had brief outlines of the bureaucracy and the main administrative divisions of the Empire.

These works form an important source on popular religion and attitudes, social practices, and the economy not found in other extant sources. See Sakai Tadao 酒井忠夫 , "Encyclopaedias for Daily Use and popular education in the Ming dynasty" (Ming-dai no jitsuyō ruisho to shomin kyōiku 明代の日用類書と庶民教育), in **Kinsei Chūgoku kyōikushi kenkyū** (Tokyo, 1958), pp. 26-154; also Niida Noboru 仁井田陞 , "Village regulations and wage laborer contracts in the Yuan and Ming as seen in twenty Encyclopaedias for Daily Use" (Gen Min jidai no mura no kiyaku to kosaku shōsho nado, nichiyō hyakka zensho no rui nijushū no naka kara 元明時代の村の規約と小作證書など日用百科全書の類二十種の中から), in his *Collected Papers on Chinese Legal History* (**Chūgoku hōseishi kenkyū** 中国法制史研究), vol. 3 (Tokyo, 1962). One of the popular encyclopaedic manuals of letter writing has recently been photographically reproduced in Japan: **Xinbian shiwen leiyao qizha qingqian** 新編事文類要啓劄青錢 (Tokyo, 1963).

27. Literary Anthologies and Collected Works

27.1   Introduction

Very large Literary Anthologies (*zongji* 總集) are extant from the sixth century onwards. They contain memorials, letters, and commemorative biographies as well as many other types of source material useful to the historian. By the Tang dynasty the practice of collecting together the prose and poetry of individual authors (called *bieji* 別集 to distinguish them from the general collections or *zongji* 總集 ; also called *wenji* 文集) was widespread and several have survived. After the Tang dynasty many hundreds of individual Collected Works are extant and the importance of the anthologies for the historian declines as a result. The three most important anthologies of Tang and pre-Tang literature (leaving out collections of poetry only) are introduced below as well as some of the reference tools for getting at the Collected Works of individual authors in the post-Tang period.

27.2   Anthologies

1.   Xiao Tong 蕭統 (Prince Zhao Ming 昭明太子, A.D. 501-531), comp., *Anthology of Literature* (**Wenxuan** 文選). Divided into poetry and prose with the prose further subdivided into 37 genres. Writing from earliest times to fifth century. A model for later anthologies. See Shiba Rokurō 斯波六郎, *A Concordance to Wenxuan* (**Monzen sakuin** 文選索引), T'ang Civilization Reference Series, 4 vols. (Kyoto, 1957-1959), which supersedes H-Y Index 25 to authors, titles, and works quoted in the anthology.

2.   Yan Ke-jun 嚴可均 (1762-1843), comp., *Complete Collection of Prose Literature from Remote Antiquity through the Qing and Han*

Dynasties, the Three Kingdoms, and the Six Dynasties (**Quan shanggu Sandai Qin Han Sanguo Liuchao wen** 全上古三代秦汉三国六朝文 ;
Peking, 1958). This huge anthology contains works by more than 3,400
writers living prior to the Tang. Use the H-Y Index to authors (Index 8,
Peking, 1932; Peking, 1965 [with corrections]; Taipei, 1966).

3. Xu Song 徐松 (1781-1848), comp., *Complete Prose Literature
of the Tang* (**Quan Tangwen** 全唐文 ; 1814; Shanghai, 1887). Contains
prose works of some 3,500 Tang authors. Use T'ang Civilization Reference
Series index: Hiraoka Takeo 平岡武夫 , *Tang Prose Authors* (**Tōdai no
sambun sakka** 唐代の散文作家 ; Kyoto, 1954) which gives alternate
names, floruit of author, and reference to his works in **Quan Tangwen** and
its continuations.

27.3 Collected Works

Collected Works of individual authors (*wenji* 文集 , *quanji* 全集),
usually contain (1) prefaces to the collection, (2) author's poetry, (3) letters
and prefaces, (4) memorials and other official writings, (5) commemorative
biographies and other commemorative writings.

There are at least 3,000 Collected Works of Qing authors, about 1,500
extant Collected Works by Ming authors, and an unknown but far smaller
number of extant Collected Works by Yuan, Song, and Tang authors. The
following reference works should be of some help in locating an author's
Collected Works and also in using them rapidly. (Titles of an author's
Collected Works are usually mentioned in his biography.)

Song

1. Tokyo Kyōiku Daigaku bungakubu tōyōshigaku kenkyūshitsu and
the Ajiashi kenkyūkai, comps., *Catalogue of Collected Works of Song Authors*
(**Sōjin bunshū mokuroku** 宋人文集目録; Tokyo, 1959).

2. B. E. McKnight, comp., *An Index to Sung Dynasty Titles Extant
in Ts'ung-shu* (Research Aids Center, Taipei, forthcoming). Lists 6,500 titles
in Song works; author index.

3. *Concordance to Ten Song Collected Works,* compiled under the direction of Saeki Tomi 佐伯富 (**Sōdai bunshū sakuin** 宋代文集索引 ; Kyoto, 1970). Contains 70,000 entries to names, places, technical terms, key words, etc. in ten important Song Collected Works.

3. R.M. Hartwell, comp., *A Guide to Sources of Chinese Economic History, A.D. 618-1368* (Chicago, 1964). Annotated index to materials of interest to the economic historian drawn from Collected Works of Tang, Song, and Yuan authors mentioned in the *Imperial Catalogue* (q.v.).

Yuan

1. Yamane Yukio 山根幸夫 and Ogawa Takashi 小川尚 , comps., *Catalogue of Collected Works by Yuan Authors Extant in Japanese Libraries* (**Nihon genzon Genjin bunshū mokuroku** 日本現存元人文集目録 ; Tokyo, 1970).

2. *Index to Historical Materials in Yuan Collected Works* (**Genjin bunshū shiryō sakuin** 元人文集史料索引 ; Jimbun kagaku kenkyūjo, mimeo, 1960). Indexes some 4,000 proper names and historical terms from 23 Yuan Collected Works.

Ming

1. Yamane Yukio and Ogawa Takashi, comps., *Catalogue of Collected Works by Ming Authors Extant in Japanese Libraries* (**Nihon genzon Minjin bunshū mokuroku** 日本現存明人文集目録 ; Tokyo, 1966). Lists the titles of Collected Works of 1,400 Ming authors; author index.

2. Franke lists Ming Collected Works only if they contain three or more memorials; the selection was not intended to be exhaustive.

Qing

1. Wang Zhong-min 王重民 , comp., *Subject Index to Titles in Qing Collected Works* (**Qingdai wenji bianmu fenlei suoyin** 清代文集編目分類索引 ; Peking, 1935; Taipei, 1965). Indexes titles in 428 Collected Works of Qing authors; arranged by broad subject categories.

2. *Catalogue of Collected Works by Qing Authors Extant in Japanese Libraries* (**Nihon genzon Shinjin bunshū mokuroku** 日本現存清人文集目録 ; Kyoto, 1972).

28. <u>Miscellanous Notes</u>

The practice among scholars of keeping notebooks had already begun after the Han dynasty but it only became widespread in the Tang and the Song. These notebooks (*biji* 筆記 or *suibi* 隨筆) contain a great quantity of very uneven jottings on a huge range of subjects. Sometimes they were based on a scholar's wide and curious readings; sometimes they were based on direct observations and often they reported gossip and rumor. Items considered unfit for more formal works found their way into a scholar's Miscellanous Notes. They form an important corrective to the Standard Histories and other works of official and Confucian historiography. As they cover every conceivable subject they were frequently classified into different categories of the old catalogues. Students of any post-Han period should make sure that they have found out the most important Miscellanous Notes of the period and glanced over them: it is often surprising what these works contain. In the Southern Song, for example, much of the intimate detail of city life in the capital is drawn from several Miscellanous Notes (heavily used in J. Gernet's *Daily Life in China on the Eve of the Mongol Invasion, 1250-1276* (London, 1962), while in the Qing, many of the great scholars, including Gu Yan-wu 顧炎武 , Zhao Yi 趙翼 , and Wang Ming-sheng 王鳴盛 , recorded some of their most interesting observations in their Miscellaneous Notes, often culled from a lifetime of reading and reflection.

Miscellaneous Notes are discussed by H. Franke in "Some Aspects of Chinese Private Historiography in the Thirteenth and Fourteenth Century," in Beasley and Pulleyblank, pp. 115-134, while Franke, pp. 98-118, contains a whole section on this type of writing by Ming authors, arranged with brief notes according to broad subject categories. The best general introduction to some sixty Miscellaneous Notes of the Ming and Qing is by Xie Guo-zhen 谢国祯 , *Collection of Notes on Ming-Qing Miscellanous Notes* (**Ming-Qing biji tancong** 明清笔记谈丛 ; Shanghai, 1962). Xie deliberately chose those works which he considered to have materials of interest to the social and economic historian and he devotes a page or two to describing and quoting from each.

Two indexes compiled under the direction of Saeki Tomi 佐伯富 are particularly useful: **Chūgoku zuihitsu sakuin** 中国隨筆索引 and **Chūgoku zuihitsu zatsusho sakuin** 中国隨筆雜著索引 ; Kyoto, 1954, 1960). Altogether the chapter headings, key words, and important nouns found in 206 Miscellaneous Notes were indexed. Among the works indexed the following are particularly worth noting:

Tang

Wang Ding-bao 王定保 , **Zhiyan** 摭言 .

Feng Yan 封演, **Fengshi wenjian ji** 封氏聞見記 (also H-Y Supplement 7).

Song

Hong Mai 洪邁 , **Rongzhai suibi** 容齋隨筆 (also H-Y Index 13).

Meng Yuan-lao 孟元老 , **Dongjing meng hua lu** 東京夢華錄 (see section 18.7).

Wu Zi-mu 吳自牧 , **Meng liang lu** 夢梁錄 (see section 18.7).

Zhou Mi 周密 , **Zhaidong yeyu** 齊東野語.

Li Fang 李昉 , **Taiping guangji** 太平廣記. Not strictly speaking a *biji* but containing similar materials, this work is more like a collectanea of *biji* (see section 27.2).

Shen Gua 沈括 , **Mengqi bitan** 夢溪筆談 ; 1089-1093.

Jin

Liu Qi 劉祁 , **Guiqian zhi** 歸潛志 . See Hok-lam Chan, "Liu Ch'i and his Kuei-ch'ien chih," in his *The Historiography of the Chin Dynasty: Three Studies* (Wiesbaden, 1970), pp. 121-188.

Yuan

Tao Zong-yi 陶宗儀, **Zhuogeng lu** 輟耕錄 (also Centre Franco-chinois d'Études sinologiques concordance 13).

Quan Heng 權衡, **Gengshen waishi** 庚申外史 . Not in Saeki, but translated by H. Schulte-Uffelage, *Das Keng-shen waishih* (Berlin, 1963).

Ming and Qing

Lu Can 陸粲 , **Gengsi bian** 庚巳編 ; c. 1520.

Zhou Hui 周暉 , **Jinling suoshi** 金陵瑣事 (see section 18.7).

Tan Qian 談遷 , **Zaolin zazu** 棗林雜俎 .

Shen De-fu 沈德符 , **(Wanli) Yehuobian** (萬曆)野獲編 .

Yu Huai 余懷 , **Banqiao zaji** 板橋雜記.Not in Saeki, but translated by H.S. Levy, *A Feast of Mist and Flowers* (Yokohama, 1966). See section 18.7.

Gu Yan-wu 顧炎武 , **Rizhilu** 日知錄.

Wang Ming-sheng 王鳴盛 , **Shiqishi shangque** 十七史商榷 (see section 16.3).

Qian Da-xin 錢大昕 , **Shijiazhai yangxin lu** 十駕齋養新錄.

Zhao Yi 趙翼 , **Nianer shi zhaji** 廿二史劄記 (see section 16.3).

Zhao Yi 趙翼 , **Gaiyu congkao** 陔餘叢考.

Yuan Mei 袁枚 , **Zi buyu** 子不語 .

Wang Qing-yun 王慶雲 , **Shiqu yuji** 石渠餘記.

Xu Ke 徐珂 , **Qingbai leichao** 清稗類鈔.

Note that many works on this type were included in special collectanea such as Tao Zong-yi's massive compilation **Shuo fu** 說郛 and its seventeenth century continuation, **Xu shuo fu** 續說郛 or the later **Biji xiaoshuo daguan** 筆記大觀. .

29. Confucian Classics and Philosophical Works

29.1   Confucian Classics

Not only are the Classics important primary sources for pre-Qin (i.e. pre-third century B.C.) history, but they are also of continuing importance in later periods in a society whose elite constantly studied and quoted them as the repositories of correct teachings on the moral and political life. The Classics and Chinese philosophical works in general have probably been more translated than any other group of texts.

Here it will be sufficient to give the titles of the Classics at the same time as indicating available indexes and concordances, bibliographies of translations, studies, and introductions.

By the Han dynasty there were five works which were supposed to have been edited by Confucius and which were counted as Classics (*wujing* 五經): (1) the *Book of Changes*, (2) the *Book of History*, (3) the *Book of Songs*, (4) the *Book of Rites*, and (5) the *Spring and Autumn Annals*.

Gradually, however, the number rose to nine (the *Book of Rites* and the *Spring and Autumn Annals* were each split into three constituent parts), and then by the Song dynasty, with the inclusion of the *Analects of Confucius*, the *Classic of Filial Piety*, the **Erya**, and finally the *Book of Mencius*, the number rose to thirteen (*shisanjing* 十三經). See Table 5 on following page.

TABLE 5

The Thirteen Classics

	Title		Index/Concordance
1.	*Book of Changes*	**Yijing** 易經 (**Zhouyi** 周易)	*H-Y Supp. 10
2.	*Book of History* (also called *Classic of Documents*)	**Shujing** 書經 (**Shangshu** 尚書)	*Gu Jie-gang (Shangshu tongjian 尚書通檢; Peking, 1936)
3.	*Book of Songs* (also called *Classic of Odes*)	**Shijing** 詩經 (**Maoshi** 毛詩)	*H-Y Supp. 9; H-Y Index 31
4.	*Rites of Zhou*	**Zhouli** 周禮 (**Zhouguan** 周官)	H-Y 37
5.	*Book of Etiquette and Ceremonial*	**Yili** 儀禮	H-Y 6
6.	*Book of Ceremonial*	**Liji** 禮記	H-Y 27
7.	*Spring and Autumn Annals*	**Chunqiu** 春秋	*H-Y 11; H-Y 29
8.	*Commentary of Zuo*	**Zuozhuan** 左傳	*H-Y 11; H-Y 29
9.	*Guliang Commentary*	**Guliangzhuan** 穀梁傳	*H-Y 11; H-Y 29
10.	*Analects of Confucius*	**Lunyu** 論語	*H-Y Supp. 16
11.	*Classic of Filial Piety*	**Xiaojing** 孝經	H-Y Supp. 23
12.	**Erya**	**Erya** 爾雅	*H-Y Supp. 18; H-Y 38
13.	*Book of Mencius*	**Mengzi** 孟子	*H-Y Supp. 17

The H-Y Indexes and Supplements often include important introductions; those which are starred (*) also include punctuated texts.

In the Song, the *Analects of Confucius,* the *Book of Mencius,* and two portions of the *Book of Ceremonial* (the *Great Learning,* **Daxue** 大學 , and the *Doctrine of the Mean,* **Zhongyong** 中庸) were linked together as the *Four Books* (**Sishu** 四書) and made the foundation of a Confucian education.

There are many editions of the *Thirteen Classics;* of these the Kaiming Shudian punctuated edition (photolith of **Shisan jing zhu shu** 十三經注疏, 1815) also appeared with an index (1934) and has been reprinted with corrections (Peking, 1957).

A full concordance of the *Five Classics* was published in Tokyo (**Gokyō sakuin** 五經索引), 4 vols. (1935-1944) and also for the Four Books

178

(**Shisho sakuin** 四書索引), 2 vols. (1933).

Translations

Listed in C.O. Hucker, *China: A Critical Bibliography* (Tucson, 1962), pp. 80-81; T. De Bary and A.T. Embree, eds., *A Guide to Oriental Classics* (New York, 1964); Chun-shu Chang, *Premodern China: A Bibliographical Introduction* (Michigan, 1971), pp. 81-89. See also translations listed in Wing-tsit Chan below.

29.2   Philosophical works

See Wing-tsit Chan, *An Outline and an Annotated Bibliography of Chinese Philosophy* (rev. and expanded ed., New Haven, 1969).

Feng Yu-lan 馮友蘭, *First Draft Studies on Materials for the History of Chinese Philosophy* (**Zhongguo zhexueshi shiliaoxue chugao** 中国哲学史史料学初稿 ; Peking, 1962).

Works listed under Philosophers in the *Imperial Catalogue* cover a broad range:

1. Confucian writers (see section 29)   *rujia* 儒家
2. Military experts (see section 21)   *bingjia* 兵家
3. Legalists (see section 20)   *fajia* 法家
4. Writers on agriculture (see section 25.1)   *nongjia* 農家
5. Writers on medicine   *yijia* 醫家
6. Writers on astronomy and mathematics   *tianwen suanfa* 天文算法

7. Divination   *shushu* 術數
8. Arts, painting, calligraphy etc.   *yishu* 藝術
9. Treatises on miscellaneous subject
        (coins, cooking, etc.)   *pulu* 譜錄
10. Miscellaneous writers (see section 28)   *zajia* 雜家
11. General Encyclopaedias (see section 26)   *leishu* 類書
12. Novels and incidental writing (see section 31)   *xiaoshuo* 小說
13. Buddhists (see section 30.1)   *shijia* 釋家
14. Taoists (see section 30.2)   *daojia* 道家

For later Confucian philosophers see the collections compiled by Huang Zong-xi 黃宗羲 , *Major Schools of Song and Yuan Confucians* (**Song Yuan xue-an** 宋元學案 ; 1750) and *Major Schools of Ming Confucians* (**Mingru xue-an** 明儒學案; 1700). There is a name index for the former: **Song Yuan xue-an renming suoyin** 宋元學案 人名索引 ; Shanghai, 1936; Taipei, 1971).

30. Buddhist and Taoist Writings

30.1   Buddhist writings

The skills required by the Buddhologist (Sanskrit, doctrinal knowledge, etc.) are unlikely to be possessed by the student of Chinese social and economic history. Nevertheless Buddhist historical writing and Buddhist sources generally are important not only for the history of Buddhist thought and institutions in China, but also for their value as supplementary sources to Confucian historical works. Unfortunately there is no guide to Buddhist historiography, but see Chen Yuan 陈垣 , *An Outline of Chinese Buddhist Historical Books* (**Zhongguo fojiao shiji gailun** 中国佛教史籍概论 ; Peking, 1955). On the first extant collection of biographies of Buddhist monks, Hui Jiao 慧皎 , **Gao seng zhuan** 高僧傳 (sixth century), see A.F. Wright, "Biography and Hagiography: Hui-chiao's *Lives of Eminent Monks*," in *Silver Jubilee Volume of the Zimbun-Kagaku Kenkyusyo* (Kyoto, 1954), pp. 383-432; also Jan Yün-hua, "Hui Chiao and His Works, a Reassessment," *Indo-Asian Culture* (New Delhi, 1964), pp. 177-190. In his "Buddhist Historiography in Sung China," *Zeitschrift der Deutschen Morgandländischen Gesellschaft* 64:360-381 (1964), Jan provides a good general account of the important changes in Buddhist historical writing in this period as it became increasingly influenced by departures in Confucian historical writing. This article contains a useful "Chronological Table of Buddhist Historical Works Written during the Sung Period" (pp. 379-381).

Jan also has a study of an important thirteenth-century history of the Tiantai sect composed in Standard History form: "Fo-tsu t'ung-chi: A Biographical and Bibliographical Study," *Oriens Extremus* 10:61-82 (1963). H. Franke discusses Buddhist historiography in passing in his "Some Aspects of Chinese Private Historiography in the Thirteenth and Fourteenth Centuries," in Beasley and Pulleyblank, pp. 115-134. The later history of Buddhist historical writing, as indeed the later history of Buddhism in imperial China, remains to be studied.

The main repository of all branches of Buddhist scriptures as well as historical writings is the *Buddhist Tripitaka* (sometimes called the *Buddhist Canon*), **Da zangjing** 大藏經 . Use the Taishō Tripitaka, **Taishō shinshū daizōkyō** 大正新修大藏經 (Tokyo, 1922-1936), with H-Y Index 11 and the index in Supplementary fascicle 1 of the *Hōbōgirin* (French dictionary of Buddhism cited below). There is a full concordance for each section: **Taishō shinshū daizōkyō sakuin** (Tokyo, in process). It is arranged by detailed subject categories, and is well indexed.

For a discussion of the printed versions of the **Da zangjing**, see P. Demiéville, "Les versions chinois du Milindapanha," Appendix 1, "Sur les editions imprimés du canon chinois," *BEFEO* 24:181-218 (1924); also K. Ch'en, "The Tibetan Tripitaka," *HJAS*, vol. 9, no. 2 (1946).

For dictionaries elucidating Buddhist terms, use W.E. Soothill and L. Hodous, *A Dictionary of Chinese Buddhist Terms* (London, 1937); also P. Demiéville and Takakusu Junjirō, ed., *Hōbōgirin, dictionnaire encyclopaedique du Bouddhisme d'après les sources chinoises et japonaises* (Tokyo, 1927- , in progress). The best dictionary is Mochizuki Shinkō 望月信亨 , *The Large Buddhist Dictionary* (**Bukkyō dai jiten** 佛教大辞典; Tokyo, 1932-1964).

The basic comprehensive reference on Buddhist works is Ono Gemmyō 小野玄妙 , *Great Dictionary of Buddhist Works with Explanations* (**Bussho kaisetsu daijiten** 佛書解説大辞典), 12 vols. (Tokyo, 1933-1936).

Note that the Dunhuang manuscripts (see section 24.3) are an important source for Tang and pre-Tang Buddhism and also that sources for the institutional history of Buddhism in Chinese society are not necessarily included in the Buddhist Tripitaka, e.g. the Monograph on Buddhists and Taoists

in the *Standard History of the Northern Wei* (the only such Monograph in
the Standard Histories); the temple gazetteers and also the extensive sections
on temples found in most Local Gazetteers (see section 18.5).

The best single work for finding the dates and also for locating biographical materials on Buddhist monks is Chen Yuan 陈垣 , *Resolved
Doubts and the Dates of Birth and Death of Buddhist Monks* (**Shishi yinian
lu** 释氏疑年录   ; Peking, 1964) which includes materials on 2,800
monks from the fourth to the seventeenth century.

Some of the general indexes to biographical materials of single periods
listed in section 17.5 include biographies of Buddhist monks.

Bibliographies

Hanayama Shinsho, *Bibliography on Buddhism* (Tokyo, 1961). Arranged
by author; covers Western literature to 1935.

Classified Bibliography of Books and Articles on Buddhism
(**Bukkyōgaku kankei zasshi rombun bunrui mokuroku** 佛教学関係
雑誌論文分類目録   ). 2 vols. (Kyoto, 1931; 1961). Up to 1955:
author/subject indexes at end of each volume.

30.2   Taoist writings

A huge quantity of not only Taoist writings but also many works
considered unorthodox were brought together in the **Daozang** 道藏
(sometimes called the *Taoist Canon*), which as a result contains many
materials not found elsewhere. The **Daozang** has the sources for both philosophical and religious Taoism and it is also an important supplement to the
various categories of Confucian historical and biographical writing.

The **Daozang** in use today dates from the fifteenth century with an
additional seventeenth-century portion: **Zhengtong daozang** 正統道藏
(1445) plus **Wanli** 萬曆 continuation (1605); reprinted under the title
Daozang, 1,120 vols. (Shanghai, 1924-1926; Taipei reprint, 1962).

There is an author/title index to the **Daozang** (and also to a supplementary
Taoist collection): H-Y Index 25 (1935).

On the various versions of the **Daozang** from the post-Han period down, see Chen Guo-fu 陈国符 , **Daozang yuanliu kao** 道藏源流考 , rev. ed., 2 vols. (Peking, 1963); and also Ōbuchi Ninji, "How the Tao Tsang Took Shape," paper for the Bellagio conference on Taoist Studies, mimeo (1968).

For a dictionary of Taoist terms, see Dai Yuan-chang 戴源長, **Xianxue cidian** 仙學辭典 (Taipei, 1962).

Some of the indexes to biographical materials of single periods listed in section 17.5 contain biographies of Taoist monks.

Note the Dunhuang catalogues of Taoist materials (section 24.3), and also M. Soymié, "Bibliographie du Taoisme: études dans les langues occidentales, le. partie," **Dokyō kenkyū** 3:1-72 (1968).

31. Oral and Popular Traditions

Although the Chinese literati neglected oral sources (on legends, cults, popular beliefs and popular arts, festivals, and customs) in their historical works, they were by no means uninterested in recording oral traditions and data on customs and festivals in their miscellaneous and literary writings; thus vestiges of popular customs and folk literature may be found preserved in the elite literature. (Literati gossip and rumor went often into a scholar's Miscellaneous Notes; see section 28.)

On folk literature, see Zheng Zhen-duo 鄭振鐸, *History of Chinese Popular Literature* (**Zhongguo suwenxue shi** 中國俗文學史 ; Shanghai, 1938; 1954) and also Yang Yin-shen's 楊蔭深 brief but more comprehensive *Outlines of Chinese Popular Literature* (**Zhongguo suwenxue gailun** 中國俗文學概論 ; Shanghai, 1946; Taipei, 1961). Note also the type of sources from which Du Wen-lan 杜文蘭 (1815-1881) drew his enormous *Ancient Songs and Sayings* (**Gu yaoyan** 古謠諺), punctuated edition (Shanghai, 1958); and likewise note that Zhang Yuan 張援 based

his fascinating *Selection of Poems from the Fields* (**Tianjian shi xuan** 田間
詩選 ; Shanghai, 1932) mainly on works of literati poets. Although the
Chinese Literature Department of Peking University covered a broader range
of topics in their anthology of *Literary Materials on Peasant Problems in
Chinese History* (**Zhongguo lidai nongmin wenti wenxue ziliao** 中国历代
农民问题文学资料 ; Peking, 1959) they too drew mainly from
literati works for reasons which are perfectly clear; the recorders in traditional China were the literati.

Not only did the literati record folk literature and use folk themes in
their writing (and one should not exaggerate the extent to which they did
so), but as officials they were particularly interested to find out what was
going on in the villages:

> *Xiao-shuo* 小說 (literally, the talk of lowly folk) were the talk of
> the streets. Thus the **Zuozhuan** quotes chair-bearers' chants, while
> the *Book of Songs* praises the ruler who consulted the peasants. In days
> of old when a sage was on the throne. . .clappers sounded in early
> spring as a search was made for folk songs, while officials on tours of
> inspection understood local customs from the popular songs, and if
> mistakes had been made these were rectified. All the talk of the streets
> and the highways was recorded. . .officials in charge of civil affairs
> reported local sayings and customs. . .
> (**Hanshu**, quoted in Lu Xun, *A Brief History of Chinese Fiction*
> [Peking, 1959], p. 4).

The *Book of Songs,* which was traditionally supposed to have been
collected in this way, contains 300 folk and ritual songs which have been
used as primary sources for the popular beliefs and customs of the Zhou
period.

From the second century on, the central government continued to set
up agencies to collect popular tunes; some of the ballads, love songs, laments,
etc. which were collected have survived, and contain important materials
for the study of the popular culture.

After the Tang many more works of popular literature have survived,
starting from the works found at Dunhuang; see A. Waley's selection *Ballads
and Stories from Tun-huang* (London, 1960). One of the most important of
the new types of popular literature to emerge in the post-Tang period was
the novel which was rewritten in many different versions from storyteller's

prompt book to finished literary product. On this process, see for example R.G. Irwin, *The Evolution of a Chinese Novel: Shui-hu-chuan* (Cambridge, Mass., 1953). For an outline see Lu Xun, *A Brief History of Chinese Fiction* (Peking, 1959); and for a bibliography see Sun Kai-di 孫楷弟, *Catalogue of Chinese Popular Novels* (**Zhongguo tongsu xiaoshuo shumu** 中國通俗小說書目 ; Shanghai, 1932; 1957); also the comprehensive work by Li Tien-yi, *Chinese Fiction: A Bibliography of Books and Articles in Chinese and English* (New Haven, 1968); and the cumulative bibliography of works in all languages on all aspects of Chinese literature published at the end of each issue of **Chūgoku bungakuhō** (Kyoto, 1954-   ). Translations into English up to 1950 are listed in M. Davidson, *A List of Published Translations from Chinese into English, French and German,* vol. 1: *Literature Exclusive of Poetry;* vol. 2: *Poetry* (New Haven, 1953; 1957). On the novels and stories as historical sources, see H.F. Schurmann, "On Social Themes in Sung Tales," *HJAS* 20:239-261 (1957); J. Prusek, "Les contes chinoises du Moyen Age comme source de l'histoire economique et sociale sous les dynasties des Song et des Yuan," reprinted in his *Chinese History and Literature* (Prague, 1970), pp. 467-494.

Not only did the literati record folk literature in their own works or rewrite popular works, but they also recorded their observations of popular customs and festivals in works on Annual Festivals (*suishi* 歲時 , *suishi* 歲事 , *shiling* 時令 , etc.) and on Popular Customs (*fengsu* 風俗, *fengtuji* 風土記). Such works were either printed separately for a locality or region or frequently were included as a chapter or two of the Local Gazetteer. A late Qing example of the genre was translated by D. Bodde, *Annual Customs and Festivals in Peking as Recorded in the Yen-ching Sui-shi-chi* (New York, 1965). Not infrequently members of the literati recorded their observations of popular cults or festivals in their miscellaneous writings or notes; see for example Chao Wei-pang's translation of a late Ming scholar's description of the dragon-boat festival in Hunan: "The Dragon Boat Race in Wuling, Hunan," *Folklore Studies* 2:1-18 (1943). A particularly fascinating work is *Compendium of Customs* (**Tongsu bian** 通俗編) compiled by Zhai Hao 翟灏 in the eighteenth century (punctuated reprint, Peking, 1958, plus a four-corner index). It is based on the author's personal observations and notes on proverbs, customs, and idioms which he came across in his travels and later traced down in books.

Turning to popular beliefs, there is a huge body of sources on Buddhism and Taoism (see section 30), as well as on the various syncretisms of the later empire; some of these latter sources have been introduced by Sakai Tadao 酒井忠夫 in his *Collected Studies on Chinese Popular Morality Books* **(Chūgoku zensho no kenkyū** 中国善書の研究 ; Tokyo, 1960), as also in his "Confucianism and Popular Educational Works," in W.T. De Bary, ed., *Self and Society in Ming Thought* (New York, 1970), pp. 331-366. A popular morality tract was translated by T.D. Suzuki and F. Carus, *T'ai-shang kan-ying p'ien: Treatise of the Exalted One on Response and Retribution* (London, 1926). Sakai has also drawn attention to the importance of the Encyclopaedias for Daily Use as sources for Chinese popular education (see section 26.3), while Zhang Zhi-gong 張志公 has contributed an important study on another type of source on the same subject: *A Preliminary Study of Traditional Language Primers* **(Chuantong yuwen jiaoyu chutan** 传統语文教育初谈), rev. ed. (Shanghai, 1962). Note also such collections of anecdotes and stories as the **Taiping Guangji** (q.v.) and Xu Ke's 徐珂 **Qingbai leichao** 清稗類鈔 (1917; Taipei, 1966).

The above sources may be divided into four types: (1) vestiges of popular literature and legends in the elite literature; (2) extant works of popular literature (mainly from the late Tang down); (3) popular tracts, devotional and other works of the popular religions; and (4) the records and direct observations of literati of "manners and customs," temples, cults, festivals, etc.

While the four types of source have by no means been fully utilized by modern historians, it would be misleading to suggest that the sources for the study of oral traditions and "folk culture" are rich, for they are not. As has already been pointed out, the recorders in traditional China were the Confucian literati who had scant respect for oral traditions. Nevertheless, these sources may be checked with and filled out using the reports and field studies of modern folklore researchers and anthropologists.

Early folklore research in China was the work of the missionaries or their converts. See for example J.J.M. De Groot, *Les fêtes annuellement célebrés à Emoui [Amoy], étude concernant la religion populaire des chinois*, 2 vols., Annales du Musée Guimet, vols. 11-12 (Paris, 1886); J.J.M.De Groot,

The Religious System of China, 6 vols. (Leiden, 1892-1910); and E. Doré, *Researches into Chinese Superstitions* (Shanghai, 1914-1938), which was based on data originally published by Pierre Hoang 黄伯祿 under the title **Jishuo quanzhen** 集說詮真 (Shanghai, 1878).

After the May Fourth Movement there developed considerable interest among Chinese researchers into folklore collection and anthropological studies. Special societies were set up and journals and reports were published; see Chao Wei-pang, "Modern Chinese Folklore Investigation," *Folklore Studies* 1:55-76 (1942), 2:79-88 (1943); and also L.A. Schneider, *Ku Chieh-kang and China's New History* (Berkeley, 1971), "The Folkstudies Movement and its Populist Milieu," and "Popular Culture as a Modern Alternative," pp. 121-152 and 153-187. Many of the publications of this period have recently been reprinted in Taiwan, where the original folk song and folk literature collections of the Institute of History and Philology are also located. Note W. Eberhard's translations, *Chinese Fairy Tales and Folk Tales* (New York and London, 1937 and 1938); and *Folktales of China* (Chicago, 1965).

A handful of Western folklorists and anthropologists also began field studies in this period (to 1949), concentrating on general community studies (see M. Fried, "Community Studies in China," *FEQ* 14:11-36 [1954-1955]), or on the popular religion (notably the group from the Catholic University in Peking led by W.A. Grootaers). Japanese studies are summed up in Gotō Kimpei, "Studies on Chinese Religion in Post-War Japan," *Monumenta Serica* 19:384-402 (1960).

During the 1950s and 1960s in China extensive oral history projects were launched and considerable attention was also paid to the recording of legends, popular tales, etc. See Yen Chung-chiang, "Folklore Research in Communist China," *Folklore Studies* 26.2:1-67 (1967). Many interesting materials were published in collections such as Cheng Ying's 程英 *Selection of Modern Chinese Anti-imperialist and Anti-feudal Songs and Ballads* (**Zhongguo jindai fandi fanfengjian lishi geyao xuan** 中国近代反帝反封建历史歌谣选 ; Peking, 1962), and A Ying's 阿英 series beginning with *Collection of Literary Materials on the Opium War* (**Yapian zhanzheng wenxueji** 鸦片战争文学集), 2 vols. (Peking, 1955).

For materials on popular uprisings and secret societies, see the large number of collections published in China, many of which are listed in Feuerwerker and Cheng; and also in J. Chesneaux, ed., *Popular Movements and Secret Societies in China, 1840-1950* (Stanford, 1972), "Bibliography," pp. 279-288.

Note: E.T.C. Werner, *A Dictionary of Chinese Mythology* (Shanghai, 1932; and later reprints); also Lu Dan-an 陸澹安 , *Collected Explanations of Phrases Found in Chinese Novels* (**Xiaoshuo ciyu huishi** 小说词语汇释; Shanghai, 1964; Hong Kong reprint, 1968).

32. Foreign Writings

Travelers to China, whether from other Asian countries, from the Arabic or Persian empires, or from Europe, frequently left records of their journeys and observations which make fascinating reading. Some of the most important examples of this type of writing up to the seventeenth century are listed here. After the seventeenth century the volume of foreigners going to China and writing about it, whether as missionaries or as traders, travelers, diplomats, or officials, increased enormously. Their writings will be found listed in the standard bibliographies given in sections 10.4 and 10.5.

Ninth century

Japanese monk: *Ennin's Diary,* tr. E.O. Reischauer (New York, 1955). See also E.O. Reischauer, *Ennin's Travels in T'ang China* (New York, 1955).

Arab merchant: *Voyage du marchand arabe Sulayman en Inde et en Chine, redigé en 851, suivi de remarques par Abu Zayd Hasan (vers 916),* tr. G. Ferrand (Paris, 1922). Also *Relation de la Chine et de l'Inde redigée en 851,* tr. J. Sauvaget (Paris, 1949).

Twelfth century

Arab merchant: *Sharaf Al-Zaman Tahir Marvazi on China, the Turks and India,* tr. V. Minorsky (London, 1942).

Thirteenth century

Early European travelers: See L. Olschki, *Marco Polo's Precursors* (Baltimore, 1943).

Franciscan diplomat: *The Journey of William of Rubruck to the Eastern Parts of the World, 1253-55,* tr. W.W. Rockhill (London, 1900).

Venetian merchant: *Marco Polo: The Description of the World,* tr. A.C. Moule and P. Pelliot, 2 vols. (London, 1938). Also R.E. Latham, tr., *The Travels of Marco Polo* (London, 1958).

Fourteenth century

Islamic traveler: *Ibn Battuta: Travels in Asia and Africa,* tr. H.A.R. Gibb (London, 1929).

Papal diplomats and priests: *Cathay and the Way Thither, being a Collection of Medieval Notices of China,* tr. H. Yule, 4 vols. (London, 1913-1916; Taipei reprint, 1966).

Fifteenth century

Shipwrecked Korean official: *Ch'oe Pu's Diary: A Record of Drifting Across the Sea,* tr. J. Meskill (Tucson, 1965).

Sixteenth century

Japanese monk: *Diary of Trips to Ming China,* reprinted in Makita Teiryō 牧田諦亮, **Sakugen nyū Minki no kenkyū** 策彦入明記の研究, 2 vols. (Kyoto, 1955; 1958).

Jesuit missionary: *China in the Sixteenth Century: The Journals of Mathew Ricci: 1583-1610,* tr. L.J. Gallagher (New York, 1953).

Shipwrecked Portuguese and Spanish travelers and clerics: *South China in the Sixteenth Century,* tr. C.R. Boxer (London, 1953).

There is a very full list of Western writings on China up to 1700 (and through the nineteenth century as well) in Cordier's *Bibliotheca Sinica* (see section 10.4), the second part of which is devoted to an exhaustive annotated list of "Les Étrangers en Chine, Connaissance des Peuples étrangers sur la Chine" (vol. 3, columns 1917-2091), which cover foreign writing on China from Strabo to 1700; the remainder of the volume deals with the eighteenth and nineteenth centuries.

Many of the earlier European accounts of China are illustrated as well as analyzed in D.F. Lach's *Asia in the Making of Europe, The Century of Discoveries,* 2 vols. (Chicago, 1965), and *A Century of Wonder,* 2 vols. (Chicago, 1970).

For an introduction to such non-Chinese sources as treaty-port newspapers, diplomatic series, national archives, missionary reports, etc., see A.J. Nathan, *Modern China, 1840-1972: An Introduction to Sources and Research Aids* (Michigan, 1973).

SUBJECT INDEX

AUTHOR–TITLE INDEX

Note: Chinese personal names not written in *pinyin* are marked with an asterisk (*).

200

202

HARVARD EAST ASIAN MONOGRAPHS

18. Frank H. H. King (ed.) and Prescott Clarke, *A Research Guide to China-Coast Newspapers, 1822–1911*

19. Ellis Joffe, *Party and Army: Professionalism and Political Control in the Chinese Officer Corps, 1949–1964*

20. Toshio G. Tsukahira, *Feudal Control in Tokugawa Japan: The Sankin Kōtai System*

21. Kwang-Ching Liu, ed., *American Missionaries in China: Papers from Harvard Seminars*

22. George Moseley, *A Sino-Soviet Cultural Frontier: The Ili Kazakh Autonomous Chou*

23. Carl F. Nathan, *Plague Prevention and Politics in Manchuria, 1910–1931*

24. Adrian Arthur Bennett, *John Fryer: The Introduction of Western Science and Technology into Nineteenth-Century China*

25. Donald J. Friedman, *The Road from Isolation: The Campaign of the American Committee for Non-Participation in Japanese Aggression, 1938–1941*

26. Edward Le Fevour, *Western Enterprise in Late Ch'ing China: A Selective Survey of Jardine, Matheson and Company's Operations, 1842–1895*

27. Charles Neuhauser, *Third World Politics: China and the Afro-Asian People's Solidarity Organization, 1957–1967*

28. Kungtu C. Sun, assisted by Ralph W. Huenemann, *The Economic Development of Manchuria in the First Half of the Twentieth Century*

29. Shahid Javed Burki, *A Study of Chinese Communes, 1965*

30. John Carter Vincent, *The Extraterritorial System in China: Final Phase*

31. Madeleine Chi, *China Diplomacy, 1914–1918*

32. Clifton Jackson Phillips, *Protestant America and the Pagan World: The First Half Century of the American Board of Commissioners for Foreign Missions, 1810–1860*

33. James Pusey, *Wu Han: Attacking the Present through the Past*

34. Ying-wan Cheng, *Postal Communication in China and Its Modernization, 1860–1896*

HARVARD EAST ASIAN MONOGRAPHS

49

THE HISTORY OF IMPERIAL CHINA
A RESEARCH GUIDE